The Church, Then and Now

 **McMaster Divinity College Press**
McMaster New Testament Studies Series

Patterns of Discipleship in the New Testament (1996)

The Road from Damascus: The Impact of Paul's Conversion on His Life, Thought, and Ministry (1997)

Life in the Face of Death: The Resurrection Message of the New Testament (1998)

The Challenge of Jesus' Parables (2000)

Into God's Presence: Prayer in the New Testament (2001)

Reading the Gospels Today (2004)

Contours of Christology in the New Testament (2005)

Hearing the Old Testament in the New Testament (2006)

The Messiah in the Old and New Testaments (2007)

Translating the New Testament: Text, Translation, Theology (2009)

Christian Mission: Old Testament Foundations and New Testament Developments (2010)

Empire in the New Testament (2011)

The Church, Then and Now

edited by
STANLEY E. PORTER
and
CYNTHIA LONG WESTFALL

☙PICKWICK *Publications* · Eugene, Oregon

THE CHURCH, THEN AND NOW

McMaster New Testament Studies Series

Copyright © 2012 Wipf and Stock Publishers. All rights reserved. Except for brief quotations in critical publications or reviews, no part of this book may be reproduced in any manner without prior written permission from the publisher. Write: Permissions, Wipf and Stock Publishers, 199 W. 8th Ave., Suite 3, Eugene, OR 97401.

McMaster Divinity College Press
1280 Main Street West
Hamilton, Ontario, Canada
L8S 4K1

Pickwick Publications
An Imprint of Wipf and Stock Publishers
199 W. 8th Av.e, Suite 3
Eugene, OR 97401

www.wipfandstock.com

ISBN 13: 978-1-61097-921-4

Cataloging-in-Publication data:

The church, then and now / edited by Stanley E. Porter and Cynthia Long Westfall

xiv + 260 p. ; 23 cm. — Includes bibliographical references and indexes.

McMaster New Testament Studies Series

ISBN 13: 978-1-61097-921-4

1. Church. I. Porter, Stanley E., 1956–. II. Westfall, Cynthia Long. III. Title. IV. Series.

BX1746 C51 2012

Manufactured in the U.S.A.

Copyrights

Revised Standard Version of the Bible, copyright © 1952 (2nd edition, 1971) by the Division of Christian Education of the National Council of the Churches of Christ in the United States of America. Used by permission. All rights reserved

New Revised Standard Version Bible, copyright © 1989, Division of Christian Education of the National Council of Churches of Christ in the United States of America. Used by permission. All rights reserved.

Scripture taken from the Holy Bible, Today's New International Version™ Copyright © 2001 by International Bible Society. All rights reserved.

"Eleven Misconceptions Explored" in the article by Michael Pawelke is from "Megachurches Today 2005: Summary of Research Findings" by Warren Bird, Scott Thumma, and Dave Travis, used by permission of the authors and of Leadership Network, www.leadnet.org.

Contents

Preface / ix
Contributors / xi
Abbreviations / xiv

Introduction: The Church Then, Now, and for the Future
—*Stanley E. Porter* and *Cynthia Long Westfall* / 1

1. The Least, the Lost, and the Last: Christ's Church in the Gospels—*Michael P. Knowles* / 12

2. Saints and Sinners: The Church in Paul's Letters —*Stanley E. Porter* / 41

3. The Church and the Synagogue: Continuity and Discontinuity—*Cynthia Long Westfall* / 68

4. When the Blood of the Martyrs Was Not Enough: A Survey of the Places Where the Church Was Wiped Out —*Gordon L. Heath* / 97

5. The Local Church: Postmodern Possibilities—*Lee Beach* / 134

6. Adapting the House Church Model —*Bruxy Cavey* and *Wendy Carrington-Phillips* / 151

7. The Megachurch in Canada: Promising Future or Passing Fad?—*Michael Pawelke* / 178

8. The Role and Identity of the Church in the Biblical Story: Missional by Its Very Nature—*Michael W. Goheen* / 190

9. Reflections on the Church *Then* and *Now* —*Steven M. Studebaker* / 218

Ancient Sources Index / 241
Modern Author Index / 255

Preface

THE 2008 H. H. Bingham Colloquium in the New Testament at McMaster Divinity College in Hamilton, Ontario, Canada was entitled "The Church, Then and Now." The Colloquium was the fourteenth in a continuing series held here at the College. This conference was somewhat different from previous ones. For this Colloquium, we invited practitioners—those engaged in various forms of active church ministry—to join biblical and historical scholars to present and discuss important perspectives on the issue of the church, perspectives found both in the New Testament and in the contemporary church in its various manifestations. An interested public attended, heard the papers, and responded with insightful questions and comments. There was spirited interest among the participants as well. We hope that this volume will be of interest to general readers and serve as a useful textbook or supplemental source for the study of the context, content, and interpretive approaches of the New Testament, and, at least as importantly, for the study of ecclesiology, or the church in its historical and contemporary contexts.

The Bingham Colloquium is named after Dr. Herbert Henry Bingham, who was a noted Baptist leader in Ontario, Canada. His leadership abilities were recognized by Baptists across Canada and around the world. His qualities included his genuine friendship, dedicated leadership, unswerving Christian faith, tireless devotion to duty, insightful service as a preacher and pastor, and visionary direction for congregation and denomination alike. These qualities endeared him both to his own church members and to believers in other denominations. The Colloquium has been endowed by his daughter as an act of appreciation for her father. We are pleased to be able to continue this tradition.

The volumes in this series are published by McMaster Divinity College Press, in conjunction with Wipf & Stock Publishers of Eugene, Oregon. We appreciate this active publishing relationship. Previous Colloquia published in this series include the following: *Patterns of*

Discipleship in the New Testament (1996), *The Road from Damascus: The Impact of Paul's Conversion on His Life, Thought and Ministry* (1997), *Life in the Face of Death: The Resurrection Message of the New Testament* (1998), *The Challenge of Jesus' Parables* (2000), *Into God's Presence: Prayer in the New Testament* (2001), *Reading the Gospels Today* (2004), *Contours of Christology in the New Testament* (2005), *Hearing the Old Testament in the New Testament* (2006), *The Messiah in the Old and New Testaments* (2007), *Translating the New Testament: Text, Translation, Theology* (2009), *Christian Mission: Old Testament Foundations and New Testament Developments* (2010), and *Empire in the New Testament* (2011).

Finally, we would like to thank the individual contributors for accepting the assignments, for all their efforts in the preparation and presentation of papers that make a significant contribution of benefit to New Testament scholars, students of the Bible, and believers concerned about the historic context of the church and its various modern outworkings. We would also like to thank the staff and student helpers and volunteers at McMaster Divinity College, all of whom were integral in creating a pleasant environment and a supportive atmosphere. Thanks go to Justin Comber for his work on the manuscript. Both of us were co-chairs of the conference and edited this volume with the hopes that it will further the important discussion on that unique and divinely ordained organization and organism, the Christian church.

Stanley E. Porter
Cynthia Long Westfall

Contributors

LEE BEACH (PhD McMaster Divinity College) is Assistant Professor of Christian Ministry and Director of Ministry Formation at McMaster Divinity College in Hamilton, Ontario. He pastored for seventeen years with the Christian and Missionary Alliance in Canada and continues to serve with the Alliance as a Minister at Large.

WENDY CARRINGTON-PHILLIPS (MDiv McMaster Divinity College) is currently working on an MA in Christian Studies at McMaster Divinity College in Hamilton, Ontario. Her areas of interest are social-scientific criticism of the Gospels and linguistics. She has a ministry of teaching the Bible to new—and not-so-new—believers. She is a member of The Meeting House, a home-church based church that is part of the Brethren in Christ denomination.

BRUXY CAVEY (MTS Tyndale Seminary) is the Teaching Pastor of The Meeting House. This multi-site community in the Greater Toronto area shares the same teaching and vision: to create safe places for spiritual seekers to ask questions and develop thoughtful faith. Beyond The Meeting House, Bruxy teaches at the university level on Evangelism and the Local Church and is the author of *The End of Religion: An Introduction to the Subversive Spirituality of Jesus*.

MICHAEL W. GOHEEN (PhD University of Utrecht) is Geneva Professor of Worldview and Religious Studies at Trinity Western University in Langley, British Columbia, and Teaching Fellow in Mission Studies at Regent College, Vancouver. He has authored or coauthored four books, most recently *A Light to the Nations: The Missional Church and the Biblical Story*.

GORDON L. HEATH (PhD St. Michael's College) is Associate Professor of Christian History at McMaster Divinity College in Hamilton, Ontario, and also serves as Director of the Canadian Baptist Archives. His publications include *A War with a Silver Lining: Canadian Protestant Churches and the South African War, 1899–1902, Doing Church History: A User-friendly Introduction to Researching the History of Christianity*, and (co-authored with Stanley Porter) *The Lost Gospel of Judas: Separating Fact from Fiction*.

MICHAEL P. KNOWLES (ThD University of Toronto) is Professor of Preaching and holder of the George F. Hurlburt Chair in Preaching at McMaster Divinity College in Hamilton, Ontario. Ordained in the Anglican Church of Canada, he teaches courses that seek to integrate sound biblical exegesis and Christian spirituality with practical engagement in the life and ministry of the church. He has published a number of articles, an edited volume of sermons and essays, and two monographs. His most recent study, *The Unfolding Mystery of the Divine Name: The God of Sinai in Our Midst*, is scheduled for publication in 2012.

MICHAEL PAWELKE (DMin Gordon-Conwell Theological Seminary) serves as the Senior Pastor of Compass Point Bible Church in Burlington, Ontario. Michael first came to serve in Burlington in 1994. Prior to that, he served as a church planter in Winnipeg and, before that, as an associate pastor in Toronto.

STANLEY E. PORTER (PhD University of Sheffield) is President and Dean and Professor of New Testament at McMaster Divinity College in Hamilton, Ontario. He has taught for over twenty-five years in post-secondary institutions in Canada, the USA, and the UK. His publications include eighteen authored books and over 250 authored journal articles, chapters, and related publications; he has also edited over seventy volumes. Porter has wide-ranging interests in New Testament and related studies, including Greek grammar and linguistics, Pauline studies, the Gospels and historical Jesus, and papyrology. He recently authored, with Jason Robinson, *Hermeneutics: An Introduction to Interpretive Theory*.

STEVEN M. STUDEBAKER (PhD Marquette University) is Assistant Professor of Systematic and Historical Theology and holder of the Betall

Chair in Evangelical Thought at McMaster Divinity College, Hamilton, Ontario. He has taught at the College for six years, having previously taught in Georgia. His research interests include Pentecostalism, the Trinity, pneumatology, and Jonathan Edwards. He recently published *The Trinitarian Theology of Jonathan Edwards*, his third monograph on Edwards. Studebaker has also edited several volumes, and has published a number of important journal articles.

CYNTHIA LONG WESTFALL (PhD University of Surrey) is Assistant Professor of New Testament at McMaster Divinity College in Hamilton, Ontario. Her areas of interest include discourse analysis of the New Testament, the Book of Hebrews, Jewish Christianity, the General Epistles, Johannine literature, and gender in ministry. She has published a number of articles, and the book *A Discourse Analysis of the Structure of Hebrews: The Relationship between Form and Meaning*.

Abbreviations

AB	Anchor Bible
ABD	*Anchor Bible Dictionary*
AJSR	*Association for Jewish Studies Review*
AnBib	Analecta biblica
BA	*Biblical Archaeologist*
BDAG	Bauer, Walter, Frederick W. Danker, William Arndt, and F. Wilbur Gingrich. *A Greek-English Lexicon of the New Testament and Other Early Christian Literature*. 3rd ed. Chicago: University of Chicago Press, 2000
BECNT	Baker Exegetical Commentary on the New Testament
BIS	Biblical Interpretation Series
BJS	Brown Judaic Studies
BBR	*Bulletin for Biblical Research*
ICC	International Critical Commentary
Int	*Interpretation*
JETS	*Journal of the Evangelical Theological Society*
JSNTSup	Journal for the Study of the New Testament Supplement Series
JSOT	*Journal for the Study of the Old Testament*
LNTS	Library of New Testament Studies
Miss	*Missiology*
MNTS	McMaster New Testament Studies
NICOT	The New International Commentary on the Old Testament
NIGTC	The New International Greek Testament Commentary
NTS	*New Testament Studies*
PTM	Princeton Theological Monograph
SBT	Studies in Biblical Theology
SNTG	Studies in New Testament Greek
ThTo	*Theology Today*
TNTC	Tyndale New Testament Commentary
WBC	Word Biblical Commentary
ZNW	*Zeitschrift für die neutestamentliche Wissenschaft*

Introduction

The Church Then, Now, and for the Future

Stanley E. Porter and Cynthia Long Westfall

What do we typically think of when someone uses the word "church"? Do we think of a building, such as the stately-spired edifice that stands prominently on a nearby street corner, or the sprawling complex of buildings of the local megachurch? Do we ever foresee the image of a widescreen movie theatre at the center of a nearby shopping mall? When we think of the word "church," what are our recollections of our church-related experiences? Are we pleasantly overwhelmed by images of comforting and edifying times with other Christians, singing songs that convey our belief in God and hearing challenging sermons, or do we instead cringe at the thoughts of music we cannot stand and the droning of incessant and impertinent words? When others talk about "church" people in our society, what are our reactions? Do we nod slowly as we ponder some of the great accomplishments of some of these people, or do we lower our eyes and shake our heads in embarrassment at some of the things that have been done at and by various churches and those associated with them?

The word "church"—even among those who should know more about its strengths and weaknesses, its great accomplishments and terrible failings, its memorable deeds and its obvious flaws—is one that is often greeted with mixed responses. These run the gamut from exultation to grave disappointment. Mentioning the word "church" in almost any circle is virtually guaranteed to elicit a visceral reaction, as people make their none-too-well hidden thoughts very publicly known. We know that many, if not most, of these reactions—whether they are positive or negative—are probably justified, as the "church" has incited and continues to arouse strong thoughts and feelings all around.

In some ways, this is to be expected, because the church is one of the few remaining cultural institutions that has endured through the ups and downs of various other cultural shifts. Church buildings continue to stand on street corners, and people sometimes drive long distances to attend the church of their choice. Even those who pay very little attention to church any other time of the year often make sure that they darken its doorway at least a couple of times a year—apart from the unexpected yet necessary funeral. In another sense, however, such a reaction is surprising, and in many ways, altogether unjustified, because they are associating "church" with something other than what it really is.

Most people associate the word "church" with a physical structure or building. If you mentally participated in the thought experiment at the beginning of this introduction, you too probably thought first of all about the church as a physical entity—one that you know or are in some way familiar with. That, however, is certainly one manifestation of what we rightly think of as the "church," but it is only an incidental characteristic of it, and one that is increasingly more and more diverse in today's culture. Those who associate the church with people, even if unfortunately often in negative terms, are getting closer to the mark of what is meant by the church, but, even then, the fact that there are people in the church is not what defines the institutional church but what characterizes its constituency.

The church, we would contend, is one of the most intriguing and significant institutions, and one that merits serious and prolonged study for a number of reasons. One of these reasons is that it is so widely misunderstood as to its essence and character. The Christian church itself is not a mere human institution, but one founded and ordained by Jesus Christ himself, according to Matt 16:18.[1] In this passage, Jesus, speaking with his disciples and with Peter in particular at Caesarea Philippi, has just heard Peter's confession of who Jesus is—"You are the Christ, the

---

1. We realize that there is serious scholarly discussion regarding whether these words of Jesus instituting the church are authentic. We believe that a highly convincing case can and has been made that they are in fact authentic. Nevertheless, even if they are not, Matthew's Gospel, as a first-generation record of early church belief, contains the incident, which attests that early Christians believed that Jesus Christ had inaugurated the church. See Porter, *Studies in the Greek New Testament*, 121–23.

son of the living God" (Matt 16:16)—and he responds by telling Peter that it is on Peter that he will build his church.[2]

There are several things to note in these words of inauguration of the church. The first is the christological and, if you will, divine, origins of the church.[3] The church is inaugurated and founded by none other than Jesus Christ himself. This is not an act to be taken lightly or to be dismissed too quickly. It implies that the church was seen by Jesus Christ as an important part of his salvific economy, and that he had a conception of the continuing role of the church even after his earthly departure and before his second coming. As the passage makes clear, the church has incredible roles and responsibilities attached to it, including a relationship to the kingdom of heaven (Matthew's favorite term for the kingdom of God) and an instrumental role to play in fulfilling the divine purpose in the absence of Jesus Christ himself. The church, therefore, has a divine commission to fulfill an ordained task in the world, and this task must be performed in the absence of the church's own founder.

A second observation to make is that there is nothing in this passage that associates the church with any type of organizational model or physical structure. In fact, there is nothing organizational or physical about the church as inaugurated by Jesus Christ. All of the elements of organization and location came about as the church developed and attempted to fulfill its divine mandate. The divine mandate necessitated that there be certain ways of organizing the church and types of locations in which the church performed its functions, but none of them was institutionalized at its founding. These all came later, as the church grew and developed from the first few people (Peter and his fellow disciples)

---

2. We know that there has been some discussion of whether Peter or something else is the foundation upon which the church is built, on the basis of this passage. We believe that most of these latter attempts are ill-conceived efforts to avoid what they seem to think is some sort of Roman Catholic ecclesial privilege. This passage was not used by the Roman Catholic Church as the basis of its foundation until long after the church was founded, and does not really enter into earliest discussion.

3. Those who would doubt the divinity of Jesus Christ will probably not be interested in this volume. In any case, more relevant issues in contemporary historical Jesus discussion are Jesus' own level of self-awareness of his divine character, when such divinization occurred, and whether Matthew's Gospel understands Jesus as divine. We will not argue this here, but believe that the New Testament makes clear that Jesus was pre-existent as God, that Jesus had an understanding of his divine nature, and that even the writer of Matthew's Gospel, on the basis of his presentation of Jesus, makes clear that he understood him as divine.

and spread throughout the world—as Acts says, from Jerusalem to all Judea and Samaria and to the ends of the earth (Acts 1:8).

A third observation, however, is that the one element of the church constituent from its inception was human membership. Jesus Christ instructed Peter to be the foundation of the church, and said that this humanly inclusive institution was to perform specified tasks. The word "church" in Greek is the same word that is used in a variety of ancient contexts to describe a group of people gathered for a particular purpose. The Christian church is exactly such an institution. It is a group of people gathered together to accomplish the purposes given to it by Jesus Christ. As a result of the evangelism of others, the church inevitably grew in members—in other words, membership in this church is composed simply of those who, like Peter and the other disciples, are followers of Jesus Christ. Human organizational structures and physical locations came about as a result of such growth. As the church grew, as Acts records, there inevitably needed to be a way of organizing such a vibrant and growing body, and so various organizational structures needed to be employed. As this group met together for its common purpose—that is, to worship God and his divine son Jesus Christ, the church's founder—it needed some place to do so, and so physical accommodations needed to be secured. However, these organizational and structural elements are only incidental to the true nature and purpose of the church—even though we often, though wrongly, attribute a higher status to them than is warranted or justified.

A fourth and final observation is that, as a result of this growth in the church, the concept of the church took on two important senses. One of them is that it still was the term that was used to refer to all of those people who identified themselves as followers of Jesus Christ and worshippers of the true God. These people, wherever they might be and however they might express their worship and in whatever way they governed themselves to accomplish these tasks, constituted the church as originally conceived by Jesus Christ, that is, the "church" inaugurated by him with its foundations on Peter and his confession of Jesus' true identity. However, there is a conceptual problem here. The problem is that it is impossible to think of such a church without actually thinking of the individual people who make it up, because, after all, it is the people that are the constituents of the church (Paul uses the term "body" to describe this element), not a building or an organizational structure. All of the constituent members of this inclusive body called the church are also individuals who are located in particular places and times. The church is by definition a "gathering," and the local gatherings of members take place on various days and in various places and at various times, as local personifications of the wider concept of the church. These are the congregations called by Paul "the church(es)" in places such as Galatia or Corinth or Thessalonica. The two concepts are inseparable. Just as it is impossible to think of the church as an institution without thinking of its individual members, it is impossible for an individual member of the church to exist without a physical expression of that church, in a local embodiment of the church or a congregation.

The conference that is represented in the papers presented in this volume addressed many of the issues surrounding this difficult and yet inspiring concept of the church. In this volume, we include two major types of essays. The first set comprises those by biblical and historical scholars concerned with the biblical and historical roots of the church. In the first essay, Michael Knowles treats the Gospels, including both the Synoptic Gospels and John's Gospel. Despite the Gospels being such a large amount of material, formal and explicit reference to the church is limited in this section of the New Testament. Nevertheless, as Knowles rightly notes, there is a wealth of indirect evidence that indicates important foundations for the church. He notes, first of all, that the church revolves around the name of Jesus. Jesus is the center of the church and it is worship of him around which the church revolves. In that sense, the church is distinctly "cruciform," that is, it reflects the cross—in other words, the redemptive work—of Christ. More than that, however, is that the church reflects a fictive kinship with God as the father. The family was a central institution in ancient society, including both Roman and Jewish society, and the church is in a major sense a surrogate family for its constituent members. The concept of the family became one of the important and dominant metaphors for relationships within the early Christian community. The reality of Christian existence, however, is that the church as family becomes more than simply a surrogate for biological family; the relationships have a deeper spiritual reality as well. It is this world that constitutes the church.

The second essay, by Stanley Porter, treats Paul's letters. In order to formulate a Pauline view of the church, Porter utilizes all thirteen letters attributed to Paul. In addressing the issue of normative versus occasional teaching, Porter attempts to define the major features of the Pauline church, and contends to be able to identify a significant number of such characteristics. These are eight in number, and run the gamut from individual to corporate belief and behavior. The distinctives of the Pauline church are that it is a community that confesses Jesus as Lord, a community built around faith, a community that is both universal and local in scope, an egalitarian community not given to accidental distinctions such as gender, race, or status, one that maintains practices of worship, including baptism, the Lord's supper, and communal expression, and is charismatic in its organization, one that demands ethical behavior, and a community that is evangelistic and eschatological in its outward look. As comprehensive as such a description attempts to be, it is also admittedly reductionistic, in that the Pauline church as a living spiritual organism is always going to be larger and more dynamic than any distillation can adequately convey.

The third essay, by Cynthia Westfall, argues that the Jerusalem church and the Jewish Christian mission were central in the birth and foundation of the early church and the writing of the New Testament. She takes the position that the book of James represents the Jewish-Christian church in Jerusalem before AD 70. Until the destruction of the temple, the Jerusalem church was the "authoritative center" of Christianity and the Jewish Christians in Jerusalem were a "party" of Judaism. The book of James illustrates the Jerusalem church's supervisory role of the extended Christian community, a zeal for the Law, and a close association with the synagogues. The Jewish-Christian mission planted churches all over the Diaspora. The Jewish-Christian corpus, identified as Matthew, John, James, Jude, 1 and 2 Peter, the Johannine Epistles, and Revelation, contributed eyewitness testimony and their interpretation of the Old Testament. The further Jewish-Christian interpretation of the Old Testament in Hebrews as well as the General Epistles made essential contributions to the identity of Jesus (Christology) and the identity of the church as the people of God (ecclesiology). Communities represented by the Gospel of John and Revelation represent the process of the parting of the ways of the church and synagogue by illustrating a growing alienation and eviction of the Jewish Christians from the synagogues, but still maintain the priority of the Jews in salvation history. This study changes the context in which we read the New Testament. It suggests that the model for the early church is Jewish-Christian, and that the "biblical model" of the New Testament church incorporates the kind of diversity illustrated by both the Gentile and Hebrew missions.

The final essay of this group is by the church historian, Gordon Heath. There are many who are heralding, and even gladly welcoming, the post-Christian era in which we are supposedly now living. Heath cautions the church to be careful what it seeks because of what has happened to churches that have encountered their own post-Christian persecution, and suffered extinction as the result. In tracing this account over 1,300 years and on three continents, Heath identifies a number of significant indigenous churches that have disappeared from history. These include the churches of the Nubians of Africa, who had not known previous occupation by Rome, the North African Christians formerly under Roman rule, the Moravian church of the tenth century, and the Nestorian church of central Asia, which spread to China. Similarly, there were once thriving churches in Asia Minor (now Turkey) and Japan. All of these churches have now disappeared, for a variety of interesting and often complex reasons—but disappeared they have. Some were eradicated because of military defeat, others because of persecution, still others on account of immigration, some because of genocide, and finally some because of conversion to other religions, such as Islam. Heath's timely warning is to be cautious what one wishes for, because there have been numerous places where the church under attack has become the church out of existence.

One of the major features of this Bingham conference, and now this volume, is that the papers not only were focused historically on the biblical origins and development of the church, from New Testament times to recent history, but also addressed a representative range of current ecclesial practices. We were fortunate to have those involved in a number of the major types of church practices as participants and contributors to the conference. The second group of essays is from this group.

The first chapter, by Lee Beach, addresses the possibilities opened to the postmodern church. Beach begins by recognizing the many and diverse challenges that the church today faces, such as perceived irrelevance, the fact that it is seen as a contributor to our problems, and its own failure to adjust to changes in culture. Rather than despairing, Beach sees this situation as presenting significant opportunities. One of these is the chance to address societal dislocation and the sense of rootlessness felt by many postmoderns. Postmoderns tend to reject grand metanarratives and focus upon the local. The church can gain their trust by living out locally some of its foundational beliefs, such as its emphasis upon relationships and the relational nature of God, embodying a Trinitarian theology that encompasses God as initiator, the Son as the incarnation of divine life, and the Holy Spirit as providing inspiration for contextualized ministry. The local church, Beach believes, can step in and constructively and relationally address the issues of postmodern society, with an appeal to the church's fundamental nature of witnessing to God at work in the world.

Along somewhat similar lines, Bruxy Cavey and Wendy Carrington-Phillips argue that the recent revival of the house church movement has much to offer in the kind of situation that Beach has described. Finding its roots in the New Testament itself, with the words and practice of Jesus and his earliest followers, Cavey, teaching pastor of The Meeting House, and Carrington-Phillips identify several features of the earliest house gatherings that are worth emulating, including a love ethic, meaningful relationships, and time spent with other individuals in mentoring. Acts 2:42 provides a template for such behavior, where four characteristics of the early house churches are identified. These include early followers of Christ meeting daily and devoting themselves to the apostles' teaching, fellowship with each other, the breaking of bread or eating together, and prayer. This is not, of course, a comprehensive and inclusive list of behavior or practices, but one that finds support and expansion throughout the rest of the New Testament, such as in the letters of Paul, and his emphasis upon forming a familial community. Nevertheless, such examples provide a model for the contemporary house church. The house church movement—which is growing in significance worldwide—includes those who gather in local groups of believers to engage in community, the study of the Bible, and evangelism. Comparison is often made to a family, because of the close and relational nature of such gatherings and groups. As with any family, however, there is potential for difficulties, in this case doctrinal deviation or insularity, and steps must be taken to ensure that such do not occur. Cavey and Carrington-Phillips suggest a model that combines home churches with larger central meetings to address these concerns. Recent efforts have shown that such a model can thrive as a model of church in reflection of the New Testament model.

By contrast, the megachurch is a phenomenon that has also shown surprising resilience and growth in recent times, to the point where there are now megachurches on several continents in addition to North America. In many ways similar to the other church models, as well as the New Testament evidence noted above, the megachurch looks to the New Testament as its basis. Michael Pawelke is the pastor of such a megachurch, and he notes that the origins of the church are in its being an organic community that has structure, leadership, and common practices. The book of Acts itself reflects the kind of situation that we find in the contemporary church when we note that in addition to small house churches there was also the church in Jerusalem that may have had up to 20,000 members, the first megachurch. Rather than seeing the situation as that of choosing between one or the other, Pawelke believes that there is a place for both small house churches and also large megachurches, and that these megachurches play an important function in the contemporary church scene, including the church scene in Canada. There has been much criticism of megachurches here and elsewhere, but Pawelke wishes to dispel many of these criticisms, by noting that these churches are often quite different from each other despite their common element of being large, with a diversity of programs and appeal. These churches are not all the same and engaged in the same kinds of practices for which they are often (too often?) criticized, but are instead individual churches, usually with significant resources to provide the kinds of programs that their parishioners both desire and need.

In the penultimate chapter of the book, Michael Goheen addresses the question of the missional church, or the church that is, as he describes it, a church with "missionary theology." That is, the church must be engaged in the mission of God in the world (the so-called *missio Dei*), and the church best functions when it discerns and then functions in harmony with the redemptive work of God in the world. Rather than missionary work being one of the works or efforts of the contemporary church, mission becomes the sole and governing work of the church. What this means for ecclesiology is that the church is chosen by God to do his work in the world. As a result, there is both discontinuity and continuity between the church and Old Testament Israel, as the church remains faithful to the promise made to Abraham in Genesis to create a nation. The nation came together in Exodus to either follow or depart from God's call. Those of God's people in the Old Testament who were obedient reflect his missional call. This call is brought to fruition, Goheen believes, in the arrival of Jesus Christ as the one who brings

God's kingdom, at least in part if not fully. Jesus is the fulfillment of the message of the Old Testament and its prophets, and his restored community of the new Israel is responsible for spreading the message of God's redemption to the world. The missional church—a people that are not geographically or ethnically limited—is this body that is now empowered to bring the good news to the ends of the earth.

Steven Studebaker concludes this volume with a reflective critique of the various contributions. As a theologian, he brings into comparison and contrast the biblical and practical papers. By doing so, he reinforces many of the findings of the contributors, but along the way he also asks a number of important and searching questions.

The format of this volume may in some ways be unusual in that it combines academic biblical studies with contemporary ecclesiological analysis—all with the design to shed light on this entity we call the church. However, as we traced the various threads during the course of the day of the conference (and as these threads can now be traced anew through the reading and contemplation of these essays) we came to realize that we were not talking about two dissimilar or unrelated entities. The church of the New Testament, though with one root and founding, was itself diverse in its manifestations. Similarly, the church of today is not a monolithic entity or organism, but a diverse and ever-changing and adapting body—this word being appropriate in light of one of the metaphors used in the New Testament (see 1 Cor 12:13 and following)—that is, in its best and proper manifestations, seeking to accomplish God's purposes in the world, of bringing men and women to him and providing living communities of fellow followers in which to live out and fulfill their redeemed lives. These two entities—the church ancient and modern—together form a trajectory that, if not forecasting, at least suggest the future of the church in contemporary society. We of course cannot predict what the society and hence the church of tomorrow will look like in its particulars, but we can be certain that there will be both continuity with the past and change as this divinely instituted yet also very human institution continues to respond to its mandate. Whereas we may at this time think that various manifestations of the church exhaust the permissible and possible New Testament embodiments, we would be surprised—were this conference to be repeated a number of years in the future—if there were not other, unanticipated models of what the church means that would arise and be functioning as Christ's proxies in the world.

BIBLIOGRAPHY

Porter, Stanley E. *Studies in the Greek New Testament*. New York: Lang, 1996.

1

The Least, the Lost, and the Last

Christ's Church in the Gospels

Michael P. Knowles

INTRODUCTION

The task of summarizing material from the canonical Gospels on the subject of the church that composed and received them faces at least two significant challenges. The first is that direct references to or descriptions of the church are exceedingly rare in these narratives, as a result of which most evidence must be inferred indirectly. But just as it is inappropriate to read the Gospels in a pre-critical manner, neither may the disciples serve as mere ciphers or symbols for communities to which the evangelists are presumed to have written.[1] The fact that the Gospels say so little about the church *per se*, focusing instead on discipleship and the relevance of Jesus, surely argues against the view that this material primarily reflects the priorities of a settled and structured community. In any event, we cannot know whether the Gospel accounts relate positively or negatively—as affirmation or correction—to the congregations that first received and transmitted them.[2] Yet it nonetheless seems self-evident that Jesus' words and example indeed provided the

---

1. A recent example tending in this direction is Coloe, *Household of God*, 194: "The Gospel text is the product of [the church's] experience and theological interpretation of the Jesus event."

2. Cf. Houlden, *Public Face*, 46.

model for the early church's identity and way of life, whatever degree of influence his teaching succeeded in exercising upon the lives of particular recipients. That each evangelist gives disproportionate attention to the twelve apostles suits such an approach since they, as representative disciples, might be expected to reflect more closely Jesus' intentions for the church.

A second difficulty emerges out of the distinctive literary and theological contexts within which Jesus' teaching now appears. Conflating—even comparing—texts drawn from John and the Synoptic accounts, or from different Synoptists, risks betraying a fundamental methodological principle of contemporary Gospel studies. Redaction criticism encourages a meticulous sensitivity to the distinctive features of each evangelist's literary and theological artistry. Yet the brevity of the present study allows room for little more than identifying common themes and principles—despite the risk of oversimplification and the necessary omission of much detail relevant to the communities behind specific accounts. At a minimum, delineating lines of continuity and contiguity between the four Gospel narratives will allow us to postulate a broad yet historically and theologically plausible series of characteristics for Christian communities of the first century.

With these cautions in mind, we will focus primarily on the kinds of people with whom Jesus interacts and on passages which, by describing the conditions of discipleship, may plausibly indicate the intended character of the post-resurrection church.

"IN MY NAME"

The first and most obvious characteristic of disciples is their close association and identification with Jesus, a premise reiterated via a wide range of pronouncements and metaphors. This dynamic emerges with particular clarity from Mark's account of the "Unknown Exorcist":

> John said to him, "Teacher, we saw someone casting out demons in your name [ἐν τῷ ὀνόματί σου], and we tried to stop him, because he was not following us." But Jesus said, "Do not stop him; for no one who does a deed of power in my name [ἐπὶ τῷ ὀνόματί μου] will be able soon afterward to speak evil of me. Whoever is not against us is for us. For truly I tell you, whoever gives you a cup of water to drink because you bear the name of Christ [ἐν ὀνόματι ὅτι Χριστοῦ ἐστε] will by no means lose their reward." (Mark 9:38–41; cf. Matt 10:42, Luke 9:49–50)

Here we observe, first, that followers are said (at least in the wording of the NRSV) to "bear the name of Christ," with his "name" indicating the essence of their Teacher's identity, and therefore theirs as well. Of similar import are the many passages in which disciples are variously said to trust (John 1:12; 2:23; 3:18), pray (John 14:13-14; 15:16; 16:23-24, 26), welcome others (Mark 9:37 *par.*; cf. John 13:20), gather (Matt 18:20), forsake family and friends (Matt 19:29), cast out demons (Luke 10:17), preach (Luke 24:47), make disciples (Matt 28:19), receive life (John 20:31), and in particular to be persecuted (Luke 21:12; cf. Matt 10:17-18; Mark 13:9; John 15:21) and hated (Mark 13:13 *par.*)— all in, through, or on account of the "name" of Jesus.³ In this respect they imitate Jesus himself, whom they acclaim as coming ἐν ὀνόματι κυρίου (Mark 11:9 *par.* // John 12:13; cf. Q 13:35; John 5:43; 10:25), since the latter title can refer equally to God or to God's messianic emissary. Even deceivers and false disciples know that appeal to the messianic name is a distinguishing mark of Jesus' followers (Mark 13:6 *par.*), so much so that discernment of authentic discipleship must in some cases await the day of judgement (Matt 7:22-23).

Notwithstanding the degree of uncertainty that Mark's scenario introduces, Jesus' response to the disciples' complaint suggests that the identification of disciples with their teacher is primarily concrete and practical rather than nominal or a matter of mere profession. In this regard the episode at hand is especially ironic, since the "unknown exorcist" succeeds in his appeal to Jesus' name where the disciples themselves have only recently failed (Mark 9:17-19 *par.*). Nonetheless, the principle still holds: "the tree is known by its fruit" (Matt 12:33; cf. Matt 7:16-20; Luke 6:43-44). Indeed, so close is this identification that Jesus assures his followers (although the saying is formulated differently in Q and John), "Whoever welcomes you welcomes me, and whoever welcomes me welcomes the one who sent me" (Q 10:16 // John 13:20).

Whereas Jesus' first call is for the twelve "to be with him" (Mark 3:14), so that discipleship is expressed by literally "following" in his footsteps (e.g., Mark 1:17-20 *par.* // John 1:43; Mark 2:14 *par.*; Q 9:57-62; 14:27),⁴ subsequent expressions of allegiance will have been character-

---

3. Here and subsequently, the shorthand form of reference "Mark 9:37 *par.*" will indicate Markan tradition with significant parallels in Matthew and Luke, while "Q 10:16," etc., will designate putative Q material via Lukan verse numbering.

4. So (with reference to Mark) Houlden, *Public Face*, 48-49.

ized instead by close adherence to his teaching (Q 6:47–49; Matt 28:20; John 14:15, 21–24; 15:10, 14). John's Gospel expresses this principle in terms of direct and intentional dependence: "Just as the branch cannot bear fruit by itself unless it abides in the vine, neither can you unless you abide in me. I am the vine, you are the branches" (John 15:4–5). Nor are we to think of Jesus as somehow "absent" from the post-resurrection church, for the evangelists clearly understand matters in quite the opposite sense. In Matthew's Gospel the themes of obedience and presence are interconnected, as Jesus' concluding instructions indicate: "Make disciples of all nations . . . teaching them to obey everything that I have commanded you. And remember, I am with you always, to the end of the age" (Matt 28:19–20; cf. 18:20).[5] The same conviction of Jesus' risen presence at the gathering of his followers is also operative—albeit implicitly and notwithstanding numerous texts that speak of Jesus' departure or foretell the return of an "absent" master (e.g., Mark 13:29–37; Matt 24:42–51; 25:14–30; Luke 12:35–48)—in post-resurrection narratives that suggest Jesus' participation in the table fellowship of the Christian community.[6]

Ongoing association with Jesus takes the form not only of direct obedience but also of conscious and consistent imitation, suggesting that the life and ministry of the Christian church will be essentially Christomorphic, "Christ-shaped." This premise is evident, for instance, in the Q saying behind Luke 6:40 ("A disciple is not above his teacher, but everyone when he is fully taught will be like his teacher" [RSV]) and Matt 10:25a ("It is enough for the disciple to be like the teacher, and the servant like his master" [RSV]). Accordingly, just as Jesus' mission is impelled by the Spirit of God (e.g., Mark 1:10, 12 *par*.; John 1:32–33), so also is the teaching and testimony of his disciples (e.g., Mark 13:11 *par*.; John 7:39; 14:26; 16:23). More concretely, the ministries of Christ and church alike are characterized by their respective proclamations of the "kingdom of God/heaven" (Mark 1:14 *par*. with Matt 10:7 // Luke 9:2), particularly as expressed in signs of God's saving intervention such as healing and exorcism (Mark 3:14; 6:7 *par*.; 6:13). We have already observed that, at least in Mark and Matthew, the disciples are noted more for their failure in this regard than for their spiritual authority or

---

5. Hagner, "Holiness and Ecclesiology," 51.

6. So Cullmann, *Early Christian Worship*, 14–18, recalling especially Luke 24:30, 35, 42; John 21:12–13; Acts 1:4; 10:40; cf. Rev 3:20.

abilities. The Matthean disciples are never shown actually carrying out these instructions, while their Markan counterparts, notwithstanding some initial success (Mark 6:12–13), soon afterward fail spectacularly (Mark 9:17–19 *par.*). Yet "deeds of power" continue to be manifested in the post-resurrection community (so Matt 7:22, together with numerous instances from the Book of Acts), indicating that the church of the New Testament era accepted ongoing responsibility for proclaiming and manifesting the divine reign after the manner of their master. Conversely, the suffering and rejection of the disciples also reflects that of their Lord (Mark 13:9–13 *par.*; Q 11:49; John 15:18–21), even to the point that, in Q, Jesus warns they will have to shoulder the same cross that is the instrument of his own death (Q 14:27; cf. John 19:17; *pace* Mark 15:20b–21 *par.*). Finally, Jesus commissions the disciples for post-resurrection ministry and mission in terms that directly echo his own divine mandate. This dynamic is most succinctly expressed in John 20:21: "As the Father has sent me, so I send you" (cf. 17:18, etc.). In the Synoptic tradition Jesus likewise speaks of having been "sent" (Mark 9:37 // Luke 9:48 // John 13:20; cf. 12:44–45; Matt 10:40; 15:24; Luke 4:18, 43), even as he sends out his own followers in turn (Mark 3:14; 6:7 *par.*; Q[?] 10:3; Luke 10:1, cf. 11:49; Matt 23:34). Accordingly, neither master nor disciples are theologically self-motivated or self-authenticating: each in turn derives their mission and—above all—authority from the "Lord" who thus commands them (cf. Mark 6:7; 11:27–33 *par.*; Matt 28:18).

"FATHERHOOD" AND FICTIVE KINSHIP

In terms of piety and devotion—whether the inspiration for this derives from Jesus himself (Q 10:21–22) or from τὸ πνεῦμα τοῦ πατρός (e.g., Matt 10:20; cf. John 14:26; 15:26)—disciples imitate their master's address to God as αββα ὁ πατήρ (Mark 14:36; cf. Matt 26:39; Luke 22:42; John 12:27–28), especially so in the course of prayer (Q 11:2, 13).[7] This key devotional category and term of address appears to have shaped both the practical discipline and the community ethos of the early church. Both premises are illustrated by the Triple Tradition pericope concerning Jesus' true kindred:

> Then his mother and his brothers came; and standing outside, they sent to him and called him. A crowd was sitting around him;

---

7. This closely parallels the teaching of Paul (Rom 8:15; Gal 4:6).

and they said to him, "Your mother and your brothers and sisters are outside, asking for you." And he replied, "Who are my mother and my brothers?" And looking at those who sat around him, he said, "Here are my mother and my brothers! Whoever does the will of God is my brother and sister and mother." (Mark 3:31–35 par.)[8]

If this passage is indeed reflective of conditions in the early church (notwithstanding the influence of competing structures and models), it suggests a social entity organized around theological convictions expressed in terms of common, concrete behaviors ("whoever *does the will* of God"). Even clearer in this regard is Matt 5:48 // Luke 6:36: "Be perfect/merciful, just as your [heavenly] Father is perfect/merciful." Implicit also in Mark 3 is Jesus' role as authoritative interpreter and executor of the divine will, for it is in relation to him that affiliation must be understood ("*my* brother and sister and mother"). Matthew fills out the remaining dimensions of this fictive kinship structure by naming the one missing relationship: "whoever does the will *of my Father* in heaven" (Matt 12:50, for Mark's "the will of God").[9] Not only is this a characteristic expression of Jesus in Q and Johannine traditions, the Gospel narratives portray Jesus describing God to his followers as, for instance, "*your* Father in heaven" (Mark 11:25 // Matt 6:14–15; similarly Q 11:13, and frequently), or, in the unmistakable language of John 20:17, as "my Father and your Father . . . my God and your God" (cf. Matt 10:29, "your Father," with 10:32, "my Father").[10]

Incidentally, the primacy of this theological construct among the community of Jesus' followers likely accounts for a notable omission in his explanation, from Mark 10:29–30, of the consolations that compensate for the cost of discipleship:

> Truly I tell you, there is no one who has left house or brothers or sisters or mother or father or children or fields, for my sake and

---

8. Hagner's assertion ("Holiness and Ecclesiology," 52) that in his adaptation of this tradition, "Matthew alone among the Synoptics specifies the 'disciples,'" is potentially misleading, for while it is true that the actual word appears only in Matthew, the intended meaning is no less obvious in Mark and Luke.

9. Although appearing too late for detailed consideration here, this theme is explored more fully by Pattarumadathil, *Your Father in Heaven*.

10. Since Jesus' opponents in John's Gospel also claim divine filiation, the metaphor of spiritual paternity is presumably a key point of community identity, and therefore also of inter-communal conflict (John 8:19, 37–47).

for the sake of the good news who will not receive a hundred-fold now in this age—houses, brothers and sisters, mothers and children, and fields, with persecutions—and in the age to come eternal life.

The one recompense they will *not* receive is "fathers," for as the Matthean Jesus elsewhere commands, "Call no one your father on earth, for you [already] have one Father—the one in heaven" (Matt 23:9). So too, he insists, πάντες δὲ ὑμεῖς ἀδελφοί ἐστε (Matt 23:8). Although this particular saying is unique to Matthew, ἀδελφός refers to Jesus' followers elsewhere in Synoptic material, especially in Q (6:41–42; 17:3; cf. Matt 5:22–24). Of particular interest is the fact that in Matthew's context, the Q term ἀδελφός is unmistakably associated with ἐκκλησία, "assembly, congregation, church" (Matt 18:17 [*bis*]; cf. 18:15b, 21, 35). Conversely, its feminine counterpart ἀδελφή, "sister," occurs nowhere else with this sense in the Gospels (notwithstanding Rom 16:1; 1 Cor 7:15; 9:5; Phlm 2; James 2:15, etc.), making its attribution to Jesus all the more distinctive.

As implied already in the passage from Mark 3, the community that forms around Jesus defines its kinship structures separately from—even in opposition to—the obligations of blood or marital relationships, according to Q.[11] We may infer as much from Jesus' warning, even more radical within a social matrix much more tight-knit in its own day than in ours:

> For I have come to set a man against his father, and a daughter against her mother, and a daughter-in-law against her mother-in-law; and one's foes will be members of one's own household. Whoever loves father or mother more than me is not worthy of me; and whoever loves son or daughter more than me is not worthy of me . . . (Matt 10:35–37; cf. Luke 12:52–53; 14:26)

This radical reorientation is graphically illustrated by Jesus' response to the would-be disciple who sought leave to bury his father. Whether or not the man's father is already deceased, the answer he receives is uncompromising in the extreme: "Follow me, and let the dead bury their own dead" (Q 9:60). Yet if the relativizing or rejection of family ties seems a harsh requirement for discipleship, it will be more than reciprocated, according to Synoptic tradition, by mortal opposition from kith and kin:

---

11. Kee, *People of God*, 60.

> Brother will betray brother to death, and a father his child, and children will rise against parents and have them put to death. (Mark 13:12 *par.*)

Even if the extent to which this bleak prospect actually materialized remains uncertain, neither the reaction of Jesus' family—"they went out to seize him" (Mark 3:21)—nor Jesus' repudiation of them in turn—"A prophet is not without honor, except in his own country, and among his own kin, *and in his own house*" (RSV; Mark 6:4 // Matt 13:57)—would have encouraged a more positive estimation of blood kinship on the part of later followers.

Other images and metaphors contribute to the religious identity and social cohesion of the early church. Primary among these, of course, is Jesus' provocative choice of twelve disciples (Mark 3:14 *par.*; John 6:67–71) to symbolize a new or renewed covenant community with strong eschatological overtones (e.g., Q 22:30, "You will sit on [twelve] thrones judging the twelve tribes of Israel"). That this remained an operative structural symbol in the post-resurrection era, at least among the Jerusalem believers, is indicated by that church's haste in choosing a disciple to assume the responsibility abandoned by Judas (Acts 1:15–26).[12] Along the same lines, just as the symbolism of twelve apostles implies a certain social cohesion around the concept of the church as a new Israel, so—albeit less obviously—does shepherding imagery, given the prominence of this motif in Hebrew Scripture.[13] Synoptic material—e.g., Mark 14:27 *par.* ("I will strike the shepherd and the sheep will be scattered" [citing Zech 13:7]); Q 10:3 ("sheep/lambs amidst wolves"); Luke 12:32 ("little flock"); or the parables of the lost sheep (Q 15:4–7) and of the sheep and goats (Matt 25:31–46)—employs such language in general terms to describe the community of the faithful. The fourth Gospel, by contrast, applies the metaphors of sheep and shepherd directly to the life of the future church: "I have other sheep that do not belong to this fold," declares Jesus; "I must bring them also, and they will listen to my

---

12. Further afield, cf. (variously) Gal 6:16; James 1:1; Rev 7:4–8; 21:12.

13. The identification of God's people as a "flock" (and its leaders as shepherds) is part of the common stock of biblical imagery: e.g., Ps 77:20; 78:52; 79:13; 80:1; 95:7; 100:3; Jer 23:1–4; 31:10; Ezek 34:2–10; Mic 2:12, and frequently elsewhere. Compare Jesus' use of this metaphor: "the lost sheep *of the house of Israel*" (Matt 10:6; 15:24; cf. 2:6, citing 2 Sam 5:2 = 1 Chron 11:2).

voice. So there will be one flock, one shepherd" (John 10:16; cf. 10:1–15, 26–27; 21:15–17).

Whichever of these metaphors we emphasize—fictive kinship moderated by God as "Father," Jesus' followers as "new" Israel, and/or the Christian community as Jesus' "flock"—it appears that, notwithstanding the unavoidable particulars of specific social and cultural contexts, the identity of the church in the Gospels is fundamentally theological and Christocentric in character: at least as portrayed by the evangelists, the church's theological character gives rise to its social identity, and not *vice versa*.

BOUNDARY ISSUES: OPEN OR CLOSED?

The episode of the "Unknown Exorcist" introduces another puzzle. In Mark 9:40 (and similarly, Luke 9:50), Jesus explains to the disciples that they must not impede whoever performs works of power in his name (no matter what their formal affiliation) because "Whoever is not against us is for us." From this it would be reasonable to infer that whatever community preserved the saying did not sense a need for definitive—much less defensive—boundaries: absence of opposition could be construed as tacit affirmation. Reconciling this statement with Jesus' warning, elsewhere in the same Gospel, that they will be "hated by all [ὑπὸ πάντων]" (Mark 13:13) is only the first difficulty to be faced. More pressing and precise is the problem of the Q logion, "Whoever is not with me is against me, and whoever does not gather with me scatters" (Q 11:23).[14] On any reading, Mark's ὃς γὰρ οὐκ ἔστιν καθ' ἡμῶν, ὑπὲρ ἡμῶν ἐστιν and Q's ὁ μὴ ὢν μετ' ἐμοῦ κατ' ἐμοῦ ἐστιν express diametrically opposite sentiments and social orientations. Aside from competing arguments for the authenticity or inauthenticity of one or the other version, that the two sayings are addressed to committed followers and decided enemies, respectively, provides one possible explanation.[15] Yet the real difficulty for our purposes lies in trying to imagine what

---

14. The evidence of this saying qualifies Kee's otherwise helpful observation that "A pervasive feature of the image of the community in the Q tradition is the inclusiveness of [its] membership, in sharp contrast to the careful—even forceful—delineation of boundaries of the covenant people in the Qumran and Pharisaic traditions, and later in the rabbinic documents of the second and subsequent centuries C.E." (Kee, *People of God*, 60–61).

15. So Baltensweiler, "Bemerkungen zu Mk 9,40 und Lk 9,50," 131–32.

either or both would have meant for the life of the post-resurrection community.

As noted already, evidence of strong opposition from rival religious communities, implying if not encouraging a reciprocal antagonism on the part of early Christians, is not hard to come by in Gospel tradition. Characteristic of John's Gospel, for example, is a radical dichotomy between the followers of Jesus and those who are of "the world," encapsulated in the question posed by Judas, "Lord, how is it that you will reveal yourself to us, and not *to the world* [τῷ κόσμῳ]?" (John 14:22); his subsequent explanation, "Because you do not belong to the world . . . the world hates you" (John 16:19), or the words of Jesus' prayer, "They do not belong to the world, just as I do not belong to the world" (John 17:16). Albeit less frequent, similar language in Synoptic material expresses an equally explicit dualism (Mark 4:19 *par*.; 8:36 *par*.; Q 4:5; Luke 12:30). No more subtle is the distinction Jesus draws between the disciples as recipients of revelation, on the one hand, and unenlightened outsiders on the other: "To you has been given the secret of the kingdom of God, but for those outside, everything comes in parables" (Mark 4:11 *par*.; similarly Mark 4:33–34 // Matt 13:34). Matthew's narrative takes these words literally, clearly distinguishing between the parabolic teaching Jesus utters in the open air, seated by the sea, and the explanation he offers only to disciples once he is back inside the house from which he first emerged (Matt 13:1, 36). Matthew is only making explicit what Mark implies, for the immediate antecedent to the parables of the kingdom in both accounts is the episode in which Jesus' human family likewise stands "outside [ἔξω]" and sends for him (Mark 3:31–32 *par*.), only to have Jesus respond by disowning them in favor of his followers (Mark 3:33–35).[16]

The opposition and social dislocation that Jesus both models and foretells makes any opposite inclination all the more momentous: "Whoever is not against us is for us." Openness to those outside the circle of confirmed disciples is elsewhere expressed in terms of willingness both to give to and to receive from those whose allegiance to the Messiah is, at best, less clear or certain than the disciples' own. Jesus himself consistently models such generosity in his ministry of healing,

---

16. The contrast is all the more striking if we understand Jesus (from Mark 3:20, καὶ ἔρχεται εἰς οἶκον) to be inside his own home, with his mother and siblings standing outside.

and especially in feeding both the multitudes at large (Mark 6:32–44 // John 6:1–15; Mark 8:1–10 *par.*) and his own betrayer in particular (Mark 14:20 // John 13:26). A similar openness and generosity is to undergird the disciples' subsequent ministries of healing and deliverance (Mark 3:14–15; 6:6 *par.*), a premise Matthew makes explicit in Jesus' monitory aphorism, δωρεὰν ἐλάβετε, δωρεὰν δότε (Matt 10:8b). In no less obvious terms, the parable of the Good Samaritan (Luke 10:29–37) advocates radical "compassion" (Luke 10:33), expressed in the form of hospitality towards ethnic rivals and religious enemies: "Jesus said to them, 'Go and do likewise'" (Luke 10:37). Indeed, Jesus imposes on his followers an absolute obligation to forgive those who oppose and injure them, just as they themselves have been forgiven (Mark 11:25 *par.*; Q 6:27–36; Matt 18:21–35, etc.).

Given Jesus' promise of universal hatred and rejection (so also Q 12:2–9, 51–53; 14:25–27, etc.), perhaps the most remarkable feature of the disciples' mission is not their responsibility for offering hospitality, but their obligation to receive it. The Synoptic Evangelists, at least, concur in reporting various forms of Jesus' command that his missionary followers are to take with them no provisions of any sort (Mark 6:8–11 *par.*). Rather, they must depend on the charity of any who may invite them into their homes. Knowing from the outset that they will be widely opposed, they must not only remain open to the possibility of a generous welcome, but rely on it absolutely. That such instructions reflect theological priorities and adverse social conditions relevant to the life of the early church seems at least as likely as postulating here a series of coded references to "safe houses" that will shelter itinerant evangelists at some later stage of ecclesiastical development.[17]

The evidence outlined above appears sharply contradictory. The social and political circumstances of a difficult discipleship require firm social boundaries: unmistakable lines of demarcation between "insiders" and "outsiders." Yet Jesus commands both generosity and openness to non-adherents, illustrating these characteristics in his own conduct. The circle of his followers is, paradoxically, both radically open and firmly closed; vulnerable and generous yet demanding and distinctive. Such characteristics serve, presumably, as clues to the intended origin and nature of the church. Although it is necessarily a social entity of sorts, the community's paradoxical character reflects something more

---

17. As proposed by Robinson, "From Safe House to House Church."

than social or sociological principles alone, as Jesus—in a passage from Q that we have cited already—indicates by reminding the disciples of the proper source and referent for their identity and conduct alike:

> Love your enemies, do good, and lend, expecting nothing in return. Your reward will be great, and you will be *sons of the Most High*; for he is kind to the ungrateful and the wicked. Be merciful, *just as your Father is merciful.* (Luke 6:35–36 // Matt 5:44–48)

Just as the people of Israel are repeatedly commanded, "Be holy, for I the Lord your God am holy" (Lev 19:2; cf. 11:44–45; 20:26; 21:8, etc.), so Jesus insists that a primary characteristic of his followers must be their intentional imitation and reflection of the generous character of God (cf. Matt 5:9, 45).

While his circle of followers identifies with Jesus in name and deed, in the opprobrium they suffer and the ministry they perform, Jesus himself orients their identity and conduct toward God. They constitute a fictive kinship group that calls on God as "Father," and by their actions live out that claim of spiritual filiation by virtue of an intentional *imitatio dei*. This key principle of imitating the character and characteristics of God explains Jesus'—and the disciples'—persistent association with and attention to those whom we may alliteratively designate the "least," the "lost," and the "last."

THE LEAST, THE LOST, AND THE LAST

Jesus' association not only with the identifiably sinful but also the socially marginalized is so characteristic of him as to be proverbial. He consistently demonstrates concern for people like lepers (Mark 1:40–45 *par.*; Luke 17:12), demoniacs (Mark 1:32–34; 5:1–20; 7:24–30 *par.*, etc.), prostitutes (Matt 21:31–32; cf. Luke 7:37–39), a ritually unclean woman (Mark 5:24–34 *par.*), and impoverished widows (Mark 12:41–44 // Luke 21:1–4; Luke 7:12–15), even composing a parable with a wronged and needy widow as its main character (Luke 18:1–7). Jesus' summary of his ministry to the followers of John the Baptist is especially telling: "the blind receive their sight, the lame walk, the lepers are cleansed, the deaf hear, the dead are raised, the poor have good news brought to them" (Q 7:22). Likewise he heals (Mark 5:21–23, 38–43; 7:25–30; 9:17–27 *par.*; John 4:46b–54) and welcomes little children (παιδία) in particular (Mark 10:13–16 *par.*), those whose humility models the qualities required for submission to the reign of God: "Unless you become as little children [παιδία], you will never enter the kingdom of heaven" (Matt 18:3–4).[18]

Similar principles apparently govern his choice of followers, whom he describes as νήπιοι, "infants":

> I thank you, Father, Lord of heaven and earth, because you have hidden these things from the wise and the intelligent and have revealed them to infants; yes, Father, for such was your gracious will. (Luke 10:21 // Matt 11:25–26)

That such language indeed refers to their lowly status is confirmed by his subsequent address to the disciples, a Q saying that (in Luke) follows immediately (although Matthew includes it elsewhere):

> Blessed are the eyes that see what you see! For I tell you that many prophets and kings desired to see what you see, but did not see it, and to hear what you hear, but did not hear it. (Luke 10:23–24 // Matt 13:16–17)

The disciples are, after all, the very antithesis of the great, the powerful, and the holy. The passage that follows in Matthew's narrative sequence is no less relevant, for as Donald Hagner explains, it announces Jesus' invitation to just this sort of disciple:

> The invitation of 11:28–30 is applicable to all who would be disciples of Jesus—not just the twelve, not just the disciples in Matthew's church, but all the disciples of Jesus throughout the history of the church: "Come to me, all who labor and are heavy laden, and I will give you rest. Take my yoke upon you, and learn from me; for I am gentle and lowly in heart, and you will find rest for your souls. For my yoke is easy and my burden is light."[19]

Jesus refers to his followers by means of diminutives expressive of this insignificance and low social status: "children" (τέκνα, Mark 20:24), "little children" (τεκνία, John 13:33; παιδία, John 21:5), or "little flock" (μικρὸν ποίμνιον, Luke 12:32). Likewise he speaks of them in the third person as οἱ μίκροι, "little ones" (Mark 9:42 *par.*; Matt 10:42; 18:10, 14;

---

18. "The point, of course, is not that children are self-consciously humble but that they are, as part of society at large, without much status or position" (Davies and Allison, *Matthew*, 2:757). Here we may perhaps be justified in reading semantic force in the use of the diminutive, παιδίον ("*little* child"), in place of παῖς.

19. Hagner, "Holiness and Ecclesiology," 51–52.

Luke 17:2); even as the eschatological king in Matthew's parable of the sheep and goats refers to crypto-disciples as "the least" or "the least of these my brothers" (Matt 25:40, 45). Jesus' explanation in Mark 9:37 and parallels aptly captures this dynamic, using a little child (παιδίον) as its point of reference: "Whoever welcomes one such child in my name welcomes me, and whoever welcomes me welcomes not me but the one who sent me." Luke 9:48 adds: "for the least among all of you is the greatest" (cf. Matt 18:4). Of similar import is the Q aphorism, "All who exalt themselves will be humbled, and those who humble themselves will be exalted" (Q 14:11; 18:14b; cf. Luke 1:52), as is the Matthean beatitude, "Blessed are the meek [οἱ πραεῖς]" (Matt 5:5). We have already seen how the Matthean Jesus describes himself in similar terms—πραΰς εἰμι καὶ ταπεινὸς τῇ καρδίᾳ (11:29)—an assessment the evangelist confirms by adding a quotation from LXX Zech 9:9 ("*humble* and mounted on an ass") to interpret Jesus' entry into Jerusalem (Matt 21:5).

Jesus addresses practical instructions to his followers (together with, presumably, the post-resurrection church) as those who are already in—or must now adopt—a position of powerlessness, and thus must submit to reviling and mistreatment:

> Bless those who curse you, pray for those who abuse you. If anyone strikes you on the cheek, offer the other also; and from anyone who takes away your coat do not withhold even your shirt. (Luke 6:28–29 // Matt 5:39, 44)

Cursing, assault, and robbery appear to be realistic, rather than hypothetical possibilities. The same expectation is especially prominent in Luke's formulation of the Beatitudes:

> Blessed are you who are poor . . .
> Blessed are you who are hungry now . . .
> Blessed are you who weep now . . .
> Blessed are you when people hate you, and when they exclude you, revile you, and defame you on account of the Son of Man
> . . . (Luke 6:20–22)

Luke's judicious use of νῦν ("now") and ὅταν ("when") again bespeaks a series of actual, factual conditions.[20] Most telling of all—and central to all four Gospels—is the nature of Jesus' death, since crucifixion was the most humiliating form of execution in current practice, a despicable fate

---

20. Cf. Kee, *People of God*, 59–60.

reserved for criminals, traitors, and slaves.[21] Nor, therefore, should the terrible cost and difficulty of Jesus' call for disciples to deny themselves and take up crosses of their own (Mark 8:34 *par.*) be underestimated. Once we rightly question our own preference for reading this challenge metaphorically, no single saying of Jesus more clearly delineates the shame, scandal, and utter impotence attached to Christian discipleship. Matthew's wording of a Q saying to similar effect is especially ironic: "Whoever does not take up their cross and follow me is not worthy [ἄξιος] of me" (Matt 10:38 // Luke 14:27). By any measure, Jesus' estimation of "worth" runs directly counter to that of Mediterranean culture in general: following him entails not "worth" so much as absolute lack of it. The life *and* death of Jesus are thus characterized by humility and humiliation, slurs that taint disciples by association even should they balk at his command to follow suit.

Since there is, as noted already, a universal consensus that Jesus welcomed the morally unfit and those who were socially as well as religiously outcast, it is difficult to imagine that this would not have continued to be one of the chief characteristics of the earliest Christian community. The evangelists are not shy about reporting the dubious character of certain disciples, and the controversy to which it gave rise:

> When the scribes of the Pharisees saw that he was eating with sinners and tax collectors, they said to his disciples, "Why does he eat with tax collectors and sinners?" When Jesus heard this, he said to them, "Those who are well have no need of a physician, but those who are sick; I have come to call not the righteous but sinners." (Mark 2:16–17 *par.*)[22]

More caustic is the rebuke, reported by Q 7:34, "Behold, a glutton and a drunkard, a friend of tax collectors and sinners!" (RSV), whose

---

21. So Hengel, *Crucifixion*, 6–7: "to believe that the one pre-existent Son of the one true God, the mediator at the creation and the redeemer of the world, had appeared in very recent times in out-of-the-way Galilee as a member of the obscure people of the Jews, and even worse, had died the death of a common criminal on the cross, could only be regarded as a sign of madness. The real gods of Greece and Rome could be distinguished from mortal men by the very fact that they were *immortal*—they had absolutely nothing in common with the cross as a sign of shame (*aischunē*) (Hebrews 12:2), the infamous stake (*infamis stipes*), the 'barren' (*infelix lignum*) or 'criminal wood' (*panourgikon xulon*), the 'terrible cross' (*maxima mala crux*) of the slaves of Plautus, and thus of the one who, in the words of Celsus, was 'bound in the most ignominious fashion' and 'executed in a shameful way.'"

22. On this passage see further Brower, "The Holy One," 66.

invocation of Deut 21:20 implies that Jesus' association with reprobates merits punishment by death.[23] Remarkably, Jesus responds to this challenge by making it a key point of contention with his contemporaries. Matthew records the master's assessment of his opponents—"Truly I tell you, the tax collectors and the prostitutes are going into the kingdom of God ahead of you" (Matt 21:31)—while Luke reports the other side of the debate: "the Pharisees and the scribes were grumbling and saying, 'This fellow welcomes sinners and eats with them'" (Luke 15:2; cf. 7:39). In the latter context, the complaint serves to introduce that Gospel's best known triad of parables, concerning a sheep, a coin, and a son, each said to have been "lost" (Luke 15:4, 6, 9, 24, 32). Or as Jesus observes regarding Zacchaeus (another dubious table companion), "The Son of Man came to seek out and to save the *lost*" (Luke 19:9). While each of these sayings is unique to Luke, they nonetheless correspond to the Matthean conviction that Jesus and his disciples are sent (at least initially) only to "the *lost* sheep of the house of Israel" (Matt 10:6, 15:24).

That such conditions apply equally to the later church is implied by Matthew's parables of the wheat and weeds (Matt 13:24–30, 36–43) and of the fisherman's net (Matt 13:47–50). Both imply that the earthly manifestation of "the kingdom of heaven" includes both "good" and "bad"; the "righteous" on the one hand and "sin and . . . evil-doers" on the other. Only "at the close of the age" will these be sorted apart: in the meantime, the church's openness to sinners necessitates a complex and demanding sort of discernment. This is precisely the balance of obligations envisaged by Matthew's formulation of the parable of the marriage feast (another eschatological metaphor). Whereas Luke's version has the servants inviting "the poor, the crippled, the blind, and the lame" (Luke 14:21), Matthew 22:10 depicts the servants gathering "all whom they found," πονηρούς τε καὶ ἀγαθούς, "bad *and* good." Sinners, it would seem, are welcome at the banquet table. Even so, invitation alone does not obviate the ultimate requirements of God's righteousness, as the subsequent expulsion of at least one guest seems to imply (Matt 22:11–14).[24]

---

23. Cf. Kee, *People of God*, 57–58, 61.

24. Insofar as Paul wrestles with a similar difficulty in 1 Cor 6:9–11, the concern Matthew addresses is evidently more than theoretical. The complementary aspects of this dynamic may be clarified by appeal to Sanders's illuminating distinction between "getting in" and "staying in" (*Paul and Palestinian Judaism*, 17). While other treatments of New Testament ecclesiology (e.g., the essays in Brower and Johnson, *Holiness and Ecclesiology*), focus primarily on conditions for "staying in" as descriptive of the early

One issue that seems largely resolved by the time the Gospels were composed—in Greek!—is that of Gentile inclusion. Matthew's Jesus initially represents a traditional Jewish outlook, using "Gentile" (ἐθνικός) as a term of disparagement (Matt 5:47; 6:7; 18:17; cf. 6:32), and forbidding ministry to non-Jews (Matt 10:5-6; 15:4). Yet, in an encounter drawn from Mark, Jesus contravenes his own principles, as a Canaanite woman convinces him to heal her daughter (Matt 15:21-28 // Mark 7:2-30). From Q, similarly, comes Jesus' praise of a centurion's faith and his healing of the man's servant (Q 7:1-10; cf. John 4:46-54). All four Gospels speak in one form or another of testimony to and by these religious outsiders, whether in the words of Simeon from Luke 2:32, Matthew's creative citation of Isaiah (Matt 4:14-16 of Isa 9:1-2; Matt 12:18-21 of Isa 42:1-4), John's record of how "some Greeks" approached Jesus in Jerusalem (John 12:20-21), or, supremely, the words of the centurion at the cross (Mark 15:39 *par.*).[25]

From a different perspective, Jesus' many acts of healing can be taken to imply openness to those who are tainted by sin, at least for readers and onlookers who share the popular theodicy reported by John: "His disciples asked him, 'Rabbi, who sinned, this man or his parents, that he was born blind?'" (John 9:2; cf. 9:24). If, with such a view, all physical affliction is a direct recompense for personal wrong-doing, then every healing or deliverance is of essentially ethical and soteriological significance.

While our review of the metaphor of being "lost" illustrates its narrower social and moral dimensions, such language equally describes the broader orientation required for discipleship as a whole, although still implying the requirement of humility and an abandonment of the presumption of religious or soteriological self-determination. In this case, three closely similar proverbs concerning "lostness" as a condition of Christian discipleship appear variously in the triple tradition ("For whoever would save his life will lose [ἀπολέσει] it; and whoever loses [ἀπολέσει] his life for my sake and the Gospel's will save it"; Mark 8:35 *par.*); in Q (so Matt 10:39: "He who finds his life will lose

---

church, this study places greater emphasis on conditions for "getting in" and their implications for Christian community.

25. To this corresponds, in John, the multilingual *titulus* that proclaims Jesus' true identity to all nations (John 19:19-22; cf. Mark 15:26). The inclusion of Gentiles and other marginalized groups is especially prominent in Luke, on which see Kee, *People of God*, 187-92.

[ἀπολέσει] it, and he who loses [ὁ ἀπολέσας] it for my sake will find it"; cf. Luke 17:33); and in the Gospel of John ("He who loves his life loses [ἀπολλύει] it, and he who hates his life in this world will keep it for eternal life"; John 12:25). Most clearly by virtue of John's reference to "eternal life," being not only "least" but also "lost" appears here as an enduring characteristic of Jesus' followers.

Most compelling in this regard, not least by virtue of its importance for subsequent Christian practice, is the prayer that Jesus taught his disciples. We may note, first of all, its structural centrality within Matthew's "Sermon on the Mount," which can only indicate its significance for the Evangelist, and likely for his readership as well.[26] In particular, Jesus instructs them to ask the Father, "Do not put us to the test" (Q 11:4). Against an understanding of religious experience that expects God to assay and thus prove the fidelity of the righteous, this petition seeks to be excused such an exercise, on the simple grounds that the petitioners have no fidelity to demonstrate, and so must be admitted on some other basis.[27] This is, inescapably, a "sinner's prayer."

The third in our set of alliterative qualities, perhaps encapsulating the first two, emerges from Jesus' admonition, "Whoever wants to be first must be *last* of all and servant of all" (Mark 9:35), which directly anticipates the terms of future judgment: "Many who are first will be last, and the last will be first" (Mark 10:31 *par.*). Matthew and Luke each repeat this aphorism in separate contexts (Matt 20:16; Luke 13:30); Luke in particular adds the parable concerning places of honor at a marriage feast, which graphically illustrates the same principle (Luke 14:7–12; esp. v. 11, "For all who exalt themselves will be humbled, and those who humble themselves will be exalted"). Here too, eschatological reward is directly in view, by virtue not only of the nuptial imagery, but also of the sapiential conclusion, which addresses the listeners/readers as much as those within the parable: "When you give a banquet, invite the poor, the crippled, the lame, and the blind. And you will be blessed, because they cannot repay you, for you will be repaid at the resurrection of the righteous" (Luke 14:13–14). The conditions of divine dominion—incumbent on the community of the faithful as much in the immediate as in their ultimate future—thus constitute a radical inversion of contemporary

---

26. Knowles, "Reading Matthew," 64–65.
27. See further Knowles, "Once More."

values (at least for those who view physical suffering as retribution for sin).

The force of this observation is underscored by the fact that Jesus' first disciples were not, in fact, all drawn from the lowest strata of Galilean society.[28] Zebedee, father of James and John, is evidently wealthy enough to have "hired servants" who fill in when the two brothers abandon their nets to follow Jesus (Mark 1:20). Likewise Luke's parable of the "unprofitable" servant is addressed to slave-owners: "Who among *you* would say to *your* slave [δοῦλον] . . . " (Luke 17:7). Yet the point of the parable is that before God, even slave owners must confess, "We [also!] are worthless slaves; we have done only what we ought to have done!" (Luke 17:10). To be in the company of Jesus reconfigures norms and inverts values that are otherwise integral to contemporary social order.

Thus, being "last" consists not simply of associating with those of low social status but also, as Mark 9:35 indicates, of becoming "last of all and servant [διάκονος] of all"—that is, of acting accordingly. This saying constitutes one half of a rare Markan doublet, and its counterpart is equally instructive. Notable in the following passage is, first, the counter-intuitive inversion of contemporary social values; second, the explicit contrast with non-Jewish culture; third, Jesus' own exemplary role; and, fourth, the location of that example in relation to Jesus' soteriological mission. This fourth element makes the principles in question especially relevant and applicable to the later church:

> So Jesus called them and said to them, "You know that among the Gentiles those whom they recognize as their rulers lord it over them, and their great ones are tyrants over them. But it is not so among you; but whoever wishes to become great among you must be your servant [διάκονος], and whoever wishes to be first among you must be slave [δοῦλος] of all. For the Son of Man came not to be served but to serve [διακονῆσαι], and to give his life a ransom for many." (Mark 10:42–45 // Matt 20:25–28; cf. Luke 22:25–27; Matt 23:11)

If we may stray momentarily outside the bounds of the canonical Gospels, Paul's conduct in Corinth provides at least one instance in which the early church follows this injunction to the letter. In keeping

---

28. So Kee, *People of God*, 66–67; thus qualifying the remark by France (*Mark*, 94), that the earliest disciples are "a group of socially insignificant people in an unnoticed corner of provincial Galilee."

with Jesus' direction to avoid domineering conduct (κατακυριεύουσιν, Mark 10:42), so the apostle to the Gentiles defends his leadership in Corinth: "I do not mean to imply that we lord it [κυριεύομεν] over your faith; rather, we are workers with you for your joy, because you stand firm in the faith" (2 Cor 1:24; cf. also 1 Pet 5:3).

Of similar (and, once more, eschatological) import to Mark 10 is Jesus' parabolic commendation of that "blessed slave" who is declared faithful upon his master's return, precisely because he has served the other members of the household (Q 12:42–44). And even prior to Jesus' eventual self-oblation, one striking enactment of this outlook, from John's Gospel, is the Master's own discomfiting insistence on washing his disciples' feet, together with his disturbing injunction for them to do the same:

> You call me Teacher and Lord; and you are right, for so I am. If I then, your Lord and Teacher, have washed your feet, you also ought to wash one another's feet. For I have given you an example, that you also should do as I have done to you. Truly, truly, I say to you, a slave [δοῦλος] is not greater than his master; nor is he who is sent greater than he who sent him. If you know these things, you are blessed if you do them. (John 13:13–17 [RSV, mg.])[29]

To characterize the Messiah's disciples as among the least, the lost, and the last is to describe not three distinct aspects of their identity, but a single characteristic viewed from three different perspectives. The Gospels convey this key feature of their identity not only discursively, but also by means of image and symbol. The disciples are thus not only a "little flock," but also "salt" (Matt 5:13), disproportionately pungent considering their small numbers and low social rank. Just so, the message they embody and bear forth is like a mustard seed, "which, when sown upon the ground, is the smallest of all the seeds on earth; yet when it is sown it grows up and becomes the greatest of all shrubs" (Mark 4:31–32 par.); it is like leaven (Q 13:20–21), again of disproportionate effect compared to its volume, and like "treasure hidden in a field" or a fine "pearl" (Matt 13:44–46) whose worth far outweighs their obscurity or small size. Exploiting another dimension of agricultural imagery, Jesus conveys much the same sense of contrast in his mission charge to the

---

29. Cf. Matt 10:24: "A disciple is not above the teacher, nor a slave above the master" (// Luke 6:40a).

disciples: "The harvest is plentiful, but the laborers are *few*; therefore ask the Lord of the harvest to send out laborers into his harvest'" (Q 10:2).

Seed imagery—central to five parables in the canonical corpus[30]—is particularly appropriate for representing the nature and identity of the community of disciples, insofar as the inheritors of God's promises are frequently identified in biblical and post-biblical literature as the "seed" (LXX σπέρμα) of Abraham, of Isaac, and of Jacob, or indeed of all three.[31] Seeds are, after all, at once tiny, inherently generative, and the instrumental gifts of a life-giving God, embodying potential for growth, fruit-bearing, and nourishment that far outweighs their physical insignificance. As such, seed imagery appropriately encapsulates the paradoxical nature and contradictory character of the earliest church,[32] which takes its cue both from the conduct of Christ and from the generous compassion of a God who, appropriately enough, "makes his sun rise on the evil and on the good, and sends rain on the righteous and on the unrighteous" (Matt 5:45).

RITUAL AND COMMUNAL IDENTITY

In what specific contexts might such principles have become operative or evident? Here we must once more acknowledge, as at the outset of our discussion, both the limits of our historical knowledge and the need to distinguish the situation of the disciples from that of the communities that succeeded them. Yet certain formal features of congregational life—what the church will much later term "liturgical actions"—nonetheless emerge as characteristic of the post-resurrection community, actions that conform to and even reinforce the convictions and characteristics

---

30. The parables of the sower (Mark 4:1–9 *par.*), the seed growing secretly (Mark 4:26–29), the mustard seed (Mark 4:30–32 *par.*), the wheat and the weeds (Matt 13:24–30), faith compared to a mustard seed (Q 17:6).

31. Abraham: Gen 12:7; 15:3–5, 13, 18; 17:9; Exod 33:1; Josh 24:3; 2 Chron 20:7; Ps 105:6; Isa 41:8; 3 Macc 6:3; 4 Macc 18:1; *Pss. Sol.* 9:9; 18:3; so Rom 4:13–18; 9:7–8; 11:1; 2 Cor 11:22; Gal 3:16–29; *m. Ned.* 3:11, etc.; Isaac: Gen 26:3–4, 24; Jacob: Gen 28:3–4; 35:12; Num 23:10; Ps 22:24; Isa 45:19; 65:9; Jer 33:26; Ezek 20:5; 4 Ezra 8:16; combined: Exod 32:13; 33:1; Deut 1:8; 34:4; Tob 4:12; *m. B. Qam.* 8:6; *m. B. Meṣ'ia* 7:1, etc. See further Wright, *Jesus and the Victory of God*, 232 n. 128.

32. Such imagery would retain its force, of course, primarily among those of Jewish heritage, since ignorance of its history and background on the part of Gentile believers would likely render it a dead metaphor.

we have traced thus far.³³ Four rites that were surely practiced in one form or another by the earliest Christian communities (at least three by virtue of their dominical origin) are baptism, foot-washing, the "holy kiss," and the eucharist or Lord's supper.³⁴

Baptism doubtless constitutes the primary rite of admission into the community, as we may deduce both from Jesus' post-resurrection mandate to baptize "all nations . . . in the name of the Father and of the Son and of the Holy Spirit" (Matt 28:19) and from widespread evidence in Acts (Acts 2:38, 41; 8:12, 36–39; 9:18; 10:48, etc.), the letters of Paul (Rom 6:3–4; 1 Cor 1:13–16; Gal 3:27; Eph 4:5, etc.), and elsewhere. As an exception to this rule, Martin Connell argues that foot-washing may have served the same function within the earliest Johannine community.³⁵ Washing is, in any event, the normal prelude to table fellowship, at least in a Jewish context.³⁶ Once admitted into the community, members re-enact Jesus' last meal, which by invoking the precedent of Passover constitutes his followers as God's people and partakers of a new covenant.³⁷ More specifically, as Paul explains it, "the fellowship [κοινωνία] of . . . Jesus Christ our Lord" (1 Cor 1:9) is ritualized through sharing the cup and bread that symbolize "fellowship [κοινωνία] in the blood [and] body of Christ" (1 Cor 10:16), even to the exclusion of competing claims (1 Cor 10:20–21). Here, correspondences between Lukan and Pauline words of institution (Luke 22:19–20 // 1 Cor 11:23–25) are especially significant, since they demonstrate—if only for Paul—the direct relevance of Synoptic material for the actual practice of the Christian community, all the more so as the apostle is simply reminding his congregants of what they already know (1 Cor 11:23a). Finally, the φίλημα

---

33. Thus, in a manner analogous to Wright's functional Christology (*Jesus and the Victory of God*, 137–44), we want to investigate the interplay between "beliefs and aims" and "consequent actions."

34. Here I employ lower-case titles so as to avoid entering into debate about the connection between specific New Testament-era forms of practice and later liturgical developments. On baptism and eucharist in particular, see the fuller treatment in the ensuing article by Stanley E. Porter, "Saints and Sinners: The Church in Paul's Letters," 54–56.

35. Connell, "*Nisi Pedes*," esp. 525–26.

36. For which purpose βαπτίζειν and νίπτειν may serve interchangeably (so Mark 7:3–4 and Luke 11:38, with the ironic intent of the latter noted by Thompson, "Gathered at the Table," 87).

37. Brower, "The Holy One," 69.

ἅγιον or φίλημα ἀγάπης also provides a sign of Christian fellowship, demonstrably so within both Pauline and Petrine communities (Rom 16:16; 1 Cor 16:20; 2 Cor 13:12; 1 Thess 5:26; 1 Pet 5:14).

The currency of such ritual actions poses some immediately practical questions: who would have been accepted for baptism, or at the table of the Lord? Whose feet would have been washed, and what might washing them imply? Who would have shared the "holy kiss"? The evidence is sparse but, for our purposes, significant.

The washing of feet is, by all accounts, normally beneath the dignity of any but a slave, from which derives the force of John the Baptist's comment about the coming Messiah, "I am not worthy to stoop down and untie the thong of his sandals" (Mark 1:7 *par.* // John 1:27).[38] Likewise it is the source of Peter's entirely proper protest, "You will never wash my feet" (John 13:8). If the early church indeed obeyed their Lord and, as Connell contends, this action demarcated entry into the community, it would have constituted a gesture of conscious self-abasement on the part of the member who administered it, an act of humble—even humiliating—service to one whose position as a newcomer would otherwise have marked him or her as "least" in the community.

Baptism, by comparison, addresses moral character more than social status. Perhaps among early generations of Jewish believers, baptism retained overtones of Gentile conversion. But its predominant significance is as an act of symbolic and ritual purification. "Repent and be baptized," declares Peter on the day of Pentecost, "so that your sins may be forgiven" (Acts 1:8); "baptism . . . now saves you," adds 1 Pet 3:21, "not as a removal of dirt from the body, but as an appeal to God for a good conscience." It is a ritual fit only for sinners, those in need of forgiveness and moral cleansing. Or to adopt the language of our study, it is a ritual that, by definition, marks its recipients as among "the least, the lost, and the last." More broadly, both baptism and foot-washing (whatever the role of the latter) are social rituals that place recipients and administrators (respectively) in positions of humility. That these are, precisely, initiation rituals surely speaks to the intended character of the community as a whole. What then of rituals of Christian fellowship?

The most notable, indeed notorious kiss in the New Testament canon is a mark of grave betrayal (Mark 14:44–45 *par.*), that of Judas. In Luke, this gesture is elsewhere offered by "a woman of the city who was a

---

38. So Marcus, *Mark 1–8*, 152.

sinner" (Luke 7:38), as well as by a father to his penitent son (Luke 15:20).[39] According to William Klassen, public kissing was generally avoided by Jews and treated with considerable reticence in the Greco-Roman world, "although a special place seems to have belonged to the kiss exchanged by slaves who discovered their spiritual kinship as slaves."[40] Each of these instances associates kissing with persons or circumstances of low social standing and/or dubious moral character. Granted, the Pauline practice is a specifically "*holy* kiss" (Rom 16:16; 1 Cor 16:20; 2 Cor 13:12; 1 Thess 5:26), while in Petrine communities it is a "kiss of love" (1 Pet 5:14). Yet in either case this ritual emphasizes the radical character of Christian community. As Klassen concludes: "The 'holy kiss' is a public declaration of the affirmation of faith: 'In Christ there is neither male nor female, Jew nor Greek, slave nor free' (Gal 3:28)."[41] Precisely so, this sign of Christian fellowship is singularly appropriate for and open to the socially disenfranchised and otherwise disregarded sort of disciples that the Gospels consistently describe.

The fullest available evidence, by far, concerns the eucharist, the ritual of the Lord's table, for the New Testament includes a comparatively rich amount of detail pertaining to its institution and administration. Here Judas comes once more to the fore. Notwithstanding the pronouncement of woe against this particular disciple, Jesus nonetheless shares his symbolic last meal with his betrayer (Mark 14:17–21 *par.*). According to John, Jesus even accords Judas a mark of special favor (John 13:21–30). Yet the Master is equally clear that every one of his dinner companions will deny or abandon him in the face of danger, despite their indignant protests to the contrary (Mark 14:26–31 *par.*).[42] To underscore the disciples' unworthiness and lack of understanding, Luke sets the dispute about precedence and greatness within this context (Luke 22:24–27; *diff.* Mark 10:41–45 // Matt 20:24–28). Even in the case of his closest followers, then, Jesus continues to practice the same table fellowship with sinners that has characterized his entire ministry. Judging only from the Synoptic accounts and the example set by Jesus'

---

39. Luke 7:45 may imply that the kiss of fellowship was typical of Jesus, and so may also claim dominical origin.

40. Klassen, "Kiss," 90–91.

41. Ibid., 92.

42. Thompson, "Gathered at the Table," 90.

first followers, it would surely have seemed difficult thereafter to set any higher standard for admission to the Lord's table.

The evidence of 1 Corinthians bears this out in practice. Wayne Meeks, following Gerd Theissen, observes that the Corinthian believers appear to organize communal meals in a manner typical of their day, reinforcing social hierarchies through inequitable distribution of food and drink:

> When you come together, it is not really to eat the Lord's supper. For when the time comes to eat, each of you goes ahead with your own supper, and one goes hungry and another becomes drunk. What! Do you not have homes to eat and drink in? Or do you show contempt for the church of God and humiliate those who have nothing? (1 Cor 11:20–22)[43]

Paul's specific charge is that in so doing, they "eat and drink without discerning the body" (1 Cor 11:29). It is not only that they fail to recognize, in principle, the meal's symbolic reference to their crucified Messiah, but perhaps also that they fail to discern the revolutionary social characteristics of the "body" of Christ, which is "the church of God." Given this example, neither adequate understanding of its meaning nor initial obedience to its implications can possibly constitute preconditions for admission to the community table (for if they had, there would have been no misunderstanding for Paul to correct). Rather, admission to the table of those who, precisely, require instruction and correction graciously enacts Christ's own generosity to the wayward, fractious, and uncomprehending.

Nor are such problems limited to Corinth: the letter of James indicates that members of his "synagogue" also observe social distinctions at the expense of Christian identity (Jas 2:1–4). They of all people should know better, James insists, on social if not theological grounds: "Is it not the rich who oppress you? Is it not they who drag you into court?" (Jas 2:6). Poverty—being among "the least, the lost, and the last"—should present no barrier to participation, no basis for discrimination, since they themselves evidently fare no better. In fact, poverty might actually qualify them for admission, if (as Cullmann contends) it is at the table set in honor of him that the risen Christ now presides as host, offering blessing and refreshment to the physically and spiritually famished (so

---

43. Cf. Meeks, *The First Urban Christians*, 67–70.

Matt 5:6; Luke 1:23; 6:21; John 6:35, etc.) for whose sake he has poured forth his life.

Thus, however imperfectly the disciples—either before or after Jesus' death and resurrection—may have appropriated the social and theological implications of such practices, it is nonetheless clear that all four rites are intended to fashion a Christomorphic community. These ritual actions, inaugurated by Jesus, act out the meaning of his mission and thereby enact the identity of the church that performs them. By reflecting—whether directly or indirectly—Jesus' own ministry, they express allegiance to the Messiah, imitate him, and establish a distinctive social identity. Properly understood, they also maintain Jesus' radical openness to those whom we have designated "the least, the lost, and the last."

CONCLUSION: THE SIGNIFICANCE OF INSIGNIFICANCE

Why do the Gospels offer so little direct evidence for the nature of the church? It cannot be that the subject was irrelevant, given the range of social and cultural settings in which apostolic teaching took early root. Nor is such relative silence due to disinterest: it seems highly improbable that the difficulties of social organization and conduct so evident, for instance, in the Pauline and post-Pauline correspondence, had all been resolved by the time the Gospel narratives were codified. If nothing else, that the only explicit references to the ἐκκλησία ("church") in the Gospels (Matt 16:18; 18:17 [bis]) occur alongside definitions of apostolic authority to "bind" and "loose" suggests otherwise. The simplest explanation is that the focus of these accounts lies elsewhere: with the cause and origins of Christian confession, rather than its consequences or subsequent circumstances. The identity, ministry, and purpose of Jesus take precedence over proto-ecclesial concerns, insofar as the identity, ministry, and purpose of the church are all understood to derive from and depend on those of Jesus. In theological terms, to speak of "church" or "Christian community" is to designate an entity that is by definition derivative, rather than inherently substantive or self-authenticating, "responsive, not originative."[44] Thus Ferreira's observations regarding Johannine ecclesiology apply in due measure to the Synoptic Gospels also:

---

44. Scott, "Eucharistic Place," 161.

Ecclesial office, church order, or sacraments do not feature prominently in Johannine ecclesiology as they do in Pauline ecclesiology. It appears that the author was not concerned about these things. Instead, the Gospel places the emphasis on the community's relationship with the Johannine Jesus. The community does not exist for itself, nor is [it] an end in itself, but rather exists for the purpose of continuing the sending of Jesus.[45]

In this sense, Jesus, his first disciples, the post-resurrection community, and even the Gospels themselves, all operate along similar lines. That is, the numerical, social, political, and cultural insignificance of this crucified Jewish rabbi and his plebeian rabble provides an initial clue to their common theological character, for he and they both testify to something greater than their own, merely human identities. Jesus may touch and be touched by the unholy and the unclean, but it is they who will come away altered, not he. He and his followers remain open to sinners, outsiders, and outcasts because their ministries are imbued (although to very different degrees!) with divine authority (Mark 2:10; 6:7 *par.*; Matt 28:18–19; John 5:27, etc.), a quality variously described as the "presence" (John 3:2), "works" (John 6:28–29), "glory" (John 11:4, 40), "majesty" (Luke 9:43), "power" (Luke 24:49), "Spirit," or "finger" of God (Matt 12:38 // Luke 11:20). Just so, the Gospel narratives are testaments not to the church itself—their portrait of the disciples is hardly flattering—but to that which creates and sustains it *as* the church.

The evidence reviewed above is neither complete[46] nor uniform, since it includes material that is unique to particular evangelists, or that varies significantly in different literary and theological contexts. Precisely for this reason, its thematic consistency appears compelling. Whether individual Gospel accounts would have functioned as affirmation, correction, or some combination of the two will no doubt have varied from one community to another, and from one era to the next. Whichever the case, accounts of the life and practice of the Messiah—all the more so as their authority was recognized and formalized in the fashioning of a scriptural canon—nonetheless delineate the intended character of the church in their depiction of those who first encountered

---

45. Ferreira, *Johannine Ecclesiology*, 201; similarly Houlden, *Public Face*, 67–68.

46. Two broad areas particularly deserving of further attention are the Evangelists' use of specific scriptural allusions and theological motifs to delineate Jesus' followers as the community of God's people, and the issue of the church's mission, whereby the faithful enact and extend Jesus' saving work.

Jesus and the ways in which that encounter proved transformative. For so many of his earliest disciples, both those of his own day and those of the church that later followed, it is precisely their own insignificance and inability—even their immorality—that testify so eloquently to Jesus as Messiah, Savior, and Lord. All four Evangelists, all four Gospels, concur in directing attention away from themselves and their communities so as to focus instead on the Messiah, for it is on his identity that the identity of their church is built.

BIBLIOGRAPHY

Baltensweiler, Heinrich. "'Wer nicht gegen uns (euch) ist, ist für (euch)!' Bemerkungen zu Mk 9,40 und Lk 9,50." *Theologische Zeitschrift* 40.2 (1984) 130–36.

Brower, Kent E. "The Holy One and His Disciples: Holiness and Ecclesiology in Mark." In *Holiness and Ecclesiology*, edited by Brower and Johnson, 57–75.

Brower, Kent E., and Andy Johnson, eds. *Holiness and Ecclesiology*. Grand Rapids: Eerdmans, 2007.

Coloe, Mary L. *Dwelling in the Household of God: Johannine Ecclesiology and Spirituality*. Collegeville MN: Liturgical, 2001.

Connell, Martin F. "*Nisi Pedes*, Except for the Feet: Footwashing in the Community of St John's Gospel." *Worship* 70 (1996) 517–31.

Cullmann, Oscar. *Early Christian Worship*. SBT 10. London: SCM, 1953.

Davies, W. D., and Dale C. Allison. *The Gospel according to Saint Matthew*. 3 vols. ICC. Edinburgh: T. & T. Clark, 1988–1997.

Ferreira, Johan. *Johannine Ecclesiology*. JSNTSup 160. Sheffield: Sheffield Academic, 1998.

France, R. T. *The Gospel of Mark: A Commentary on the Greek Text*. NIGTC. Grand Rapids: Eerdmans; Carlisle: Paternoster, 2002.

Hagner, Donald A. "Holiness and Ecclesiology: The Church in Matthew." In *Holiness and Ecclesiology*, edited by Brower and Johnson, 40–56.

Hengel, Martin. *Crucifixion in the Ancient World and the Folly of the Message of the Cross*, translated by John Bowden. Philadelphia: Fortress, 1977.

Houlden, J. L. *The Public Face of the Gospel: New Testament Ideas of the Church*. London: SCM, 1997.

Kee, Howard Clark. *Who Are the People of God? Early Christian Models of Community*. New Haven and London: Yale University Press, 1995.

Klassen, William. "Kiss (NT)." *ABD* 4:89–92.

Knowles, Michael P. "Once More 'Lead Us Not *Eis Peirasmon*.'" *Expository Times* 115.6 (2004) 191–94.

Knowles, Michael P. "Reading Matthew: The Gospel as Oral Performance." In *Reading the Gospels Today*, edited by Stanley E. Porter, 56–77. MNTS 8. Grand Rapids: Eerdmans, 2004.

Marcus, Joel. *Mark 1–8: A New Translation with Introduction and Commentary*. AB 27. New York: Doubleday, 2000.

Meeks, Wayne A. *The First Urban Christians: The Social World of the Apostle Paul*. New Haven: Yale University Press, 1983.

Pattarumadathil, H. *Your Father in Heaven: Discipleship in Matthew as a Process of Becoming Children of God.* AnBib 172. Rome: Pontifical Biblical Institute, 2008.

Robinson, James M. "From Safe House to House Church: From Q to Matthew." In *Das Ende der Tage und die Gegenwart des Heils: Begegnungen mit dem Neuen Testament und seiner Umwelt. Festschrift für Heinz-Wolfgang Kuhn zum 65. Geburtstag*, edited by M. Becker and W. Fenske, 183–99. Leiden: Brill, 1999.

Sanders, E. P. *Paul and Palestinian Judaism.* Philadelphia: Fortress, 1977.

Scott, Peter. "A Theology of Eucharistic Place: Pilgrimage as Sacramental." In *Explorations in a Christian Theology of Pilgrimage*, edited by Craig Bartholomew and Fred Hughes, 151–69. Aldershot: Ashgate, 2004.

Thompson, Richard P. "Gathered at the Table: Holiness and Ecclesiology in the Gospel of Luke." In *Holiness and Ecclesiology*, edited by Brower and Johnson, 76–94.

Wright, N. T. *Christian Origins and the Question of God.* Vol. 2, *Jesus and the Victory of God*. Minneapolis: Fortress, 1996.

2

Saints and Sinners

The Church in Paul's Letters

STANLEY E. PORTER

INTRODUCTION AND PRELIMINARY QUESTIONS

THERE HAVE BEEN MANY stereotypes of the churches founded either directly or indirectly by Paul. Some have wanted to characterize these churches as primarily charismatic communities driven by life in the Spirit. Others have found a sense of egalitarianism regarding personal roles that has liberated them from all restriction. Still others have castigated Paul for his hierarchicalism. The list could go on, but I will not. Instead, in this paper I wish to examine the Pauline letters afresh in order to grasp the nature of the church as seen in Paul's letters.

For the sake of examination in this paper, I will consider all of the thirteen letters attributed to Paul as authentic.[1] One cannot hope to get a glimpse of the Pauline conception of the church without accessing all of Paul's letters. In a similar way, to attempt a Pauline ecclesiology on the basis of letters that one does not consider genuine is to provide an inaccurate picture of such a church. It may be the notion of church as conceived by Paul's closest and quickest followers, but it cannot be a genuine view of Paul's conception of the church.

---

1. See McDonald and Porter, *Early Christianity*, 489–97, where such issues are addressed.

When we examine the corpus of Paul's thirteen letters, several significant observations come to mind. The first is that Paul's letters are conveniently divided into two parts: the church letters and the personal letters. There are nine church letters, and four personal letters. These letters are arranged in roughly descending order of length. As a result, the book of Romans is the first and longest church letter and 2 Thessalonians is the shortest. First Timothy is the longest and Philemon is the shortest of the personal letters. The reason they are arranged this way is not in terms of doctrinal, historical, or other significance, but because this is how they were placed in order when they were gathered together, a process probably instigated by Paul himself. Paul was probably the first collector of his own letters, a task that he inaugurated during his lifetime. It would not have been uncommon for him as a letter writer to have copies of his letters made at the time of their writing. These copies formed the basis of the letters that he then gathered as his collection of letters.[2] On the basis of this, it is entirely appropriate to consider all of his letters when examining the concept of the church within his writings.

This paper will rely primarily on Paul's letters in composing a picture of the Pauline church. The letters of Paul are our primary sources for knowledge of him, but I will draw in the book of Acts when appropriate. Although I use the language of "church," I do not confine myself to examination of this word, but deal with the community of those who are followers of Jesus Christ as reflected in Paul's letters.[3]

CHARACTERISTICS OF THE PAULINE CHURCH

Any attempt to describe the characteristics of the Pauline church through Paul's letters runs into the major issue of the relationship between normativity and occasionality. Previous generations of interpreters, for example during the time of Melanchthon, who considered Paul's letter to the Romans a compendium of Paul's thought,[4] viewed Paul's letters as inherently normative. Recent interpreters are more inclined to note the occasional nature of the letters.[5] If they are all seen to be normative at every turn, then we may well find that we are trying to generalize and

---

2. See Porter, "Paul and the Process of Canonization."

3. For a recent discussion of the notion of Pauline churches and how they relate to other communities in the ancient world, see Ascough, *What Are They Saying*.

4. See McDonald and Porter, *Early Christianity*, 455–56.

5. See, e.g., Beker, *Paul the Apostle*, 23–36; Beker, "Paul's Theology."

universalize comments that are clearly made for a particular occasion. As an example, Paul's instruction to Timothy to take a little wine for his stomach's sake (1 Tim 5:23) is probably not a comment that should be universalized as an injunction for all to drink wine. However, if all comments are seen to be occasional comments, only applicable to the specific context in which they are given, we run the risk of minimizing the significance of such an image as dying and rising with Christ (Rom 6:4–9). There have been many attempts to traverse this normative/occasional divide. In his *The Two Horizons*, Anthony Thiselton proposes a means by which Wittgenstein's work, especially in the *Philosophical Investigations*, could be used to parse three types of linguistic utterances: (1) neutral or universal grammatical utterances, similar to analytical or a priori statements of logical positivism; (2) statements particular to a given religious or ethical tradition; and (3) statements that recommend a new way of examining a state of affairs.[6] If a given statement of Paul could be linguistically analyzed, one could determine how to interpret the statement and hence determine its normative or occasional value. However, such a straightforward scheme so far has not proven workable,[7] and we must rely upon other means to determine what is universal and what is contingent.

This does not mean that we must despair of being able to determine normative versus occasional values in Paul's writings. It does mean that we must be less attuned simply to the grammar of a particular utterance and more attuned to the context in which such an utterance is made. As a result, I have identified what I consider a set of distinctives that define the Pauline church.

The Pauline Church Is a Confessing Community

The heart of the Pauline church is that, regardless of whatever else distinguishes it, it is a community of confessing individuals. These individuals make (and I would add, believe) certain confessions about especially Jesus, but also God and the Holy Spirit.[8] The fundamental Pauline confession is found in Rom 10:9 and 1 Cor 12:3: "Jesus is Lord."

---

6. Thiselton, *The Two Horizons*, 386–407.

7. Porter, "Wittgenstein's Classes."

8. See W. Porter, "Creeds and Hymns," including information on the passages discussed below.

In Rom 10:9, Paul states that if you (singular) confess with your lips that Jesus is Lord and you (singular) believe in your heart that God raised him from the dead, then you (singular) will be saved. There are at least five key elements of this confession to emphasize. The first is that Paul states this in the singular. This is not a corporate confession or a confession made by someone on behalf of others.[9] This is an individual confession. The second is that this confession assumes that there is a God, for Paul the God of the Old Testament. Note that this passage occurs in Romans 9–11, that somewhat awkward end to the body of the book of Romans that Paul uses to remind his readers that God is not done with the nation of Israel (Rom 11:26).[10] God is not a debatable point in Paul's church, but a fundamental assumption. If your universe of understanding does not include the God who created this universe and you in it, then you cannot be a part of Paul's church. It is this God who is the "Lord" of the Old Testament Scriptures. The third point is that Paul equates Jesus with this Lord of the Old Testament. Whereas the title "Lord" was used to translate YHWH in the Old Testament, here it is used as the predicate of who Jesus is: Jesus is Lord, i.e., Jesus also is God.[11] The fourth element is the proof of this. God raised Jesus from the dead. For Paul, this is not a communal delusion or phantasmagoric hallucination. This is the simple fact that the Jesus who was killed and dead did not remain dead, but was raised to new life. He was no longer dead, not just perceived not to be dead. This is the basis of salvation. The fifth is Paul's expansion on this statement in Rom 10:10, when he says that it is with the heart that a person believes and it is with the mouth that a person confesses. The first results in righteousness, and the second in salvation. In other words, the two are intertwined, with confession and belief going hand in hand. A related statement, perhaps also from a previously formulated confession, is found in Rom 1:3–4, which states that God's son was declared Son of God with power by the resurrection from the dead according to the Spirit of Holiness: Jesus Christ our Lord.

The second passage is 1 Cor 12:3. Paul says that no one (singular) who speaks by the Spirit of God can say "Jesus is accursed," and no one

---

9. While there are corporate elements to Paul's concept of church, it is not fundamentally corporate, contra Horrell, *Solidarity and Difference*, 99–101.

10. McDonald and Porter, *Early Christianity*, 458–59.

11. On the use of Lord in the translation of the Old Testament, and implications for use in the New Testament, see Kramer, *Christ, Lord, Son of God*, 215–19.

(singular) can say, "Jesus is Lord," except by the Holy Spirit. There are four elements to note in this confession. The first is that the confession is the same as the one found in Romans: Jesus is Lord. The second is that this is a confession made by individuals. It is a person who either curses or affirms Jesus as Lord. The third is that this passage occurs in the ethical portion of the first letter to the Corinthians, indicating that this confession was something that they already knew, or at least should have known. The reason Paul introduces it here is that the Corinthians have lost sight of it and gotten it entangled with other things, such as the issue of charismatic gifts (to which we will return below). The fourth is that the confession of Jesus as Lord (with all that this implies as stated above from Romans) is by the power of the Holy Spirit. We confess our belief, but we are empowered to make that confession by the work of God through his Holy Spirit within us. This confession constitutes the heart of Paul's evangelistic preaching ministry. As he says in 2 Cor 4:5, he preached "Jesus Christ is Lord." The Corinthian letters also have several two- and three-part affirmations that are related to this. In 1 Cor 8:6, Paul states that for us there is one God, the Father, from whom are all things and we are for him, and one Lord, Jesus Christ, by whom are all things and we are through him. In 2 Cor 13:13 (Greek), Paul states: "The grace of the Lord Jesus Christ and the love of God and the fellowship of the Holy Spirit be with all of you."[12]

These are two of the most significant and fundamental confessions found within the Pauline letters. As fundamental as they may seem, however, they are far from simple, as they imply directly and indirectly more than they at first seem to convey. These two statements encapsulate what is often confessed at greater length in other confessional passages in the Pauline letters. Throughout Paul's letters there are a number of statements formulated in creedal or confessional form. There is divided opinion on whether these statements were formulated in these memorable ways by Paul himself, or whether they were material that he incorporated because they represented the common body of material that early Christians, including Paul and his churches, would have confessed together. For the sake of my treatment here, it is not necessary to

---

12. I am tempted to say that the Pauline church was a proto-Trinitarian church. Whereas I think that Paul was what we would now call Trinitarian in outlook—recognizing three persons of the godhead in economic relationship—I am not sure that knowing this was a confessional requirement for being in the Pauline church.

resolve this question, as, in any case, Paul uses these creedal statements as memorable ways to encapsulate fundamental beliefs. Virtually all of these confessional statements are at least about Jesus, but often about more. I select several of the most significant for brief treatment.

In 1 Cor 15:3–5, Paul recognizes that he is passing on to the Corinthians material that he has received from other Christians: (1) that Christ died for our sins according to the Scriptures, (2) and that he was buried, (3) and that he was raised on the third day according to the Scriptures, (4) and that he was seen by Cephas, then by the twelve. There is a four-part confession here, both conceptually and grammatically: Christ died, was buried, was raised, and was seen.[13] I note that whereas Christ died (active voice), he was buried by others, was raised by God, and was seen by witnesses, such as Cephas and the disciples, and eventually Paul. There is a logical and grammatical shape to this passage, in that Christ is the agent of his death, that is, it was not something done to him by others, although once dead he required others to bury him (he really was dead), and God himself to resurrect him.

Perhaps the most well-known confessional statement is in Phil 2:6–11. There has been much treatment of this passage (and others) regarding whether it is a confessional or creedal statement or a hymn. There is no doubt that it is not a hymn in the classical sense.[14] However, even if it were, it could still be creedal. Paul frames the use of this passage in terms of it providing the basis for thinking the same way that Christ Jesus did. The passage in this sense may be ethical, in that it provides a norm for behavior. However, this ethical norm is grounded in the confessional belief that Paul is drawing upon, probably because the statements contained in it were recognized within the wider church. A few recent interpreters have wanted to see this passage as reflecting a two-stage christological statement, beginning with Jesus Christ as the second Adam and proceeding to his exaltation. Few have accepted this interpretation. The three-stage progression is clearly more likely. (1) Christ Jesus, being in the form of God, did not consider equality with God a thing to be grasped, (2) but emptied himself, taking the form of a servant, becoming in likeness as a human, and, being found in form

---

13. Some take this statement as a double statement: (1) died and was buried, (2) was raised and appeared. Others take this as a three-part statement: (1) died, (2) was buried, (3) was raised. The four-fold division is reflective of the grammar.

14. On these issues, see Fowl, *Ethics of Paul*, 31–45.

as a human, he humbled himself, becoming obedient to the point of death, even death on a cross. (3) Wherefore, God exalted him and gave to him the name above every name, so that in the name of Jesus every knee might bow on heaven and on earth and under the earth, and every tongue confess that Jesus Christ is Lord to the glory of God the Father.[15] As noted above, Paul does not argue for God's existence, being, or character, but wishes here to affirm statements about Jesus. Before his human existence, he existed in the form of God, but did not retain or hold onto these rights of equality. He became a human being in all ways, including form, character, and appearance, and even humiliating death. God, who by nature has such prerogatives to exercise, hyper-elevated Jesus to a restored place of pre-eminence over all realms, heavenly, earthly, and otherwise. Note that the Philippian confession ends with the very confession that we noted above. When all humans appear before him, they will be compelled to confess that Jesus Christ is Lord.

In Col 1:15–20, Paul makes a highly structured statement about Jesus. There are questions whether this statement should be divided into two major parts or a number of smaller parts. Perhaps both give the clearest idea of its structure: Paul says of Jesus (1a) that he is the image of the unseen God, firstborn of all creation, (1b) that in him all things in heaven and on earth, seen and unseen, either thrones or lordships or powers or authorities were created, all things through him stand created, (1c) and that he is before all things and all things in him hold together, (1d) and he is the head of the body, the church. He says further of Jesus (2a) that he is the ruler, firstborn from the dead, so that he might be preeminent in all things, (2b) that in him all the fullness was pleased to dwell, (2c) and through him to reconcile all things in him, establishing peace through the blood of his cross, whether things upon the earth or things under the earth. Paul here leads the Colossians in a confession of Jesus as the visible manifestation in appearance and being of the unseen God, and from this positional being he exercises authority over the world.

I will draw this section to a close with an example from 1 Timothy. In 1 Tim 3:16, Paul labels what he is going to say as "confessedly" made, and that its mystery of godliness is great. Paul gives a six-part confession regarding Jesus Christ: (1) he was manifested in flesh; (2) he was justified in Spirit, (3) he was seen by angels, (4) he was proclaimed in nations,

---

15. See Amiot, *Key Concepts*, 87–116.

(5) he was believed in the world, (6) he was taken up in glory. All six of the finite verbs in this confession are in the aorist passive, with each followed by a prepositional phrase with the preposition *en*, except for the third ("he was seen by angels"). There have been numerous attempts to equate each of these statements with a particular time or set of events in the life of Jesus. We do not need to do that here (although I think that it is possible) to realize that this creedal confession is making clear statements about Jesus as the pre-existent one who became human, was affirmed in his ministry by the Holy Spirit, was the object of proclamation and belief, and was vindicated through resurrection and ascension when he was taken up in glory.

The Pauline church is a confessing church. The church is one that confesses certain beliefs about Jesus Christ, God, and the Holy Spirit. This church confesses that Jesus is Lord or God, that he was resurrected from the dead, that he is the incarnate God, and that he is going to superintend events at the end of time. This confession of Jesus is the basic requirement for entrance into the Pauline church. In this sense, Paul's church is a confessing church, not an evangelistic church. That is, it is a church of those that confess that Jesus Christ is Lord, not one that admits those who are not able to make that confession, hoping to reach them once they are inside.

The Pauline Church Is a Faith Community

We have noted the confessional statements above. These in many ways contain the core doctrine and belief that people were required to be able to publicly state as a declaration of their assent to the essentials of the faith. However, the Pauline community was also a faith community. That is, more was required than simply a confession. The confession was to be mirrored by belief that leads to salvation. The confession in Rom 10:9 captures this well when it says that one must confess content and believe in one's heart.

Terms for belief or having faith are significant in Paul's letters. In Rom 1:16, Paul says that the gospel or good news, that is, the good news concerning Jesus Christ (what we might call the confession noted above) is the power of God for salvation to everyone who believes, to the Jew first and also to the Greek. Paul uses a variety of words to refer to what we might call salvation, including justification and reconciliation. There are three key passages that I wish to treat briefly here.

In Romans 3, Paul tells his readers that, apart from the law, God's righteousness is manifested, even though it is witnessed to by the law and the prophets. The righteousness of God comes through faith in Jesus Christ for all those who believe. There is no distinction for any human being in this regard. There has been much recent discussion about whether the phrase "faith of Jesus Christ" (v. 22; cf. Gal 2:16; 3:22) is a so-called subjective or objective genitive. The traditional position is that this is an objective genitive: faith directed toward Jesus Christ. Recent scholarship has wanted to see it as a subjective genitive: faith or faithfulness that Jesus Christ has. Recent linguistic research has shown that the use of the genitive can be deciphered if the larger phrase ("through faith of Jesus Christ") is taken into account. When the larger phrase is considered, there is no clear instance elsewhere of a subjective use of the genitive.[16] Thus, the objective genitive seems to be the best understanding. Paul is saying that those who believe are to have faith or belief in Jesus Christ. The reason for this is that all humans have sinned and fall short of God's glory (v. 23). In Romans 5, Paul says that God demonstrated his love for humans in that while they were still sinners Christ died for them. Being justified by means of the blood of Jesus Christ means that humans can be saved from God's wrath. The death of God's Son meant that we could be reconciled to God, and, if reconciled, saved. Finally, in Galatians 2, Paul says that, knowing that a person is not justified by works of the law but through faith in Jesus Christ, we have believed in Christ Jesus so that we may be justified by means of faith in Christ and not by means of works of the law (2:16).

The Pauline church is a faith community, that is, a community that puts its faith or trust in Jesus Christ for its salvation.

The Pauline Church Is a Universal and a Local Community

In his letters, Paul makes clear that he believes that the church is both a universal and a local phenomenon.[17] By this, he seems to understand that everyone who confesses that Jesus is Lord becomes a member of

---

16. Porter and Pitts, "Πίστις."

17. I do not treat all of the elements of what it means for Paul's church to be a community. On this topic, among others, see Banks, *Paul's Idea of Community*. Cf. Chester, "The Pauline Communities."

the larger body called the church, but that believers of this sort are also located in local believing communities.[18]

The best way to see this is to examine the openings of Paul's letters. In Rom 1:7, he addresses his letter to all of those who are in Rome, beloved of God, called saints. In 1 Cor 1:2, Paul sends this letter to the church of God that is in Corinth, those sanctified in Christ Jesus, called saints. In 2 Cor 1:1, Paul similarly sends this letter to the church of God that is in Corinth, with all the saints who are in the whole of Achaia. In Gal 1:3, Paul addresses his letter to the churches of Galatia. In Eph 1:1, there is the difficulty of the textual variant regarding whether the words "in Ephesus" belong in the earliest form of the letter. They almost assuredly do not. If this is the case, then probably this was a slot for a circular letter to have its particular recipient placed in the greeting. Ephesians 1:1 would read: to the saints who are "in Ephesus or Laodicea or somewhere else in western Anatolia" and faithful in Christ Jesus. Philippians 1:1 is addressed to all the saints in Christ Jesus who are in Philippi with overseers and deacons. Colossians 1:2 is sent to the saints in Colossae and faithful brothers (and sisters) in Christ. First Thessalonians 1:1 is sent to the church of Thessalonians in God the Father and Lord Jesus Christ. Second Thessalonians 1:1 is addressed to the church of Thessalonians in God our Father and Lord Jesus Christ.

If we look a little more carefully at the wording here, I think we can see that Paul has a view of how the local and universal church works. The first factor is that Paul has a variety of words for those who are members of that group that we like to call the church. He often calls them saints in the address of his letters (cf. 1 Cor 14:33, where he refers to the churches of the saints). The second is that Paul uses the term "church" for that body that is made up of those who are the saints, wherever they may be. When Paul wants the term church to refer to a local body of saints, he modifies the term church so that it is the church in a particular location (e.g., Rom 16:1, the church in Cenchrea; 1 Cor 16:1, 19; 2 Cor 8:1) or uses the plural form of the word, churches (e.g., Rom 16:16, all the churches of Christ). The third is that Paul sees the church as not simply an earthly organization of human beings, but as God's or Christ's church (cf. 1 Cor 15:9; Gal 1:13; 1 Tim 3:5, 15). In several of the openings of the

---

18. See Bruce, *Paul*, 431–32, where he notes that the universal church is implied in the local; Stephens, *Pauline Theology*, 320, but who also endorses study of the notion of the Kingdom of God as Paul's term for the community of believers in the messianic age.

letters he addresses the church as the church of God. Elsewhere he refers to the church as the body of Christ (e.g., Col 1:18, 24; Eph 5:23).[19] The fourth is that his phrasing indicates that there is a "church of God/Christ" that may be located in a particular place, such as Rome or Corinth or Ephesus or Philippi or Thessalonica. It appears that these churches were gatherings in houses (e.g., Rom 16:5; 1 Cor 16:19; Phil 4:22; Phlm 2).[20] These churches may well have had several different places in which they met, yet they were all part of the church in that particular location. Thus, there are a variety of local manifestations of the church as the body of saints. I do not think that Paul would have understood the idea of a person being a part of the church universal without being a part of a local meeting of the church. In the same way, he could not conceive of a person thinking that he or she was a member of the church without being able to make the confession that Jesus is Lord.

Although Paul writes his letters to local churches, many of his most profound statements about the church are addressed to the church universal, where he uses the analogy of the human body. For example, he notes in 1 Cor 12:12–30 that there is one body that has many members. Though the members are many, there is one body, just as Christ is one. In Col 1:18, Paul says that Christ is the head of the body, the church. Similarly, in Eph 5:23, Paul says that Christ is the head of the church.

For Paul the universal church as the body of Christ has a local manifestation. That is, all of the saints in a particular location would be part of the church or churches in that area. Paul does not address the issue of denominationalism. However, he does say something about those who draw similar kinds of distinctions. In 1 Cor 1:11–12, Paul says that he has been informed by Chloe's representatives that there are quarrels among the members of the church. He clarifies that some are saying "I am of Bill Hybels," and "I am of the Presbyterians," and "I am of the Baptists," and "I am of Christ." Has Christ been divided? Bill Hybels was not crucified for you, was he? Or were you baptized into the name of John Calvin? I think Paul makes it clear what he thought regarding incipient denominationalism.

---

19. See Amiot, *Key Concepts*, 204.

20. It appears that Paul's churches did meet in houses. On house churches, see Ascough, *What Are They Saying*, 5–9.

The Pauline Church Is an Egalitarian Community

The Pauline church was an egalitarian community in the most radical sense of the word; however, it was not necessarily egalitarian with regard to the world outside of the church.

One of the most important insights that Paul had regarding the community of saints was that it was a community for everyone. Paul recognized that Jesus Christ, as a Jew, had come first to his own people, and that his people had a role to play in the future (note Romans 9–11, including 11:26), but that he was called as the apostle to the Gentiles, that is, to extend the boundaries of those included in God's church to include people from each and every race. In several places, Paul says that the message of the gospel is to the Jew first, but also to the Greek (Rom 1:16; 2:10; 10:12).

Within the church, Paul does not see any distinction on the basis of criteria such as race, socio-economic standing, or gender. As he states in Gal 3:26–28, those who have faith (v. 25) are children of God through faith in Jesus Christ (3:6). Those baptized into Christ are clothed with Christ. There is neither Jew nor Greek, neither slave nor free person, neither male nor female—those who have faith are all one in Christ Jesus. Richard Longenecker made this set of verses the basis for an entire Christian ethic.[21] There is some merit to this, as a similar sentiment is reflected elsewhere in Paul's writings as well. In Col 3:11, Paul states that there is no Greek and Jew, no circumcised and uncircumcised person, no barbarian, Scythian, and no slave and freeman, but Christ is all and in all. Paul's social stance for those within the church is one of equality. There are no superficial grounds by which one is distinguished within the faith community.

This does not mean, however, that Paul advocated enforced equality outside of the faith community. I believe that he did think that there should be equality, but he was also a man of practical insight, so that he clearly refrained from causing any sort of social unrest that would upset the order of Roman society. However, that does not mean that he wished for such social ordering to continue in the church. Philemon gives us a good glimpse into Paul's view of social standing inside and outside the church. In the letter to Philemon, Paul sends a letter back to Philemon,

---

21. Longenecker, *Social Ethics*.

being carried by what was probably his runaway slave Onesimus.[22] In the meantime, since Onesimus went missing (whether he had failed to return from a mission or simply had run off), he had met up with Paul and had become one of the members of the faith community, one of the saints. Now Paul was returning this runaway slave, for whom the penalty under Roman law could have been death, to his master, Philemon. Note what Paul says. First, he frames the letter to Philemon with accountability for his actions before Apphia, whom Paul calls "our sister," and Archippus, whom he calls "our fellow soldier," as well as the church that (probably) met in Philemon's house (v. 2). Second, he notes the Christian virtues that Philemon displays, such as love and faith in Jesus Christ (v. 5). In other words, Philemon too is a member of the church, one of the saints. Third, Paul, who designates himself as a prisoner for the sake of Christ Jesus (v. 9), makes an appeal to Philemon on behalf of Onesimus, whom he calls his "child," whom he has begotten while in prison (v. 10). The one who was once a useless slave to Philemon now has become useful to both Paul and Philemon (v. 11). Fourth, Paul is not violating the law by harboring a slave (v. 13), but returning him to Philemon (v. 12), because he wants Philemon to do the right thing (v. 14). Fifth, Paul notes that now Onesimus is not a slave but a "beloved brother" to both Paul and Philemon, both in a physical and in a spiritual sense (v. 16). Sixth, Paul then asks Philemon to accept Onesimus back on the same terms he would accept Paul, who was the one who led Philemon to faith in Jesus Christ (v. 19). Seventh, Paul closes the letter with confidence that Philemon will do even more than he has indicated (v. 20). I agree with F. F. Bruce that by this letter Paul was indicating the end of social injustice, through a silent revolt in which, within the church, it was impossible for a person to maintain such inequities as slavery.[23] More than that, such was the faith community, the church, that Paul was promoting, that he could count on a slave owner becoming a brother or sister in Christ with a former slave. The household codes of Col 3:18—4:4 and Eph 5:21—6:9, I believe, are cast in the light of a church ethic dictating personal relations, within a larger Roman world, where there was not equality of opportunity or protection for women and children. As Paul says in Col 4:1 to masters, they are to give their slaves justice and fairness, knowing that

---

22. There are a number of questions that have been raised regarding this reconstruction. For a recent treatment of the issues, see Pearson, *Corresponding Sense*, 46–92.

23. Bruce, *Paul*, 401.

they have a master in heaven; and in Eph 6:9, that they must remember that both a slave and a master have a master in heaven, and there is no partiality with him.

The Pauline Church Maintains Practices of Worship

There were standard practices that the Pauline churches seemed to engage in regularly. These include baptism, the Lord's supper, and public worship.

Baptism[24]

Baptism is no doubt important to Paul and one of the important practices of the Pauline church. As he states in Eph 4:5, there is "one Lord, one faith, one baptism." Although some have wanted to temper what is meant by this baptism (making it spiritual, etc.), it is clear that Paul places the practice of baptism on a similar level to recognition of there being one Lord and one faith. That the three are tied together should not come as a surprise. One of the observations regularly made with regard to the confessional statements treated above is that they were often used at the time of baptism. It is entirely logical to think, with Dunn and others,[25] that the confession in Rom 10:9 was uttered by those being baptized. It may well have been the kind of statement that a person about to be baptized would be called upon to confess as a testimony of their faith, as it involved the outward confession of the inward belief regarding Jesus. The confession of Phil 2:6–11 might also be a baptismal statement, because it reflects a three-part confession—from a high exalted status, to descent, to re-exaltation—just as one might move down and out of the water. First Timothy 3:16 may also reflect this pattern, because it begins with manifestation in the flesh and ends with glorification.

Paul assumes that baptism is a practice that the saints of his churches will undergo. In the dispute over incipient denominationalism in 1 Corinthians 1, the assumption is that those involved in the dispute have been baptized (see vv. 13–17). However, the way that Paul phrases his statements seems to make clear that proclamation of the good news regarding Jesus Christ (contained in the confessions of who he is) takes precedence over baptism (v. 17)—he says that Christ did not send him

---

24. Many have written on Pauline notions of baptism. See Whiteley, *Theology of St. Paul*, 166–70; Horrell, *Solidarity and Difference*, 102–6.

25. Dunn, *Romans*, 606.

to baptize, but to preach the gospel. Nevertheless, Paul uses some significant metaphors to speak of baptism. In Rom 6:3 (see also Gal 3:27), Paul asks whether his readers know that all who have been baptized into Christ Jesus have been baptized into his death. He explicates this in v. 4 by noting that we have been buried with him through baptism into death, so that just as Christ was raised from the dead we too might walk in newness of life. This mirrors the descent and ascent framework found in Phil 2:6–11 and 1 Tim 3:16. A similar pattern is found in Col 3:1–4. Though baptism is not mentioned in this passage, Paul relies on the analogy of dying and rising with Christ in the same way as he does when speaking of baptism. The one who is baptized or dies to self and sin is then hidden with Christ in God (v. 3), and then raised up with Christ (v. 1) and will then be revealed with him in glory (v. 4).

Three important conclusions are evident from what Paul says about baptism. The first is that Paul seems to assume a water baptism, in which the person being baptized is immersed in a body of water, such as a river. The second is that baptism is for those who are able to make the confession of faith. The third is that there is no indicated preliminary instruction or teaching before baptism is to take place. In fact, the references to teaching within Paul's letters seem to indicate teaching that goes on within the believing community, and hence probably after baptism. This is consistent with Jesus' words of commission at the end of Matthew's Gospel, when he says, "going into the world, make disciples by baptizing and teaching" (Matt 28:16–20).

Lord's Supper[26]

There is only one passage in Paul that explicitly refers to the Lord's supper. It may seem as if this is not a practice that the Pauline church took very seriously. However, examination of this one passage reveals that Paul seems to have assumed that the saints in local churches gathered regularly to celebrate such a meal together. In 1 Cor 11:23–34, Paul reveals a number of important facts about the Lord's supper. The first is that there was a tradition regarding the night on which Jesus was betrayed that he has passed on to the saints. The language regarding passing on the tradition is very similar to the language used in 1 Cor 15:3–5, the confession regarding Jesus, and probably is meant to have a similar authoritative status. The second is that Paul is reflecting wording that is

---

26. See Horrell, *Solidarity and Difference*, 106–10.

found in the Gospels, in particular Luke's Gospel (see Luke 22:19–20), and so has a direct link back to Jesus himself. The third is that there is a confessional element to participation in the Lord's supper. Just as there was a confessional element to baptism, as we have noted, Paul states that those who eat and drink proclaim the Lord's death until he comes (1 Cor 11:26). Like baptism, as a public statement of dying and rising with Christ, the Lord's supper is a public proclamation of the Lord's death in expectation of his return. The fourth is that there are penalties for participating in the Lord's supper in an unworthy way. Clearly the Lord's supper has more than simply symbolic or memorial value for Paul. He says that some are weak and sick and have even died (he says sleep, using the term euphemistically) because they have participated in an unworthy manner. It is difficult to determine the exact nature of the unworthy participation. Some think that it may be simply greed (see vv. 33–34). However, I think that it is worth considering whether participating in an unworthy manner means the participation of someone who has not made the confession of faith vital to membership in the Pauline church. In 1 Cor 11:27, Paul says that those who have participated unworthily are guilty of the body and blood of the Lord. This may mean that they are still in an unredeemed state in which they are still guilty as sinners of participating in the death of Jesus Christ. In any case, unworthy participation is to be avoided at all costs. The fifth observation is that the Lord's supper is in the context of it being a regular event that is focused upon a meal. This not only mirrors the Passover meal that Jesus celebrated, but reflects the context in which the Pauline church, at least at Corinth, gathered.

Worship

We know very little about the communal worship of the early church, including the Pauline church, although we know they were to gather together (1 Cor 5:4; 11:17, 20, 33). The only passage that really seems to give insight into the actions of gathered believers is found in 1 Cor 14:26.[27] Paul says that, when they assemble, each one is to have a psalm, a teaching, a revelation, a tongue, an interpretation. This may not be an inclusive list of what was to occur at such a gathering (after all, Paul forgot the announcements, the children's sermon, and the special music).

---

27. Cf. Thompson, "Romans 12.1–2," who believes that Rom 12:1–2 is the basis, but must admit that 1 Corinthians gives more practical insight (p. 129).

What he does say, however, does give insight into communal worship in the Pauline churches. The first is that the entire gathering was communal and apparently involved participation by all of those who were gathered together in various ways. Paul's language is that each one is to have the things that are specified. The second is that there is a great variety involved in the communal time together. The psalm may refer to the reading or reciting of a psalm from the Old Testament. It may also, however, refer to the use of music in the communal gathering. In Eph 5:19 and Col 3:16, Paul may be referring to a similar communal gathering of saints. He says in Eph 5:19 that they are to speak to one another in psalms and hymns and spiritual songs, singing and making melody with their heart to the Lord. Similarly, in Col 3:16, he says that they are to admonish one another with psalms, hymns, and spiritual songs, and they are to sing with thankfulness in their hearts to God. There has been much debate regarding the distinctions among psalms, hymns, and spiritual songs. Whereas most think there is no significant distinction, I think that it is worth considering whether there was a distinction being made among psalms being cantillated (Jewish psalms that used a form of speaking and singing), hymns as songs of praise, and spiritual songs as some form of jubilant, or even ecstatic, chants.[28] These various types of songs were meant to be addressed to God but also to have an admonitory value to fellow saints. The teaching may well have involved an exposition of the Old Testament, and even be related to what we would often refer to as preaching. Preaching for Paul, however, may have involved delivering the word of God (2 Tim 4:2; Titus 1:3; cf. 1 Tim 4:5; 2 Tim 2:9) both to those within the community (Rom 12:7; Col 1:28; 1 Tim 4:13; 2 Tim 4:3) and to those outside the believing community in order to convince, rebuke, and exhort those who heard (2 Tim 4:2; 1 Thess 2:13). Revelation is distinct from speaking in tongues, as Paul makes clear in 1 Cor 14:6, where he speaks of bringing a revelation or knowledge or prophecy or teaching, and this seems to involve God giving direct knowledge to the recipient (1 Cor 14:30; Gal 1:12; 2:2; Eph 3:3). I will speak of tongues and revelation below. There is also a passage in 1 Timothy 4 where Paul in instructing his companion Timothy tells him to pay attention to reading (presumably Scripture), exhortation, and teaching (v. 13), but it does not specify whether this is in a communal worshiping context.

28. W. Porter, "Creeds and Hymns," citing Wellesz, "Early Christian Music," 2; Wellesz, *Byzantine Music*, 33–34.

The Pauline Church Is Charismatic in Its Organization

The charismatic nature of the Pauline church is reflected in a variety of ways. These include the nature of its church order and leadership.

Paul makes clear that the church is to be a place where charismatic gifts, that is, those gifts given by the Holy Spirit, are to have expression. The problems of the Corinthian church with manifestation of these gifts have detracted from the clear statements regarding order that Paul makes regarding these gifts. In 1 Cor 12:4–11, just after one of his two fundamental confessional statements, and just before one of his key metaphors for the church, Paul makes a statement about the charismatic gifts. He says that there are varieties of gifts that originate with the one Holy Spirit, and there are varieties of ministries and the same Lord. There is a question of whether the gifts and the ministries are the same, or whether Paul is making a distinction here. If he is making a distinction, he apparently does not wish to pursue it, because he goes on in v. 6 to say there are varieties of effects, but the same God who works all things. I think that Paul is identifying each member of the godhead and then attributing a manifestation to each one. Then he goes on to describe these in a non-inclusive sense, without distinguishing which ones come from which, as if such could be done. (The alternative is to say that we have gifts, ministries, and effects, when they are all effects of the work of God.) All of these are given for the common good of the church. They include "word of wisdom," "word of knowledge," "faith," "gifts of healing," "effecting of miracles," "prophecy," "distinguishing of spirits," "kinds of tongues," and "interpretation of tongues." In one sense, these are all manifestations of the work of the Spirit, and so in that sense only one gift, but manifested in various ways in each individual. Paul makes somewhat similar distinctions elsewhere in his letters. I am encouraged to think that the list in Romans 12 is to be considered in the same light, because Paul uses the analogy of the body in Rom 12:4–5 as well. In Rom 12:6–8, Paul distinguishes another non-inclusive list of gifts. They include prophecy, service, teaching, exhortation, leading, and mercy. There is significant overlap with the list given in 1 Corinthians 12. The final list to consider is found in Eph 4:11. Although Paul does not use the same analogy of the body as he does in 1 Corinthians 12 and Romans 12, he does refer to the phenomena that he cites as designed for the equipping of the saints for the work of service and for the building up of the body of Christ, until we attain unity of the faith

(vv. 12–13)—language that is not foreign to the context in 1 Corinthians 12 and Romans 12. In Eph 4:11, Paul specifies that God according to Christ's gift (v. 7) has given some to be apostles, some prophets, some evangelists, some pastors and teachers. The list is surprisingly similar to the ones already discussed.

There are several observations to be made regarding these gifts. The first is that it is difficult to see these as institutionalized positions in the Pauline church. They seem to be functions that are being performed on the basis of gifts that the saints are given. The second is that there is a wide variety of gifts to be manifested. There is no clear program of their use outlined, but it appears that Paul envisioned a widespread distribution and use of these gifts within the believing community. The third is that Paul does not establish any sort of priority or hierarchy within these gifts. This is in keeping with what we noted above regarding worship within the Pauline community. There are a number of worshipping functions to be performed, just as there are a variety of gifts to be manifested. The fourth is that these gifts are apparently to be used within the believing community, for the building up of that community. These are not public gifts, but church gifts. The fifth is that these gifts are to be used in orderly ways. Paul clearly rebukes those who are manifesting particular gifts in ways that are not suitable (1 Corinthians 14).

From what we have seen, the gifts discussed above are not a part of any sort of hierarchy within the Pauline church. That clearly does not mean that there is no order within the Pauline church, however, as we have seen how Paul talks about their orderly use in 1 Corinthians 14. Paul does entertain two positions of leadership within his churches, however. These are overseers and deacons. In Phil 1:1, Paul addresses the letter to the saints in Philippi, including the overseers and deacons. Many scholars are skeptical that these are positions of church order, because they believe that the charismatic element in the Pauline church meant that such positions were not established until later. However, all of the evidence is that Paul envisioned orderly leadership in his churches from the start. In the book of Acts, if it is to be credited (and I believe that it is), we are told in Acts 11:23 that, on their return trip through Anatolia on the first missionary journey, Paul and Barnabas appointed elders in the churches (so much for congregational government).

In the light of this, I think that it is appropriate to look briefly at the two positions of overseers and deacons as Paul outlines them in 1

Tim 3:1–7, 8–13. (I take overseers and elders as the same position, on the basis of how Paul uses the term for elder in 1 Tim 4:14 and 5:17, as well as Titus 1:5.)

Concerning overseers or elders, Paul has a number of statements to make regarding the worthiness of their work (1 Tim 3:1), their being of model character (vv. 2, 7) and behavior (vv. 3–4), and their spiritual maturity (v. 6; cf. also Titus 1:5–9). Concerning deacons, Paul says that they too must be of model character (vv. 8, 11–12) and behavior (v. 10), and of spiritual maturity (vv. 9, 13). There are several observations to make regarding these lists. The first is that, although they are usually interpreted as gender restrictive in their formulation, this is not necessarily the case. The reference to overseers and deacons may well have usually meant men, but the formulation for overseers is in terms of the generic "someone" (using the indefinite pronoun) desiring the position, and for deacons using the plural. The indefinite pronoun can be either masculine or feminine, and the Greek masculine plural would be expected for any group consisting of mixed gender. The only statement that can be clearly construed as addressed to men is the statement regarding overseers being husband of one wife (1 Tim 3:2; Titus 1:6). This does not mean that the statement is confined to men, however, as it is men in the culture of the times who were more inclined to have more than one wife in sequence, practice divorce and remarriage, have mistresses, or even possibly have multiple wives or women.[29] The specific mention of women in 1 Tim 3:11 is plausibly not to make a distinction between overseers and deacons (or deaconesses), but apparently to address a specific problem that women in Ephesus were having with being lured into various specifically Ephesus-focused religious malpractices, such as were associated with the Artemis and Dionysius cults.[30] The use of the masculine plural pronoun throughout the section on deacons may well include women (see also Titus 1:5). The second observation is that these seem to be two distinct positions to be held by multiple people in every community. The third is that they do not appear to have any direct correlation with the lists of gifts outlined by Paul elsewhere.

---

29. See Treggiari, "Divorce Roman Style," and Corbier, "Divorce and Adoption"; cf. also Ferguson, *Backgrounds*, 72–77.

30. See J. Ferguson, *Religions*, 21–22; Porter, "Ephesians 5.18–19"; Ferguson, *Backgrounds*, 259–66.

The question that naturally arises is concerned with what we today would call ordained ministry in the Pauline church. There is, to my mind, no clear position of what we would call ordained ministry, as typically conceived today, within the Pauline church. In other words, there is no designated vocational position such that the person is the only or one of a very restricted group of elders with designated and special gifts, especially of teaching and preaching. The gifts are meant to be shared by the entire church, including the other gifts that are not usually associated with ordained ministry. Furthermore, the group of overseers may have some of these gifts, but there is no one-to-one correlation with these gifts (note 1 Tim 5:17, where elders are mentioned for double honor, especially those involved in preaching and teaching). Besides, the overseers or elders are not singularly chosen but are appointed in groups within the Pauline churches.

In three places within Paul's letters, he does however refer to the laying on of hands (1 Tim 4:14; 5:22; 2 Tim 1:6). This is often taken as an indication of ordination to something similar to what we now think of as ordained ministry, or possibly as bringing back into fellowship those who have been ostracized.[31] There are a number of problems with both positions, not least that there is no collaborating interpretation before the third century AD. There is the further difficulty that the context does not indicate ordination in anything like the modern sense. As Irwin points out, the passages in 1 Tim 4:14 and 2 Tim 1:6 are in the context, not of a particular office or official function, but of giving spiritual gifts (see 1 Tim 4:13, discussed above). A passage often drawn into the discussion, Acts 13:1–3, is in the context of the same kinds of gifts mentioned above (prophets and teachers) and commissioning for service.[32] Similarly, Acts 6:1–6 does not mention a specific office, but the service of others. I believe that 1 Tim 5:22 refers to a similar context as the above. Paul has mentioned elders who work hard at preaching and teaching and how they are worthy of their wages (1 Tim 5:17–18). The accusation against an elder (v. 19) appears to be in terms of how they have violated their position as elders, and thus the admonition not to lay

---

31. I am dependent on Irwin, "The Laying on of Hands." Irwin argues that laying on of hands in 1 Tim 5:22 refers to making an accusation against another. His conclusion is unconvincing, especially as he fails to explain the use in 1 Tim 4:14 or 2 Tim 1:6, which clearly are related to appointment for a purpose.

32. As Irwin points out, Paul and Barnabas were already leaders in the church ("Laying on of Hands," 125).

hands on them too quickly. As Liefeld so ably states, "the New Testament church did not ordain people to positions of *authority*, but designated people to ministries of *service*."³³

As a last item, I raise the question of what constitutes membership in the Pauline church as an issue related to order. As noted above, Paul envisions everyone who confesses Jesus as Lord and believes in his heart as a member of the church. However, he does not recognize a person being part of the church who is not part of a local church community. In that sense, the implication is that there is no other criterion for membership in the church than confession of faith and belief in Jesus Christ.

The Pauline Church Demands Ethical Behavior

I have mentioned the confessional nature of the Pauline church. One must confess Jesus Christ as Lord as the minimal confession for membership in the community. The title of this paper is "Saints and Sinners," and it is now that we turn to the sinner part. For Paul, the church consists of those who have made their confession of Jesus Christ as Lord and who have faith in him. However, Paul also realizes that those same human beings are sinners in need of repentance.

As Paul says in Rom 3:9, all people, both Jews and Greeks, are under the power of sin, and in 3:23, all have sinned and fall short of God's glory. Instead of leaving us in this condition, Paul says that God provides a means of repentance (Rom 2:4). Those who do repent are able to be restored to the community (2 Cor 7:10), but those who do not repent are a source of mourning for their repeated impurity, immorality, and other sinful behavior (2 Cor 12:21).

Paul's letters are unfortunately filled with examples of those who have sinned and whom he calls to repentance or rejection from the community. The best known example is the immoral behavior of the man who is living with his father's wife (1 Cor 5:1). As Paul says, those in the church are not to associate with such immoral people (1 Cor 5:9).

---

33. Liefeld, "Your Sons and Your Daughters," 144. Liefeld goes further and says that some evangelical churches have an ordination to designate some called to ministry. However, "Such 'privilege' as ordination may confer is not the same as an exclusive right to preside over certain sacramental rites or to exercise governing authority over the church, practices that have no precedent in Scripture. All believers share in a spiritual priesthood, sacramental functions not being assigned to any class (or gender). Scripture uses the word priest only of Christians in general, not of an individual to the exclusion of other believers" (p. 145).

Paul clarifies that he does not mean those of the world, who are by nature immoral (1 Cor 5:10), but a "so-called brother" (NASBrev) who is immoral. The church, Paul says, is to judge those who are within it (1 Cor 5:12), while leaving God to judge those who are outside the church (1 Cor 5:13).

The ethic of the Pauline church is not one of anticipating and expecting sin, however. The ethical demand of those who are within the church is a life of holiness, sometimes referred to as sanctification, the result of life in the Spirit. There are two passages that make this especially clear. In Romans, Paul develops a trajectory that begins with human sinfulness, Christ's justification and reconciliation, and then life in the Spirit as one who is without condemnation before Christ Jesus (Rom 8:1). Those whose sins have been removed and who have set their minds not on things of the flesh but on things of the Spirit (Rom 8:4–5) are those who have the Spirit of God dwelling in them. Paul says that even though they continue to live in a sinful body their spirit is alive because of righteousness, and the Spirit of God who raised Jesus from the dead lives within them (Rom 8:10–11). In 1 Thessalonians, Paul frames this in terms of how we ought to walk in order to please God (4:1). Paul says that the will of God is that those who wish to please God be sanctified or set aside as holy. This involves refraining from immorality and controlling their own desires and passions (1 Thess 4:4–5).

There is also a social dimension to the Pauline church that demands the care of those within the church. There are two important sides to this. One of them is that Paul expects those within the Christian community to be actively involved with and for the community. One of the problems of the Pauline church appears to have been those who for a variety of reasons did not think that work was a necessity (1 Thess 4:11). Paul both sets the example for work (1 Cor 15:10; 1 Thess 2:9; 2 Thess 3:8; cf. Col 4:13) and demands that others work as well (2 Thess 3:10–12). However, there are those, especially the socially disenfranchised such as elderly widows, who are in need and for whom, if their families are not able (1 Tim 5:4, 16), the church is to provide (1 Tim 5:5). One of the common threads of Paul's demand for responsible social action is that those who are not working or busying themselves are too often prone to get into trouble (2 Thess 3:11; 1 Tim 5:11, 14).

The Pauline church therefore is an inclusive and exclusive community. It includes all of those who confess Jesus as Lord and have faith in him, including those who have sinned and repented of their sins and have been welcomed back by the community of saints. After all, this is a community of saints who are all redeemed sinners. The Pauline church also excludes those who are not a part of the community of faith. Those who have not come to make that confession are not members of the church, and I do not see them as included within the activities that Paul outlines as the functions of the church, including its worship, baptism, and celebration of the Lord's supper, but also its teaching and preaching within the community.

The Pauline Church Is an Evangelistic and Eschatological Community

The last distinctive of the Pauline church that I would like to discuss includes two related elements. These are that the Pauline church is an evangelistic and an eschatological community. This means that it is a community that attempts to proclaim the good news regarding Jesus Christ to those who have not heard or do not know of him. The primary motivation for this is an anticipation of the return of the Lord Jesus Christ, which is the eschatological dimension of the church's function and mission.

In Romans 10, Paul outlines the evangelistic imperative of the church in terms of preaching.[34] Expressing his concern for his own people (Rom 9:1—10:5), Paul speaks of the word being near to each one. As a result, if they confess with their mouth that Jesus is Lord and believe in their heart that God raised him from the dead, then they will be saved (Rom 10:9). Paul expands on these words addressed only to the Jews in Rom 9:1—10:5 by stating that whoever believes on him will not be disappointed (Isa 28:16) and whoever will call on the name of the Lord will be saved (Joel 2:32). As Paul says, there is no distinction between Jew and Gentile (Rom 10:12). However, that raises the question of how those who do not believe will be able to call on God and believe. As Paul says, "How will they hear without a preacher? How will they preach unless they are sent?" (Rom 10:14–15). They must hear the word preached before they can come to faith. This is the evangelistic mission of the Pauline church. In 1 Corinthians, Paul says that he was sent to preach the gospel (1 Cor 1:17) to a world that did not know God through its own wisdom (1 Cor 1:21). Paul says that he preached Christ

---

34. See Peerbolte, *Paul the Missionary*, 207–8.

crucified to those who thought of such a thing as foolishness (1 Cor 1:23). Furthermore, in 2 Corinthians, Paul notes that he came to Troas, a new city for outreach, to preach the gospel of Christ and a door was opened for him by the Lord (2 Cor 2:12). He preached Jesus Christ as Lord (2 Cor 4:5).

The function of the Pauline church is to be active as the community of Christian faith in anticipation of the return of the Lord Jesus Christ. The evangelistic preaching, and the preaching, teaching, worshipping, and service of those within the community, are all done in anticipation of the return of Jesus Christ. There is both a personal and cosmic eschatological dimension to this expectation (see Rom 8:18–30), with the church participating in the first. We noted above that Paul instructed the Corinthians that they were to take part in the Lord's supper as a means of proclaiming the Lord's death until his return (1 Cor 11:26). Paul continues in 1 Corinthians 15 by pointing out that Christ's being raised from the dead is the first fruits or the guarantee of resurrection for those who believe in him. He applies this to those who belong to Christ, both those who have already died and those who will still be alive at his return (1 Cor 15:20, 23).

CONCLUSION

The Pauline church is not necessarily an easy spiritual organism to describe. The evidence for it is found throughout Paul's letters, letters that were written to address particular early ecclesial circumstances. Nevertheless, there are a number of common patterns found within the letters that indicate that Paul in his writings had an overall conception of the church. It is this church that I have attempted to describe. The description no doubt will raise a number of questions. One of the major questions is how this church that I have described is related to the church of today. There are indeed a number of similarities, but there are also a number of significant differences. As broached at the outset, the question of the normativity of the Pauline letters emerges whenever one attempts to analyze and synthesize the situations described in Paul's letters. Nevertheless, knowing what Paul thought helps us at least to begin to formulate a normative position that takes the necessary evidence into account.

BIBLIOGRAPHY

Amiot, Francois. *The Key Concepts of St. Paul*. New York: Herder & Herder, 1962.
Ascough, Richard S. *What Are They Saying about the Formation of Pauline Churches?* New York: Paulist, 1998.
Banks, Robert J. *Paul's Idea of Community: The Early House Churches in Their Cultural Setting*. Rev. ed. Peabody, MA: Hendrickson, 1980.
Beker, J. Christiaan. *Paul the Apostle: The Triumph of God in Life and Thought*. Philadelphia: Fortress, 1980.
———. "Paul's Theology: Consistent or Inconsistent?" *NTS* 34 (1988) 364–77.
Bruce, F. F. *Paul: Apostle of the Heart Set Free*. Grand Rapids: Eerdmans, 1974.
Chester, Andrew. "The Pauline Communities." In *Vision for the Church: Studies in Early Christian Ecclesiology in Honour of J. P. M. Sweet*, edited by Markus Bockmuehl and Michael B. Thompson, 105–20. Edinburgh: T. & T. Clark, 1997.
Corbier, Mireille. "Divorce and Adoption as Roman Familial Strategies." In *Marriage, Divorce, and Children in Ancient Rome*, edited by Beryl Rawson, 47–78. Oxford: Clarendon, 1991.
Dunn, James D. G. *Romans*. WBC 38AB. Dallas: Word, 1988.
Ferguson, Everett. *Backgrounds of Early Christianity*. 3rd ed. Grand Rapids: Eerdmans, 2003.
Ferguson, John. *The Religions of the Roman Empire*. Ithaca: Cornell University Press, 1970.
Fowl, Stephen E. *The Story of Christ in the Ethics of Paul: An Analysis of the Function of the Hymnic Material in the Pauline Corpus*. JSNTSup 36. Sheffield: JSOT Press, 1990.
Horrell, David G. *Solidarity and Difference: A Contemporary Reading of Paul's Ethics*. London: T. & T. Clark, 2005.
Irwin, B. P. "The Laying On of Hands in 1 Timothy 5:22: A New Proposal." *BBR* 18.1 (2008) 123–29.
Kramer, Werner. *Christ, Lord, Son of God*. SBT 50. London: SCM, 1966.
Liefeld, Walter L. "Your Sons and Your Daughters Shall Prophesy." In *Women in Ministry: Four Views*, edited by Bonnidell Clouse and Robert G. Clouse, 127–53. Downers Grove, IL: InterVarsity, 1989.
Longenecker, Richard N. *New Testament Social Ethics for Today*. Grand Rapids: Eerdmans, 1984.
McDonald, Lee Martin, and Stanley E. Porter. *Early Christianity and Its Sacred Literature*. Peabody, MA: Hendrickson, 2000.
Pearson, Brook W. R. *Corresponding Sense: Paul, Dialectic and Gadamer*. BIS 58. Leiden: Brill, 2001.
Peerbolte, L. J. Lietaert. *Paul the Missionary*. Leuven: Peeters, 2003.
Porter, Stanley E. "Paul and the Process of Canonization." In *Exploring the Origins of the Bible: Canon Formation in Historical, Literary, and Theological Perspective*, edited by Craig A. Evans and Emanuel Tov, 173–202. Acadia Studies in Bible and Theology. Grand Rapids: Baker, 2008.
———. "Ephesians 5.18–19 and Its Dionysian Background." In *Testimony and Interpretation: Early Christology in Its Judeo-Hellenistic Milieu: Studies in Honour of Petr Pokorny*, edited by J. Mrázek and J. Roskovec, 68–80. JSNTSup 272. London: T. & T. Clark International, 2004.

———. "Wittgenstein's Classes of Utterances and Pauline Ethical Texts: A Study of Galatians 3:28–29 in Context." *JETS* 32 (1989) 85–97.

Porter, Stanley E., and Andrew W. Pitts. "Πίστις with a Preposition and Genitive Modifier: Lexical, Semantic and Syntactic Considerations in the πίστις Χριστοῦ Discussion." In *The Faith of Jesus Christ: Problems and Prospects*, edited by M. F. Bird and P. M. Sprinkle, 33–56. Carlisle: Paternoster, 2010.

Porter, Wendy J. "Creeds and Hymns." In *Dictionary of New Testament Background*, edited by Craig A. Evans and Stanley E. Porter, 231–38. Downers Grove, IL: InterVarsity, 2000.

Stevens, George B. *The Pauline Theology: A Study of the Origin and Correlation of the Doctrinal Teachings of the Apostle Paul*. London: Dickinson, 1892.

Thiselton, Anthony C. *The Two Horizons: New Testament Hermeneutics and Philosophical Description*. Grand Rapids: Eerdmans, 1980.

Thompson, Michael B. "Romans 12.1–2 and Paul's Vision for Worship." In *Vision for the Church: Studies in Early Christian Ecclesiology in Honour of J. P. M. Sweet*, edited by Markus Bockmuehl and Michael B. Thompson, 121–32. Edinburgh: T. & T. Clark, 1997.

Treggiari, S. "Divorce Roman Style: How Easy and How Frequent Was It?" In *Marriage, Divorce, and Children in Ancient Rome*, edited by Beryl Rawson, 31–46. Oxford: Clarendon, 1991.

Wellesz, Egon. "Early Christian Music." In *Early Medieval Music up to 1300*, edited by Anselm Hughes, 1–13. 2nd ed. London: Oxford University Press, 1955.

———. *A History of Byzantine Music and Hymnography*. 2nd ed. Oxford: Clarendon, 1961.

Whiteley, D. E. H. *The Theology of St. Paul*. 2nd ed. Oxford: Blackwell, 1974.

Wittgenstein, Ludwig. *Philosophical Investigations*. Translated by G. E. M. Anscombe. Oxford: Blackwell, 1974.

3

The Church and the Synagogue

Continuity and Discontinuity

Cynthia Long Westfall

INTRODUCTION

ONE OF THE FIELDS that have been rapidly changing in biblical studies concerns the nature of Second Temple Judaism and its relationship to early Christianity as well as Rabbinic Judaism.[1] On the one hand, it is beginning to be assumed that greater continuity exists between early Christianity and Judaism than has been previously recognized, and on the other hand, scholars have convincingly questioned the high degree of continuity between Second Temple Judaism and Rabbinic Judaism that was formerly assumed.[2] There is a growing consensus that there were many Judaisms in first-century Palestine as well as in the dispersion. There is a complementary discussion that challenges previous assump-

---

1. For example, at the 2007 Annual Meeting of the Society of Biblical Literature, the Jewish Christianity session featured a well-attended panel review of Skarsaune and Hvalvik, eds., *Jewish Believers in Jesus*, and Jackson-McCabe, ed., *Jewish Christianity Reconsidered*. The books and the panel review reflect both the changes in the field and the current relevance of the topic.

2. During the 1970s and 1980s, a challenge to the incautious use of rabbinic texts such as the Mishnah, Tosefta, and Talmuds as primary sources for first-century Jewish practice was successfully led by Jacob Neusner. See, for example, Neusner, "Use of the Later Rabbinic Evidence"; Neusner, *Formative Judaism*, 87–97; see also Alexander, "Rabbinic Judaism and the New Testament," 237–46.

tions about the nature of the synagogue in the first century involving its nature and origin.[3] Further attention has been given to "the parting of the ways" between Judaism and Christianity, and there is also a growing consensus that Jewish Christianity and Judaism were to a great degree integrated until the destruction of the temple in AD 70, and still to some degree until the Bar Kochba revolt in AD 132–135.[4] Even these dates are not considered to be associated with the sharp division that is sometimes assumed, and there is even some insistence that the ways of Judaism and Jewish Christianity never parted, in the sense that Judaism and Christianity "remained intertwined long after the Second Temple had fallen and the dust had settled from the Jewish revolts against Rome."[5] In this endeavor, there is increasing collaboration between Jewish and New Testament scholars, where at least one Jewish scholar insists that the term "Jewish Christianity" should be replaced by "Christian Judaism."[6] There is an indication that many if not most first-century and early second-century Christians who were ethnically Jewish did not voluntarily separate from Judaism.[7] Rather, any separation occurred because of external factors that were a result of a combination of pressures from Gentile Christianity and the greater Jewish community.

Burton Vitsosky describes Jewish Christianity as occupying an uncomfortable "middle ground" between Judaism and Christianity and summarizes:

> They just don't fit very neatly; they never did. Ever since it became clear that the law-free mission to the gentiles would create

---

3. Archaeological research of the first-century synagogue particularly received fresh impetus after the creation of the the state of Israel in 1948. See Catto, *Reconstructing the First-Century Synagogue*, 1, 10.

4. The revolt impacted Jewish Christianity in two ways. Because the leader of the revolt, Simon bar Kochba, claimed to be the Messiah, Jewish Christians in Judea did not support him. This sharpened the hostility of Jews toward Jewish Christians. And like all other Jews, Jewish Christians were expelled from Jerusalem.

5. Reed and Becker, "Introduction," 1–33.

6. Daniel Boyarin, University of California-Berkeley, who was a panelist in the Jewish Christianity session and addressed "Definitions, Sources, and Aims" in the panel review of Skarsaune and Hvalvik, eds., *Jewish Believers in Jesus*, and Jackson-McCabe, ed., *Jewish Christianity Reconsidered*, November 19, 2007, Annual Meeting of the Society of Biblical Literature in San Diego.

7. Here, the broad definition of Jewish Christians as Jews by birth or conversion who believed in Jesus is used as opposed to limiting the term to only those Christians who continued a Jewish way of life. For a discussion of the use of the term, see Skarsaune, "Jewish Believers in Jesus in Antiquity," 3–4.

a church and not a synagogue, Jewish-Christianity has been an uncomfortable reality with which to deal. The "Synagogue" didn't like it. The "Church Catholic" didn't like it.[8]

This may have been true during the fourth century. However, during Luke's and Paul's lifetimes, which was arguably the period in which most of the New Testament was written, their writings portray a Jewish Christianity led by the Jerusalem church, which defined the movement and provided the pillars of leadership. These pillars were those who knew Jesus and were eyewitnesses of his ministry. On the other hand, the Pauline mission to the Gentiles was an innovation that had to be defended at the Council of Jerusalem. Whatever Paul's vision was, it was not by any means clear that the "law-free mission to the Gentiles would [exclusively] create a church and not a synagogue" during the period of time in which the New Testament canon was written.[9] Whatever the discomfort that has developed historically among both Jewish and Christian movements and scholars towards Jewish Christians, it must not be anachronistically projected into the context in which the New Testament was written.[10] Before AD 70 or even perhaps AD 136, it was Pauline Christianity that did not fit neatly into the movement.

What does this have to do with the church in Hebrews and the General Epistles as well as the rest of the Johannine literature? The nature of Jewish Christianity raises new questions for the context of the parts of the New Testament that were written by Jewish Christians outside of the Pauline Mission, and impacts their exegesis.[11] Before AD 70 and

---

8. Visotzky, "Prolegomenon," 47.

9. As Skarsaune observes, the religious leadership on both sides of Judaism and Christianity eventually attempted to establish sharp boundaries. Furthermore, "in the long run the religious leadership were the 'winners,' in that their conception of an intrinsic incompatibility between 'Judaism' and 'Christianity' heavily influenced realities 'on the ground' and was destined to form them to a great extent" (Skarsaune, "Jewish Believers in Jesus in Antiquity," 8). However, this was by no means the case while the New Testament was being written, and the ways continued to intersect and overlap into at least the fifth century.

10. Craig Hill describes this anachronistic projection as the dominant approach at the popular level: "Christians such as James and Peter, both leaders of the Jerusalem church, are thought to have thrown off the shackles of their Jewish past. It is not difficult to see in this view an uncritical retrojection of modern Gentile Christianity onto the primitive church" (Hill, "Jerusalem Church," 41).

11. Generally, these texts as well as the Gospel of Matthew have been categorized as Jewish Christian literature, as opposed to the Pauline Epistles, Luke-Acts, and the

the destruction of the temple, the Jewish Christian church in Jerusalem was the authoritative center of Christianity, which was led by James for a significant span of that time period, consisted of thousands of Jews who were "zealous for the Law," and continued to be associated with the temple and the synagogue. The mission to the lost sheep of Israel went forth from Jerusalem, and planted churches through associations with the synagogues that reflected similar character and associations of the mother church, as well as adapted and responded to the conditions and challenges in the Diaspora. Throughout the first century, the apostolic core that conducted and participated in the mission from Jerusalem preserved the eyewitness accounts of Jesus' life and death, developed the Christian interpretation of the Old Testament, and contributed a high Christology and a theology of the identity of God's people rooted in Israel's story. After the destruction of the temple, a number of factors led to hostility on the part of the greater Jewish community towards the Jewish Christians. Some painful conflict and separation between the synagogues and the Jewish Christian churches occurred, not because Jewish Christians were choosing Christianity over Judaism (they did not see the two as mutually exclusive), but because the Jews wished to be distinguished from Christianity, which was coming under increasing pressure and attack from the Roman Empire. The recovery of the central role of Judaism in the birth and foundation of the early church and the writing of the New Testament canon can enhance our understanding of what it means to be a biblical church.

THE JEWISH CHRISTIAN CHURCH IN JERUSALEM BEFORE AD 70 AND THE BOOK OF JAMES

Jerusalem was not only the central city of Israel; it was also geographically, spiritually and politically the center of the Jewish Diaspora, which refers to the places outside of Israel where Jews were living. The function of Jerusalem as the religious center was assured by the location of the temple, which was the place of God's presence and the accompanying cultic worship, to say nothing of the focus of Jewish eschatological expectations. Pilgrims and temple taxes poured into Jerusalem from the Diaspora, and official letters from the Jewish authorities in Jerusalem

---

Gospel of Mark. This is not only due to the traditional views and their internal claims, and external understanding of an apostolic (Jewish) pedigree, but also due to their content.

were sent out, indicating its important political function beyond the borders of Palestine. As Richard Bauckham states, "The Jerusalem church, located at this literal and symbolic center of the Jewish world, rather naturally assumed the corresponding role of center for the renewed Israel, the Christian movement."[12]

The Jerusalem church was also "the authoritative center" of Christianity at least until the Great Jewish Revolt failed in AD 70.[13] Acts and the Pauline Epistles attest to the status of Jerusalem as the mother church of Christianity, for both Gentiles and Jews. Whatever the tension between Paul and Peter, Paul referred to James, Cephas (Peter), and John as the "the pillars" (Gal 2:9). The supervisory role of the Jerusalem church was apparent when the elders in Jerusalem sent Peter and John to assist Philip's Samaritan revival (Acts 8:14–17), and when the Jerusalem church sent Barnabas to Antioch when Gentiles began to be converted in significant numbers (Acts 11:22–24). Both Paul and Acts describe how Paul and Barnabas submitted their practice of admitting uncircumcised Gentiles into the church to the Jerusalem Council (Gal 2:1–10; Acts 15:6–29). James the brother of Jesus was the leader of the Jerusalem church, and initiated the policy towards Gentile believers that was sent out from the Jerusalem apostles and elders to the Gentile believers in the network of Christian communities in Antioch, Syria, and Cilicia.[14] The letter itself assumes the authority and practice of the Jerusalem church to send out authorized messengers and to determine requirements for the Gentile believers (Acts 15:24–29). The Epistle of James fits well into this context. It was a circular letter sent out to Jewish Christian believers

---

12. Bauckham, "James and the Jerusalem Community," 56.

13. The description "authoritative center" comes from Bauckham, ibid. A hundred year span of influence rather than a forty year span might be extrapolated from lists of Jerusalem bishops in Eusebius and Epiphanius. However, after AD 70 the "Jerusalem bishops" appear to have been in exile in Perea and, so Bauckham infers, "it would also have been in this period that it [Jerusalem] began significantly to lose its place of prominence in the world-wide Christian movement and even for Jewish Christians in the Diaspora. This must have been the consequence of the fact that there was no longer a Christian community in Jerusalem itself and that pilgrimage to the temple, which maintained the close links between the Jerusalem church and the Diaspora, will have entirely or largely ceased" (Bauckham, "James and the Jerusalem Community," 80).

14. This reflects the sphere of influence of the Judaizers, reflecting the extent of the problem at the time the letter was written. Note that the recipients of the letter from the Jerusalem Council did not include the churches that Paul and Barnabas planted during Paul's first missionary journey.

in the Diaspora, which fits the description of a missive from the leader of the mother church (James 1:1).[15] In the same way that Antioch was the home church of Paul's mission to the Gentiles, Jerusalem was the home church to the twelve disciples who were eyewitnesses of Jesus' ministry, who were conducting their own mission trips to Jews throughout the Diaspora.

Though Paul claimed an equal calling and status to Peter and the other apostles, outside of the churches he or the members of his team planted, he neither exercised nor claimed authority and status comparable to Peter, the rest of the twelve apostles, or James.[16] Furthermore, Paul taught his churches that they were indebted to the Judean churches and held the latter up as a model (1 Thess 2:14; Rom 15:25–27). Finally, according to Acts, Paul was arrested in Jerusalem because he submitted to James's request that he take part in and finance a purification ritual in the temple to demonstrate that he was living in obedience to the Law and that he did not teach Jewish Christians to reject the Law (Acts 21:20–25). Luke depicts James as claiming at that time that thousands of Jews who were zealous for the law had become Christians (Acts 21:20). This description represented the nature of the heart and center of the Christian movement until the Jewish Christians were expelled from Jerusalem after AD 135.

Our understanding of the Jewish Christian church in Jerusalem must be primarily drawn from Luke's account, which is an interesting source, since, in Acts, Luke is primarily devoted to providing a defense of Paul's mission to the Gentiles.[17] In spite of the fact that Acts argues that the Jerusalem church decided that Gentiles did not have to keep the

---

15. This assumes for the sake of argument that the authorship of James is the leader of the Jerusalem church and the brother of Jesus (Gal 1:19), though it is not the contention of most scholars. However, some, such as Patrick J. Hartin, consider James as "the source behind this letter acting as its authority figure" (Hartin, "Religious Context," 205–6). The first occurrence of James's name in Acts 12:17 is so offhand, without the expected information at the first occurrence of a new participant in a narrative, that one may conclude that the identity and authority of James was shared information with the readers of Acts as well as the Epistle of James.

16. It may be argued that his actual authority did not equal Peter's and James's even within his own churches such as Corinth.

17. As Jacob Jervell asserts, "Acts is, to a great extent, a book on Paul" (Jervell, *Theology of the Acts*, 82). See Hvalvik's brief summary about the centrality of Paul (Hvalvik, "Paul as a Jewish Believer," 121). See also Porter and Westfall, "Cord of Three Strands," 109–10.

Law, Luke portrays the Jewish Christian church in Jerusalem as maintaining a close association with the temple and cult and interacting with local synagogues. In addition, the early church met in homes, and lived in community where they held possessions in common. Luke portrays other Jews as referring to the Jerusalem church with the term "party" (αἵρεσις, *hairesis*; see Acts 24:5; 28:22). According to Bauckham, this terminology suggests that other Jews considered Jewish Christianity to be a distinctive party or sect belonging to Judaism, comparable to the Sadducees, Pharisees, and Essenes (Acts 5:17; 15:5; 26:5; see also Josephus, *Ant.* 13.171).[18]

Unlike the Essenes, such as the Qumran community who rejected the Second Temple, the Jerusalem church was less sectarian because it maintained a strong attachment to the temple. The members attended temple prayers at the time of the burnt offerings (Acts 2:46a, 47a; 3:1, 11), the apostles taught daily in the outer court (Acts 2:42, 46; 5:12),[19] and some members participated in cultic rituals such as Nazarite vows and purification ceremonies, which included offering sacrifices that were "extensive, expensive and expressive of the spirit of total commitment to the Lord."[20] As mentioned above, Paul footed the bill for four men who had presumably made a Nazarite vow.[21] He was arrested while par-

---

18. However, the occurrences may be too few to maintain with Bauckham that "it must reflect a standard Jewish Greek terminology for the various parties within first-century Palestinian Judaism, based on comparing them, as Josephus explicitly does, with Greek philosophical schools" (Bauckham, "James and the Jerusalem Community," 61).

19. The daily temple attendance that characterized the church at the time of its foundation is not expressly mentioned when the church is mentioned in Acts after chapter 5, but neither are the other practices of teaching, breaking bread, and praying, so that they may be taken to be a pattern for the early church. However, the mention of participation in cult ritual occurs much later, in Acts 21.

20. Aptly described by Allen and Barker in the *NIV Study Bible* footnotes, 199, on Num 6:13–20. In the case of the Nazarite vow, according to Num 6:1–21, the vow of separation was concluded with offering a year-old ewe lamb as a burnt offering, a year-old ewe lamb for a sin offering, a ram for a fellowship offering, and offerings of grain, drink, and unleavened bread consisting of cakes and wafers. Arguments that the temple association was mission-motivated can account for the daily teaching but it cannot account for the ritual participation. The making of offerings for sin and guilt associated with the Nazarite vow indicates either that Jesus' death was not yet understood as a once-for-all offering for sin as the book of Hebrews would eventually teach, or that the early believers did not see a conflict of significance between the sacrifice for a vow and Jesus' sacrifice.

21. In the case of Acts 21:23–24, the seven-day period of purification may indi-

ticipating in their purification ceremony located in the Court of Israel beyond the inscribed markers that forbade entrance to the Gentiles (Acts 21:28–29). Paul's arrest took place around AD 59, and since the Jerusalem church maintained this kind of close association with the temple for nearly thirty years, one may assume that similar associations continued for the next eleven years until the destruction of the temple.[22] The account in Acts indicates that the Christian Jews and their apostolic leadership in Jerusalem observed the Law.[23]

It is likely that the Jewish Christians in Jerusalem also maintained relationships with the synagogues. The "homogenous" nature of the synagogue has been assumed in much New Testament scholarship in the past, but that was largely due to assuming that the fourth-century rabbinic synagogue was the same as a first-century synagogue. It is now recognized that what was termed a "synagogue" or a place of prayer had a variety of liturgical, social, and institutional functions. A synagogue in Galilee should not be perceived as being exactly the same as a synagogue in a Diaspora city.[24] The architecture and function of the first-century synagogue varied according to its location. Furthermore, while "synagogue" came to be a term that referred to a building in which religious activities took place, in the first century the term was more flexible and wide-ranging and it could refer to the building or the community gathering, and the activities of the synagogue were not confined to a religious nature.[25]

Jesus had a custom of attending the synagogue and reading Scripture (Luke 4:16), so that a continued association of Jewish Christians with

---

cate that the four men had been in the presence of someone who had suddenly died. Therefore they may have each offered two pigeons on the first day and after seven days, each offered a year-old male lamb as a guilt offering (6:9–12), so that Paul may have "only" paid for eight pigeons and four lambs rather than the larger number of offerings for the conclusion of the vow.

22. The events in Acts were probably concluded in AD 62, and all of the Pauline corpus would have been completed with the possible exception of the Pastoral Epistles, so that this composite scenario represented the temple practices of Judean Christianity during the time that most of the New Testament was written, granting a dating for Luke-Acts that reflects the information recorded.

23. As Bauckham states, "All our evidence suggests that it was entirely taken for granted in the Jerusalem church that Jewish Christians remained Torah-observant" (Bauckham, "James and the Jerusalem Community," 65).

24. Catto, *Reconstructing the First-Century Synagogue*, 4.

25. Ibid., 7.

the synagogues should not surprise us. There were a large number of Palestinian and Hellenist synagogues in Jerusalem.[26] Groups of Hellenist Jews had their own synagogues that retained close contact with their cities of origin in which they could continue to worship weekly as they did at home, participating in familiar rituals with other Jews that shared the same background and spoke the same dialect of Greek.[27] The story of the stoning of Stephen may document an instance of a continued association of the members of the Jerusalem church with their natural networks in the local synagogues in Jerusalem (Acts 6:8–10). Stephen, who was a Hellenist, came into conflict with Jews from "the Synagogue of the Freedmen," which included Hellenist Jews from Cyrene, Alexandria, Cilicia, and Asia. It may be inferred that the conflict came because of his continued association with the synagogue, and the hostility toward Stephen did not indicate any kind of rejection of the synagogue on the part of Christians. Associations of Jewish Christians with their natural networks through the synagogues would be expected since they included familial, social, and institutional associations and activities as well as functioning as places of prayer and reading the Torah.

The church also functioned as a community apart from meeting and worshipping in the temple and synagogue. It met in smaller groups in homes and private rooms where people gathered privately, prayed, and shared common meals. Communal meals, or "breaking bread," were clearly an important part of their common life. While some see the reference in Acts 2:42 as a reference to the Eucharist, it is more likely a reference to a more general practice of sacred communal meals that were common among the communities of Diaspora Jews, sometimes in a *triclinium* (a formal dining room in a Roman building) built into the synagogue.[28] According to Luke, the early church in Jerusalem also prac-

26. The Babylonian Talmud claimed that there were 394 synagogues in Jerusalem before the destruction of the temple, whereas the Jerusalem Talmud claimed there were 480 synagogues. While Catto suggests that these numbers may be an exaggeration, he describes the archaeological evidence of one synagogue from the first century (ibid., 82–85).

27. There has been a long-held view that the synagogue originated in the Babylonian exile with the absence of the temple, but this is no longer the consensus of scholars.

28. Josephus, among others, attests to the importance and place of sacred meals in the Jewish community (*Ant.* 14:214–15). Catto suggests that the practice of sacred meals in the synagogues may have reflected an influence of Hellenistic guilds in both the architecture and form of the meals. Archaeological remains of a synagogue at Ostia appear to have incorporated some of the features of the guild buildings into the

ticed a "community of goods" where the members sold their possessions and held everything in common (Acts 2:44–45; 4:32—5:11). This practice not only continued patterns established by Jesus and the disciples who shared a common purse (Luke 8:3; John 12:6), but also paralleled practices of the Qumran community and Essene groups throughout the towns and cities of Palestine.[29] The practice modeled the early church's commitment to caring for the members who had needs. The discrete meetings of the church were framed as gatherings of an extended family that loved each other, gathered together, and took care of its own. However, the situation was not without its problems, as the young church grew and its membership reflected the cultural and linguistic variety of the synagogues in Jerusalem. There was an early conflict between the "Hebrews" who were Jewish Christians that spoke Aramaic, and the "Hellenists" who were Jewish Christians from the Diaspora that spoke Greek. The majority of Jesus' followers and the early leadership in the church were from Galilee and Judea, and the Hellenists claimed that when food was distributed daily by the Hebrew Christians, the Hellenist widows were overlooked.[30] The solution was to appoint a second tier of leadership consisting of six spiritually qualified Hellenists (all had Greek names) and a proselyte (Nicholas from Antioch) to ensure equitable food distribution and to leave the twelve apostles free to concentrate on the "ministry of the word of God" (Acts 6:1–6). This solution incorporated greater diversity into the leadership and practice of the early church, which resulted in rapid growth (Acts 6:7) and gave authority and impetus to the Hellenist leaders Steven and Philip.

Worship and community practices of the early church in Jerusalem reflected both the cultural context of Israel and influences and cultural imports from the Diaspora. The church continued in association with the temple and the synagogues and met as a discrete Christian community as well, with its own structure of leadership, so that the synagogue and the church had overlapping functions, but it does not appear that churches were converted synagogues. The relationship of the Jewish

---

synagogue building including a *triclinium* for meals (*Reconstructing the First-Century Synagogue*, 143–47).

29. Capper, "Palestinian Cultural Context."

30. There may have been a disproportionate number of needy Hellenist widows due to the practice of Jews from the Diaspora returning to die in Jerusalem, leaving widows in reduced straights.

Christians to the synagogues appears to be similar to the behavior of people today in the Charismatic Movement who, by definition, continue to attend their traditional churches and to associate with their denominations after experiencing a sign gift and a paradigm shift.

The New Testament letter most closely related to the Jerusalem church is James.[31] When read in the context of Luke's description of James and the Jerusalem church, the book of James is consistent with the church's supervisory role, the zealous relationship with the Law that is coherent within Second Temple Israel and the thousands of Jewish Christian believers, and an assumed association of Jewish Christians with the synagogue in the Diaspora.

James writes to "the twelve tribes who are dispersed abroad" (Jas 1:1), which refers to Jews in the Diaspora who also have faith "in our glorious Lord Jesus Christ" (2:1). The concerns and theology of the letter reflect identifiable issues among the peasants and merchants in first century Palestine, but are also relevant to the Hellenist Jewish communities.[32] The letter does not display an identifiable concern for a mission to the Gentiles, but is rather more concerned with critiquing economic conditions under the Roman Empire.[33]

James describes the Law as royal and perfect and refers to the Law of freedom (Jas 1:25; 2:8–12; 4:11–12) but is primarily interested in moral aspects of the Law and its social function in the community.[34] Purity is also an important concept but is primarily expressed ethically rather than ritually (1:24; 3:17; 4:4). James is often read as being consciously in opposition to and in competition with Paul in his understanding of law and faith. While there is apparent tension between Paul and James

---

31. Jude may also be read in a similar context for many of the same reasons. However, because of its content and its association with 2 Peter, it will be considered with the Jewish *Theologoumena* below.

32. Though scholars such as Martin Dibelius suggest that James lacks cohesion because it does not apply to a single audience or a single set of circumstances, its assumed association with James's leadership and his role in Jerusalem obviates such evaluations (see Dibelius, *James*, 11).

33. See Westfall, "Running the Gamut."

34. Scholars are divided on what James means by the "law" and many take it to refer to a messianic new law. See, for example, Davids, *James*, 99–100. However, if one allows Luke's description of James to be credible, then taking "law" as a reference to the biblical Torah is more convincing. Also, see Hartin, "Religious Context," 210–20.

on both sides, Patrick Hartin articulates the different approaches to law between Paul and James as focusing on different concerns:

> Paul's main concern is to oppose those who attribute any salvific function to the law; James's concern lies with the social function of the law. James is not entering the conflict in which Paul is involved. He shows that he is heir to traditions in early Christianity that still preserve a very positive understanding of the Torah.[35]

This helps to contextualize Luke's account of Paul's compliance with James's request to demonstrate his obedience to the Law in order to conciliate the thousands of Jewish Christian believers who are zealous for the Law (Acts 21:20–25). James's request that Paul participate in a purification ritual apparently did not compromise Paul's view of his relationship to the Law as a Jew. That is not to say that Paul's understanding, theology, and practice or non-practice of the Law would have been shared and articulated by Jewish Christians in Jerusalem.

James's application of the Law is directed toward, concerned for, and supportive of communities of Jewish Christians. The communities in his sphere of influence lie not only in Jerusalem, but also outside of Israel. All are addressed as "brothers and sisters," and treated as an extended family. James assumes that they have their own organizational structures that include elders with certain recognized functions and responsibilities (5:14) and teachers with specific qualifications (3:1). James also assumes that they remain in association with the synagogues (2:2), but it is not probable that the elders and teachers of the church were synonymous with the leadership of the synagogue in most cases. The Jewish Christians would meet separately as a community.

In conclusion, the Jerusalem church under James's leadership included several features: it provided authoritative and responsible leadership of the Christian movement, the Law continued to be observed by the Jews that exercised faith in Christ, Jewish Christians continued to meet in the temple and participate in the temple cult until its destruction, Jerusalem Christians continued to be associated with the synagogues, and the Christian community also gathered privately in homes and private rooms for teaching, prayer, and meals, and also had an institutional structure of leadership.[36] The mission to the Jews that went out

---

35. Hartin, "Religious Context," 216.

36. Clearly, the synagogue and the church are not the same, in terms of either the group as a whole, the assembly, or the structure. However, the range of meaning of

from the church in Jerusalem had continuity with the mother church, but also adapted and responded to the conditions and challenges of the Diaspora.

THE JEWISH CHRISTIAN MISSION AND CHURCH OUTSIDE OF JERUSALEM

The Jewish mission that planted churches all over the Diaspora originated with Jesus' ministry to Israel (Matt 15:24), his commission of the twelve apostles to preach to Israel until his eschatological return (Matt 10:6, 23), and the spread of the gospel from the mother church in Jerusalem initiated by the twelve apostles commissioned by Jesus after his resurrection (Acts 1:8). At first, the disciples had little concern for the Gentiles, except perhaps for the hope that the nations would flock to Mount Zion in fulfillment of their eschatological expectations (Matt 10:3–6, 23; 15:24; cf. 8:11–12 // Luke 13:23–30 and Mark 11:17; cf. Isa 56:7). However, the first converts to early Christianity were "God-fearing Jews" from all over the Diaspora who were exposed to Christianity through spontaneous preaching in tongues and who responded to Peter's sermon during Pentecost (Acts 2:8–12, 41). In one sense, the church became multi-cultural at this point, because these Jews were "culturally and linguistically members of many nations."[37]

Many believe that the church in Rome was planted by the "visitors from Rome" who were present at Pentecost in Acts 2:10 and brought the gospel back after spending time with the church in Jerusalem. Whatever the Roman church's origin, Reidar Hvalvik is most likely correct in stating: "It is clear that the cradle of Roman Christianity is to be found within the Jewish community."[38] More specifically, the origin of Roman Christianity was the Roman synagogue—the Roman church already existed when Paul met Priscilla and Aquila in Corinth around AD 50 after they were expelled with other Jews from Rome in AD 49 by the edict of Claudius because of riots over Christianity (Acts 18:1–2).[39] This

---

συναγωγή is very similar to the range of meaning of ἐκκλησία, and both can mean a group as a whole or the gathering. At this time, there is no evidence that ἐκκλησία meant the building as well, but the extension of the meaning to the building was a natural extension when Christians began to have buildings.

37. Keener, *Bible Background Commentary*, 327.
38. Hvalvik, "Jewish Believers," 184.
39. Support for this interpretation of "Chrestus" in the Jewish riot reported in *De*

plausible explanation fits the fourth-century writer Ambrosiaster's assertion that the gospel came to Rome through Jews so that early Roman Christians professed Christ but kept the Law, and so that their faith in Christ was practiced as a Jewish rite.[40] However, the conversion of godfearing Gentiles associated with the synagogues followed by the expulsion of the Jews from Rome would have resulted in a church that was re-formed and led by Gentiles during the five years that the Jews were absent, but included a strong minority of Christian Jews that returned from exile after Claudius's death in AD 54, including Priscilla and Aquila (Rom 16:3–16).[41] This would have been a situation rife with tensions and questions concerning the relationship between Jews and Gentiles and the future of Israel that Paul attempts to address in Romans. Both Paul and Peter are associated with the church at Rome. Paul was imprisoned there at least once, purportedly wrote the Prison Epistles from there, and was executed there. The most reliable traditions place Peter in Rome shortly after Paul's death. Rome appears to be the provenance of 1 Peter (1 Pet 5:13), and Peter was also executed there.

A second wave of church growth occurred in a similarly spontaneous way. The stoning of Stephen and the subsequent persecution (Acts 7:59—8:8) shifted the margins of the early church growth to the Jews in the Diaspora. Jewish Christianity spread through the Hellenist believers fleeing the persecution, and churches were planted in the Jewish communities outside of Palestine. Luke's account implies that the gospel first spread through the synagogues, because when Paul wished to expand his persecution of the church outside of Jerusalem, "He went to the high priest and asked him for letters to the synagogues in Damascus, so that if he found any there who belonged to the Way, whether men or women, he could take them as prisoners to Jerusalem" (Acts 9:1–3). Ironically, when Paul was converted, he immediately began to preach Christ in the synagogues (Acts 9:20). Paul's well-documented strategy during his missionary journeys of first going to the Jewish synagogue (cf. Acts 14:1) did not originate with him, but with the Hellenist evangelists.

vita Caesarum by the Roman historian Suetonius is discussed convincingly by Hvalvik, "Jewish Believers," 181. The riot was in the ninth year of Claudius's reign according to Orosius's *Historia adversus Paganos*, 417/18.

40. *Corpus scriptorium ecclesiasticorum latinorum* 81:5–6.

41. Hvalvik concludes that if the names in Romans 16 are representative of the percentage of Jews in the congregation, then close to 30 percent of the church could be Jewish (Hvalvik, "Jewish Believers," 193).

Often the portrayal of the synagogues and churches in these texts is understood solely according to the Luke-Acts account and the Pauline model(s)—Stephen Catto's criticism of the scholarly treatment of the synagogue that "the evidence of the New Testament has been used as a single source without enough recognition of the different times and communities in which any particular gospel or letter may have been written" applies equally or even more to the church.[42] However, if there is a high level of continuity between Judaism and Jewish Christianity, then our growing understanding of the synagogue may well provide a better frame of reference than our understanding of the Pauline model alone, which was a frontier mission outreach that intentionally reached across ethnic boundaries. When Paul turned from his outreach in the synagogue and focused on his outreach to the Gentiles in Corinth after reasoning at the synagogue every Sabbath in Acts 18:6, one cannot interpret this as paradigmatic for Paul, let alone a widespread policy of the early church that involved abandoning the synagogues and turning away from the Jews. In Acts 18:8, Paul converts the synagogue ruler and his household, and when Paul moves on from Corinth to Ephesus in 18:19, he again starts his ministry with the synagogue, reasoning with the Jews. One should not assume that Paul's Jewish converts abandoned association with their synagogues, and it is certain that all the other Jewish Christian first-century evangelists and believers were not abandoning the synagogue.

Paul spoke of the existence of three gospels in the Diaspora in Galatians: the gospel for the Gentiles or the uncircumcision led by Paul (Gal 2:7), the gospel for the Jews or the circumcision led by Peter (Gal 2:7), and the third gospel of the "Judaizers" that were associated with James (at least initially), the party of the Pharisees and the Jerusalem church (Gal 1:6–9).[43] Paul attacks the third gospel. When a delegation sent from James arrived in Antioch, they were astounded that the Gentile believers were not required to be circumcised. As Bauckham reasons, up until the Judaizers and Paul drew the lines in the sand, "we should probably assume that such Gentiles were required to become Jews and that initially this was uncontroversial."[44] It became a controversy in Antioch

---

42. Catto, *Reconstructing the First-Century Synagogue*, 9.

43. The conflict in 2 Corinthians sounds similar, but is centered on the concept and claim of apostleship, and conflict between personalities and leadership styles.

44. Bauckham, "James and the Jerusalem Community," 73.

when the Judaizers, without direct authorization from James or the other apostles (Acts 15:24), explicitly taught that the Gentiles in Antioch must be circumcised and keep the Law as a requirement for salvation (15:1).[45] Apparently the teaching spread through the surrounding regions of Syria and Cilicia (15:23—which indicates that a significant number of Gentiles had been converted by the Jewish mission in these areas), and found strong support with the party of the Pharisees in Jerusalem who had become believers (Acts 15:5). While there is clearly tension and conflict among Paul, Peter, and James (e.g., Gal 2:11–14), all three are depicted by Luke as ultimately recognizing each other's validity after a decision-making process at the Jerusalem Council.

Jewish Christian texts are sometimes read in the context of the Judaizing controversy, which applies to the Pauline mission. The Judaizing controversy concerned the requirements for the salvation of the Gentiles and whether Gentiles should be required to keep the Law. This was not an issue for the Jewish Christians and their own relationship to the Law and circumcision, and it cannot be assumed that there was a policy on the part of the early Jewish Christian church to disassociate Jewish Christians from the Law, the temple, or the synagogue.[46] The policy that the early church formed was that Gentiles were not required to become Jews in order to receive salvation and to be added into the people of God. However, it was expected and adamantly required that Jews continued to be Jews.[47]

According to Paul, God appointed him as an apostle to the Gentiles and God appointed Peter as an apostle to the Jews (Gal 2:7–8). This distinction seems somewhat confusing when compared with Acts, where Paul's strategy in each city starts with the synagogue, and he converts Jews as well as Gentiles. Similarly, according to Luke, it is Peter that makes the first Gentile converts when he preaches to Cornelius and his household (Acts 10). However, the distinction between the missions is one of focus rather than exclusion and segregation. One may say that the

---

45. See Dunn, *Unity and Diversity*, 23.

46. The ramifications particularly may reverse a popular reading of Hebrews that presupposes that Hebrews is a polemic against Judaism and the author is attempting to prevent Jewish Christians from "reverting back to Judaism" (see, for example, Kim, *Polemic in the Book of Hebrews*).

47. As Bauckham asserts, "Of course, the decision of the Jerusalem council made no difference to Jewish Christian obedience to the Torah, which was taken entirely for granted" (Bauckham, "James and the Jerusalem Community," 74).

literature from the Pauline circle is contextualized to communicate to "ideal" Gentile Christian readers, though historically the churches that were addressed in the Pauline epistles often included Jewish Christians. The Pauline Epistles were intended to speak to the Gentile culture of the city in which the church was located. The Jewish Christian literature is categorized primarily according to authorship—the authors of Hebrews, the General Epistles, and the Johannine literature are generally held to be Jewish believers. The question of the identity of the readers may be more complex. With the exception of 1 Peter, the content in these documents appears to be primarily relevant to Jewish Christian communities, though many scholars argue that the recipients may include Gentiles.[48] These texts are not contextualized or adapted for Gentile readers, or at least they are oriented to the Jewish worldview of the author. The author's worldview is assumed to be shared or prioritized by the readers—Gentile readers who associated with the local Jewish community that gathered at a synagogue could also conceivably be part of the readers.[49] "Going to the Jews" primarily involved working through the local synagogues, but Gentiles could be reached in the process (Acts 18:5). Like Paul, the Jewish Christian apostles would reason with Greeks as well as Jews as they evangelized through the synagogue network.

THE JEWISH THEOLOGOUMENA AND THE JEWISH CHRISTIAN CORPUS

According to Bauckham, the Jerusalem church contributed two forms of activity that were essential and were among its most important contributions to the Christian movement: handing down the traditions and sayings of Jesus, and "the development of Christian 'pesher' interpretation of the biblical prophetic texts in which the Christians read the events of eschatological fulfillment in which they were involved."[50] The Jewish Christian corpus, consisting of the Gospels of Matthew and John

---

48. The recipients of 1 Peter were either Gentiles (the general consensus, see Michaels, *1 Peter*, xlvi) or a mixed group of Jewish and Gentile believers. In Hebrews and the General Epistles, the term ἔθνος occurs only in 1 Peter (1 Pet 2:9, 12; 4:3; cf. 3 John 7).

49. According to Cohen, Gentiles often mingled with Jews to varied degrees and even observed Jewish rituals and practices without conversion or any other formal relationship (Cohen, *Beginnings of Jewishness*, 67).

50. Bauckham, "James and the Jerusalem Community," 66.

(and possibly Mark), Jude, 1 and 2 Peter, as well as the Johannine epistles and Revelation, are a representative sample of the contribution of the Jerusalem church to these two forms of activity. In addition, the author of the letter to the Hebrews claims that he and the recipients received the gospel from eyewitnesses with apostolic confirmation (Heb 2:3–4). This places the author of Hebrews and the recipients within the second generation of the Jewish Christian mission. While scholars do not all agree with the internal evidence and accompanying traditions that the Jewish Christian corpus was directly written by the apostles, pillars, and brothers of Christ, scholars are coming to a consensus that (with the exception of Hebrews) they consciously and intentionally indicate an origin in apostolic circles and their content often displays some association with the Jerusalem church.[51] One of the concerns and contributions of the Jewish Christian corpus in its activity of the interpretation of the biblical prophetic texts is about the identity of the people of God, which was closely related to the development of the identity of Jesus Christ.

The Jewish Christian documents develop a body of interpretation of the biblical prophetic texts that includes elements of identity concerning Jesus and the people of God that draw heavily from the Old Testament and the Maccabean and apocryphal traditions.[52] Second Peter and Jude respond to the infiltration of false prophets and teachers into the Jewish Christian community. The authors are drawing the boundaries of faith and the identity of the people of God so that the conflict is with adversaries who are outsiders.[53] Similarly, 1, 2, and 3 John reflect possibly early Gnostic or docetic disputes in the church concerning the genuine humanity of Christ (1 John 1:1–3; 4:2–3; 5:6; 2 John 7). Those letters also portray the adversaries who question the identity of Jesus as the Christ (1 John 2:22; 3:23; 4:2; 5:1) and the Son of God (1 John 4:15; 5:5, 10, 12) as outsiders, even "antichrists" who "went out from us" (1 John 2:18–19). There is an essential and formative missiological and ecclesial concern for the content of faith that is central for proclamation, and

---

51. The discussion of the authorship of the individual books is beyond the purposes of this paper. However, I assume an apostolic association of the Jewish Christian corpus with the mission to the Jews that was directly associated with Jerusalem until AD 70.

52. Concerning John, D. Moody Smith wrote, "It is in the interest of the evangelist not to destroy or negate Judaism, but to remain in dialogue with it. . . . John holds traditional Jewish messianism and his own distinctive Christology in creative tension" (Smith, "John," 109).

53. Westfall, "Hebrew Mission," 192.

for membership in the church that is the eschatological people of God. Clearly, the lines of membership and the circle of community are drawn in such a way that Jewish believers in Jesus are distinguished from the rest of Judaism.

Both Hebrews and 1 Peter demonstrate continuity between Israel and the church. This argument permeates Hebrews, and much of the argument of Hebrews rests on explicit parallels between the Israelites in the Exodus and wilderness generation and the readers (Hebrews 3–4). The association between Christian believers and their Jewish ancestors comes to a climax in chapter 12. The characters from the Old Testament, the apocryphal traditions, and Jewish tradition are examples of faith in chapter 11. They have neither received the promises, nor have they been made perfect because they have been waiting for the Christian believers (11:39–40). They are now avidly witnessing the believers' "race"; they are joined together in a festival assembly and are being made perfect together with the "church of the firstborn" (12:1–2, 22–24).[54]

In 1 Peter, Old Testament imagery for Israel is utilized in the description of the church as God's flock (1 Pet 5:2–4) and the house of God (1 Pet 4:17). However, it is 1 Pet 2:1–10 that is particularly marked in transferring to the church a number of phrases that describe Israelites in the Old Testament, particularly in v. 9: "a chosen people, a royal priesthood, a holy nation, God's special possession." As Marshall states:

> We have one of the most powerful statements in the New Testament identifying the company of believers as the people of God; language used to describe the privileged position of the Jews as the people of God in the Old Testament is now deliberately applied to the readers so that they are identified as this people.[55]

What is remarkable about 1 Peter is the fact that, as a Jewish Christian interpreter, the author consciously applies the identity of Israel to Gentiles.

The work of the Jewish Christian corpus concerning the identity of Christ and the people of God provides a major contribution to the Christian movement. These documents also indicate that the authors forged the identity of Jesus Christ and the Christian movement in the midst of and in opposition to challenges they faced within the tradi-

---

54. Westfall, *Discourse Analysis of Hebrews*, 275.
55. Marshall, *New Testament Theology*, 654.

tions and varieties of Judaism. Their work indicates a consciousness of continuity with the faithful remnant of Israel but also a development of a distinct identity and separation from Jews who did not confess Christ. The Jewish Christians saw themselves as the true Israel, and, according to Acts and 1 Peter, willingly and explicitly extended Israel's identity to Gentile believers. However, the addition of uncircumcised Gentiles was never viewed as a replacement of Israel as the people of God. Rather, Paul's description of the Gentiles as being "grafted into" Israel (Rom 11:17–24) is an apt description of the relationship of the Gentiles to the church, which remains clearly Jewish, not only in the first century, but eschatologically, as is illustrated in Revelation.

THE GOSPEL OF JOHN AND COMMUNITIES OF REVELATION PART WITH THE SYNAGOGUE IN ASIA MINOR

The Gospel of John and the book of Revelation are often associated with each other, not only or primarily because of the traditional association of the "disciple that Jesus loved" (John 13:23; 21:20–24) with the prophet John who wrote Revelation (Rev 1:1, 4, 9–20; 22:8), but because of similar background, provenances, and content. Most scholars show little hesitation in recognizing these texts as Jewish in origin.[56] While many assert that the author(s) is a Hellenist Jew, a significant number are also agreed that even if they place both documents toward the end of the first century, the author(s) shows an intimate acquaintance with Israel before the destruction of the temple. The traditional location of the recipients as Asia Minor is explicit in Revelation, and reasonably convincing for the provenance of John. The similar content that is of special interest is the hostility and polemic towards the Jews in both texts. The hostility reflects conflict between the Jewish Christian churches and the synagogues after the destruction of the temple in AD 70 and the ultimate attack on, rejection of, and expulsion of Christian Jews from the

56. The author's claim to be "the disciple whom Jesus loved" was inherently a claim to be an eyewitness and a guarantor of the tradition, which means being a Jewish Christian by definition (Bauckham, *Jesus and the Eyewitnesses*, 358–83). The Jewish orientation of Revelation can be seen in the numerous references to the Old Testament and Israel's priority in salvation history. For further discussion of the authorship of Revelation, see Hirschberg, who claims, "Among the New Testament writings Revelation bears the clearest stamp of Jewish-Christian origins" ("Jewish Believers in Asia Minor," 218–19).

synagogues. In spite of the breakdown between the synagogues and the churches, Revelation maintains the central place of the Jewish people in salvation history and the eschatological restoration of Israel that is promised in the Old Testament, though there is definitely a universal new creation where the Gentiles are fully included.

There were five developments that directly contributed to hostility between the church and the synagogue: the developing Jewish Christian views about the identity of Jesus, the temple's destruction in AD 70, the humiliating imposition of a war reparation tax on all Jews in the Roman Empire, the increasing criminalization of Christianity by the Roman Empire, and the desire on the part of the Jews to be distinguished from the Christians. The identification of Jesus as the Messiah and the development of the implications in terms of royalty, the temple, and the parousia is a particular emphasis of the Hebrew Christian texts.[57] The Gospel of John is the apex of the trajectory of this development, for it clarifies Jesus' divinity and delivers what Andrew Chester calls the most highly developed Christology in the New Testament.[58] Howard Marshall summarizes the description of Jesus in the Gospel of John:

> Jesus is presented unequivocally as the incarnate Word, through whom God created the world and communicates with it, and more personally as his Son who was with the Father before he came into the world and will return to him. His place within the divine identity is clearly depicted. This Christology is also expressed in terms of his being Messiah and Son of Man. Jesus acts as God's messenger and his mission establishes the possibility of salvation. In so doing he brings glory to God.[59]

Ultimately, in the Gospel of John, the Johannine epistles, and Hebrews, the Jewish Christian corpus countered an infiltrating theory of adoptionism with a high Christology that alienated the Jews.[60]

---

57. Westfall, "Messianic Themes." Dunn asserts, "Where the confrontation between Judaism and Christianity remained a factor of importance in the development of confessional Christianity, the confession 'Jesus is the Christ' retained its significance and importance . . . but almost nowhere else" (Dunn, *Unity and Diversity*, 44–45).

58. Chester, "Parting of the Ways," 305.

59. Marshall, *New Testament Theology*, 525. As Dunn observes, John overlapped the exalted Jesus with the historic Jesus so that "the glory that was to be his by virtue of his death, resurrection and ascension" was "already visible in his earthly life" (Dunn, *Unity and Diversity*, 27).

60. Chester stipulates, "It can of course be claimed that it is precisely the high

The Jewish-Roman war in Judea and destruction of the temple in Jerusalem in AD 70 exacerbated relations between Judaism and Jewish Christians. As John Riches argues, the temple's destruction in AD 70 was a "massive shock" to the Jewish community, followed by "an urgent need to strengthen and support their community's sense of identity." This was "an acute crisis . . . clearly precipitated by the loss of one of the key markers of Jewish identity: the Temple and its cult."[61] Before the destruction of the temple, there were many Judaisms, but after the destruction of the temple, the movement of Rabbinic Judaism that eventually won the day strove for a uniformity that would not tolerate Jewish Christianity.[62]

All Jews in Palestine and the Diaspora were required by Rome to transfer the payment of the temple taxes to the reconstruction of the temple of Jupiter Optimus Maximus in Rome, which was called the *fiscus Judaicus*. It is most likely that the collection of the tax was done centrally through the local synagogues. This had three consequences: all Jews were humiliated by paying for and participating in an idolatrous temple, the Jews who did not believe in Jesus were motivated to avoid further trouble and more severe penalties, and the synagogue became a potential battleground that the Jewish Christians would not be able to avoid while it put them at risk in a threatening climate.

It was a threatening climate because the Roman Empire was becoming increasingly antagonistic towards Christianity. Rome characterized Christian beliefs as "abominable superstitions." The insistence on monotheism was branded as "atheism," and critics misrepresented some of the Christian teachings and practices in the worst possible light, charging Christians with incest and cannibalism. In addition, Christians worshipped a Jew who was executed for being a political rebel, which associated Christianity with the Zealot movement. It is no wonder that Jews were motivated to disassociate themselves and their synagogues from the Christian movement. There was a real potential for confusion

---

Christology of the Fourth Gospel, and the nature of the claims made about Jesus, that forces the division between Judaism and Christianity, and there is surely some truth in that; but we have also to ask to what extent the formulation of a Christology of this kind was meant to work retrospectively, to justify the situation in which the Johannine community found itself" (Chester, "Parting of the Ways," 305).

61. Riches, "Introduction," 1.

62. This would particularly be true in the face of Christian prophecies of the destruction of the temple, or purported abandonment of Jerusalem by Christians when the armies surrounded it.

as long as the Jewish Christians were allowed to remain embedded in the Jewish community. The Jews would want to show that they had nothing in common with the subversive Christian movement.[63]

Therefore, one of the ripple effects of the destruction of the temple and accompanying developments was a growing alienation, rejection, and eviction of the Jewish Christians who were still living in Jewish communities all over the Empire and attending Jewish synagogues. This loss could include their occupation, their home, and their families, as well as any social position, and the support of their community and any other extended network. They would be caught between the proverbial rock and a hard place.

This provides the context for the conflict with the Jews in John and the polemic against the synagogues in Revelation. Most scholars believe that the readers of John were being evicted from the synagogue so that it motivated the author of John to include episodes of basic conflict between Jesus or Jewish believers and the Jews that threatened expulsion from the synagogue (John 9:18–22; 12:42; 16:2). The reason for expulsion was confessing Christ in public (9:22). There is a connection between the Jewish criticism and apostasy by believers, which the author counters by emphasizing abiding in Christ (8:31, 35; 6:56; 12:46; 15:4, 5, 6, 7, 9–11). The same pressures are also the context for the scathing polemics in Revelation against "the synagogue of Satan who say they are Jews but are not" (Rev 2:9; 3:9). While both of these documents may be read as polemics that reject or attack the Jews, the context must be considered. Even after the rebellion, the Jews were operating from a position of greater strength. The Jewish Christian texts record a reaction and response where Jewish Christians are the victims of persecution and eviction from their systems of life support, caught between the persecution of the Roman Empire and rejection by fellow Jews who are kicking them out of the nest, potentially to serve as the scapegoats of the rebellion.

Even in this antagonistic climate, John maintains the priority of the Jews and the book of Revelation maintains a vision of the people of God that is identified with Israel in continuity with the people of God in the Old Testament. Jesus' conversation with the Samaritan woman is particularly enlightening in this context, where Jesus responds to her theological query about the correct place of worship with, "You Samaritans

---

63. For a more detailed description of the conflict, see Hirschberg, "Jewish Believers in Asia Minor," 219–23.

worship what you do not know, we worship what we do know, because salvation comes from the Jews" (John 4:22). His caveat that the time is coming when true worshippers will worship in Spirit and truth addresses her presupposition that there must be a correct place, but the Jews retain their position as both the origin of salvation and the theological interpreters of it. John repeatedly presents Jesus as Israel's king (1:49; 12:13; 19:19). However, the sign at his crucifixion was written in Aramaic, Latin, and Greek, so it is clear that his rule was relevant for those who spoke other languages as well. Under Jesus' rule, Jews form the heart of the new community in Christ. He is the shepherd of Israel, which is his sheep pen (10:13–16). The other sheep that do not belong to the sheep pen will be brought into it or added to the pen so that they will be one flock and one shepherd (10:16). Similarly, Jesus died first for the whole nation of Israel and also for the scattered children of God, which would probably be understood as the Diaspora by a Jewish reader, but could be extended to include the Gentiles or the "other sheep" (11:50–52; 18:14). In a climate where the greater community of Jews was attempting to strip their identity from Christians, John was enabling Jewish Christians to claim that they were the true Israel, the core of the new Christian community.

According to Revelation, true Israel finds its completion in Jesus Christ and the Jewish people occupy a central place in salvation history.[64] The persecuted Jewish believers are the basis and core of the eschatological Israel, represented by the 144,000 that are sealed from the twelve tribes (Rev 7:4–8), the gates with the names of the twelve tribes (21:12), the foundation stones of the twelve apostles (21:14), and the rest of the numerous fulfillments of Old Testament prophecy and references to imagery and motifs. The author and the readers in the context of the Christian movement in the first century would have no question that these Jewish symbols and institutions referred to Jewish Christians as a faithful remnant of the people of God, but Gentiles were also clearly included in John's visions.

---

64. Though many commentators argue for the Jewish symbols representing the people of God as a whole, besides the contrasts of faithful Gentile believers with faithful Jews in the text in Revelation 7, it is highly unlikely that a first-century Jewish Christian would see this as the replacement of Israel by the church. See also Hirschberg's argument in Hirschberg, "Jewish Believers in Asia Minor," 224–26, 229–30.

On the one hand, the new Jerusalem is the eschatological restoration of Israel and Israel maintains its priority in salvation history; but on the other hand, the Gentiles are included as newcomers, represented as people from every tribe, language, nation, and race (ἐκ πάσης φυλῆς καὶ γλώσσης καὶ λαοῦ καὶ ἔθνους, *ek pasēs phulēs kai glōssēs kai laou kai ethnous*, Rev 5:9). As Hirschberg describes it:

> This Israel, in return, has opened itself to the Gentiles and they belong now—in the soteriological sense—entirely to it, but from the point of view of salvation history they are being added.[65]

The Gentiles are juxtaposed against the 144,000 Jews selected from Israel when they are introduced (Rev 7:9–10), but fully qualified to serve God in his temple and receive blessings that were promised to Israel (Rev 7:15–17); the story culminates in a universal new creation where the nations and kings walk by the light of the city and receive healing (Rev 21:24; 22:2).

Statements and descriptions of the Jews in John and Revelation have historically been read as polemical attacks on the Jews and even used as justification to persecute the Jews. However, these were insider documents that were written by Christian Jews who were a minority within the Jewish communities. Written at the end of the first century when Jews were striving to separate themselves from Christianity, the Gospel of John and Revelation make it particularly clear, regardless of the hostility and behavior of synagogues in Smyrna and Philadelphia, or the problem of Jewish Christians being expelled from the synagogues as reflected in John, that Israel still has a priority in salvation history until its eschatological renewal.

CONCLUSION

The existence of first-century Jewish Christians who kept the law, the importance of the Jerusalem church, the biblical priority of the mission to the Jews, and Israel's eschatological importance must affect our concept of the "biblical" church in the first century. Let us return to Vitsosky's comment:

---

65. Ibid., 225.

> Ever since it became clear that the law-free mission to the gentiles would create a church and not a synagogue, Jewish-Christianity has been an uncomfortable reality with which to deal.[66]

His statement is problematic for the church in the first century on two counts: First, he fails to recognize the complex nature of the Jewish Christian church, whose structure and associations extended well beyond the boundaries of the temple and synagogue, to include a vibrant church community that was held up as a model by both Luke and Paul. No doubt the structure, organization, and function of the Jewish churches were largely drawn from or influenced by the local synagogues. However, the synagogues varied from each other reflecting influences from their various locations, and it is clear that the Jewish church adapted and morphed as it met new challenges. Furthermore, there is no evidence to suggest that the customs of the churches planted by the "law-free mission to the Gentiles" led by Paul were not similarly drawn from or influenced by Paul's synagogue experiences as well as the local synagogues that he contacted on his mission trips. Second, while Paul can be credited with many important contributions, including allowing the Gentiles into the community without requiring them to be Jews, he cannot be credited with the foundation of the church. He should be credited with the successful extension of the church to the Gentiles and the practice of contextualizing the gospel when it crossed cultural boundaries.

Vitsotzky's statement assumes that a "church" must be culturally Gentile to be identified as a church, demonstrating a clear break with Judaism by definition, which is the final product of the "parting of the ways." Of course that church did not exist in the first century. This reflects the majority church's later conviction that, in effect, a Jew was required to become a Gentile in order to be saved, which is far worse in its ramifications than requiring Gentiles to proselytize to Judaism in order to be saved. As we continue to sort out the relationship between law and grace, works and faith, the Old Testament and the New Testament, and Israel and the church, we need to avoid a New Testament theology that would have required these Jewish Christians to reject and abandon their Judaism in the first century. If we read Paul over and against the rest of the New Testament as requiring Jews to cease being Jews, then we

---

66. Visotzky, "Prolegomenon," 47.

are faced with glaring inconsistencies that cannot be easily reconciled, and we make Pauline Christianity a far harsher authority and master than Jerusalem Christianity. Beyond that, we must continue to work on our biblical interpretation, theology, and historical understanding of Christianity's relationship to Judaism past, present and future, as well as listen to the dialogue that has opened up with Jewish scholars who interpret the New Testament from a Jewish context and arrive at different conclusions.

In terms of how this affects the churches now, it may expand our possibilities of what a church can look like and how models of churches can adapt as they cross various cultural and social boundaries. Searches for the "biblical model of the New Testament church" have been made to develop or support the biblically correct church that attempts to be faithful in every detail possible. But it often assumes uniformity among the churches that would only have been possible in the Pauline mission. However, Paul was gifted at contextualizing. While he clearly maintained certain consistent patterns of leadership and practice, it is likely that he allowed some diversity and adaptation among his churches like what we see in the mission to the Jews. Therefore, the glaring differences in liturgy, ritual, and community life that may have existed between a Jewish Christian church and a predominantly Gentile church are joined by any number of varieties and variations such as existed among the synagogues during the Diaspora that adapted to their local community. This could roughly parallel the varieties and differences we find among Christian denominations and movements. While I deplore denominational rivalry, competition, and ugly division, this allows me to be much more comfortable with an amicable lack of uniformity among us while we attempt to be biblical, rooted in tradition, and responsive to culture. However, one thing stands out in the early Christian movement: while there may have been diversity in structure and mission, there was still a vital familial relationship among all who called on the name of Christ across the boundaries and an attempt at mutual cooperation and recognition among the leaders as they worked through the tensions and challenges.

BIBLIOGRAPHY

Alexander, P. S. "Rabbinic Judaism and the New Testament." *ZNW* 74 (1983) 237–46.

Allen, Ronald B., and Kenneth L. Barker. Study notes on Numbers in *The NIV Study Bible*. Grand Rapids: Zondervan, 1985.

Bauckham, Richard. "James and the Jerusalem Community." In *Jewish Believers in Jesus: The Early Centuries*, edited by Skarsaune and Hvalvik, 55–95.

———. *Jesus and the Eyewitnesses*. Grand Rapids: Eerdmans, 2006.

Capper, Brian. "The Palestinian Cultural Context of the Earliest Christian Community of Goods." In *The Book of Acts in Its First Century Setting*. Vol. 4. *The Book of Acts in Its Palestinian Setting*, edited by Richard Bauckham, 323–56. Grand Rapids: Eerdmans, 1995.

Catto, Stephen K. *Reconstructing the First-Century Synagogue: A Critical Analysis of New Testament Research*. LNTS 363. London: T. & T. Clark, 2007.

Chester, A. "The Parting of the Ways: Eschatology and Messianic Hope." In *Jews and Christians: The Parting of the Ways A.D. 70 to 135*, edited by J. D. G. Dunn, 239–306. Grand Rapids: Eerdmans, 1999.

Cohen, Shaye J. D. *The Beginnings of Jewishness: Boundaries, Varieties, Uncertainties*. Hellenistic Culture and Society 31. Berkeley: University of California Press, 1999.

Davids, Peter. *The Epistle of James: A Commentary on the Greek Text*. NIGTC. Exeter: Paternoster, 1982.

Dibelius, Martin. *James: A Commentary on the Epistle of James*, translated by Michael A. Williams. Philadelphia: Fortress, 1975.

Dunn, J. D. G. *Unity and Diversity in the New Testament: An Inquiry into the Character of Earliest Christianity*. 2nd ed. Harrisburg, PA: Trinity Press International, 1990.

Hartin, Patrick J. "The Religious Context of the Letter of James." In *Jewish Christianity Reconsidered*, edited by Matt Jackson-McCabe, 203–31.

Hill, Craig C. "The Jerusalem Church." In *Jewish Christianity Reconsidered*, edited by Matt Jackson-McCabe, 39–56.

Hirschberg, Peter. "Jewish Believers in Asia Minor according to the Book of Revelation and the Gospel of John." In *Jewish Believers in Jesus: The Early Centuries*, edited by Skarsaune and Hvalvik, 217–38.

Hvalvik, Reidar. "Jewish Believers and Jewish Influence in the Roman Church until the Early Second Century." In *Jewish Believers in Jesus: The Early Centuries*, edited by Skarsaune and Hvalvik, 179–216.

———. "Paul as a Jewish Believer—According to the Book of Acts." In *Jewish Believers in Jesus: The Early Centuries*, edited by Skarsaune and Hvalvik, 121–53.

Jackson-McCabe, Matt, ed. *Jewish Christianity Reconsidered: Rethinking Ancient Groups and Texts*. Minneapolis, MN: Fortress, 2007.

Jervell, Jacob. *Theology of the Acts of the Apostles*. Cambridge: Cambridge University Press, 1996.

Keener, Craig. *The IVP Bible Background Commentary of the New Testament*. Downers Grove, IL: InterVarsity, 1993.

Kim, Lloyd. *Polemic in the Book of Hebrews: Anti-Semitism, Anti-Judaism, Supersessionism?* Princeton Theological Monograph Series 64. Eugene, OR: Pickwick, 2006.

Marshall, I. H. *New Testament Theology: Many Witnesses, One Gospel*. Downers Grove, IL: InterVarsity, 2004.

Michaels, J. Ramsey. *1 Peter*. WBC 49. Waco, TX: Word, 1988.

Neusner, Jacob. *Formative Judaism: Religious, Historical and Literary Studies*. BJS 37. Chico, CA: Scholars, 1982.

———. "The Use of the Later Rabbinic Evidence for the Study of First-Century Pharisaism." In *Approaches to Ancient Judaism: Theory and Practice*, edited by W. S. Green, 215–25. BJS 1. Missoula: Scholars, 1978.

Porter, Stanley E., and Cynthia Long Westfall. "A Cord of Three Strands: Mission in Acts." In *Christian Mission: Old Testament Foundations and New Testament Developments*, edited by Stanley E. Porter and Cynthia Long Westfall, 108–34. MNTS. Eugene, OR: Pickwick, 2010.

Reed, A. Y., and A. H. Becker. "Introduction." In *The Ways That Never Parted: Jews and Christians in Late Antiquity and the Early Middle Ages*, edited by A. Y. Reed and A. H. Becker, 1–33. Minneapolis, MN: Fortress, 2007.

Riches, John. "Introduction." In *The Gospel of Matthew in Its Roman Imperial Context*, edited by John Riches and David C. Sim, 1–8. JSNTSup 276. London: T. & T. Clark, 2005.

Skarsaune, Oskar. "Jewish Believers in Jesus in Antiquity—Problems of Definition, Method, and Sources." In *Jewish Believers in Jesus: The Early Centuries*, edited by Skarsaune and Hvalvik, 3–11.

Skarsaune, Oskar, and Reidar Hvalvik, eds. *Jewish Believers in Jesus: The Early Centuries*. Peabody, MA: Hendrickson, 2007.

Smith, D. M. "John." In *Early Christian Thought in Its Jewish Context*, edited by J. Barclay and J. Sweet, 96–111. Cambridge: Cambridge University Press, 1996.

Visotzky, Burton L. "Prolegomenon to the Study of Jewish-Christianities." *AJSR* 14 (1989) 47–70.

Westfall, Cynthia Long. *A Discourse Analysis of the Letter to the Hebrews: The Relationship between Form and Meaning*. LNTS 297. SNTG 11. London: T. & T. Clark, 2006.

———. "The Hebrew Mission: Voices from the Margin?" In *Christian Mission: Old Testament Foundations and New Testament Developments*, edited by Stanley E. Porter and Cynthia Long Westfall, 187–207. MNTS. Eugene, OR: Pickwick, 2010.

———. "Messianic Themes of Temple, Enthronement and Victory in Hebrews and the General Epistles." In *The Messiah in the Old and New Testaments*, edited by Stanley E. Porter, 210–29. MNTS. Grand Rapids: Eerdmans, 2005.

———. "Running the Gamut: Endurance in Resistance—Empire in Hebrews, the General Epistles, and Revelation." In *Empire in the New Testament*, edited by Stanley E. Porter and Cynthia Long Westfall, 230–58. MNTS. Eugene, OR: Pickwick, 2011.

4

When the Blood of the Martyrs Was Not Enough

A Survey of Places Where the Church Was Wiped Out

GORDON L. HEATH

> A great principle that we see over and over again in the book of Acts is that persecution always results in blessings. The church continued to grow despite the persecution of the Apostles in Acts chapters 4 and 5. When the church faced widespread persecution in Jerusalem under Saul in Acts 8, Christians continued to preach the gospel message no matter where they fled. Persecution brings blessing. Infiltration destroys the church. Today, people say, "The church is better than it has ever been." But Satan is probably very active in the church now because we are not being persecuted. Satan can work subtly and effectively through infiltration. Persecution is what causes the church to grow.[1]

IN A SIMILAR VEIN, in answer to the question as to why God allows the Chinese church to suffer so much, Jonathan Chao replies, "If God loves the American church so much, why doesn't He allow us to suffer so that our churches might be purified, our faith strengthened, and our relationship with Christ deepened to serve Him wholeheartedly?"[2] Such pronouncements on the benefits of persecution and the inevitability of church growth in the midst of it are quite common.[3] They also seem to

---

1. MacArthur, "How to Handle Persecution."
2. Chao, "Witness of a Suffering Church," 89.
3. One exception is Galli, "Sometimes."

have the support of the North African church Father Tertullian (ca. AD 160–ca. 225), who stated to the Roman authorities: "Your most refined cruelties are to no purpose. We become more numerous each time you reap: the blood of the martyrs is a seed" (Tertullian, *Apology* 50:13). Linked to these sentiments regarding the positive benefits of persecution is the glee that some seem to have over the disestablishment of the church and the concomitant loss of Christendom in the West. One author states that the disestablishment of the church is "God's gift to the church in our era,"[4] another that the end of Christendom "spells the beginning of a new flowering of Christianity,"[5] and yet another states that his book "celebrates the end of Christendom."[6] Craig Carter states that "Too many Christians regret the demise of Christendom; they need not."[7] Douglas J. Hall states, "[T]he end of Christendom could be the beginning of something more nearly like the church,"[8] and Stanley Hauerwas and William H. Willimon declare that the decline of Christendom is an "opportunity to celebrate. The decline of the old, Constantinian synthesis between the church and the world means that we American Christians are at last free to be faithful in a way that makes being a Christian today an exciting adventure."[9]

The purpose of this article is to challenge these two sentiments. Does persecution always lead to church growth? Does the loss of Christendom mean the future is now bright for the church? Should Christians wish for persecution and the death of Christendom? This research argues that Christians had best be careful what they wish for, for as the following survey of the church's history indicates, persecution sometimes leads to the elimination of the church and disestablishment sometimes leads to immense hardships and the very end of a Christian witness. (There needs to be a distinguishing between learning to live within a post-Christendom culture and wishing for it: this paper is concerned with the latter, not the former.)

---

4. A fuller quotation is: "I will propose that the slow demise of Christendom and the end of the Constantinian age may be God's gift to the church in our era. At least it is a challenge and an opportunity for an authenticity we may not have had for some time. It puts us on the margins again, and perhaps that is our proper location" (Bayer, *A Resurrected Church*, 2).

5. Frost, *Exiles*, 7.

6. Murray, *Post-Christendom*, 21.

7. Carter, *Rethinking Christ and Culture*, 21.

8. Hall, *End of Christendom*, 51.

9. Hauerwas and Willimon, *Resident Aliens*, 18.

Of course, the problem with surveys is that they are just that—surveys. This study looks at churches on three continents, over the course of 1300 years, and in a wide variety of cultural and linguistic contexts. Due to the breadth of material being covered, readers should direct their attention to the footnotes for the necessary extra reading required for the technicalities and particularities of each church studied. It should also be noted that historians have difficulties finding sufficient sources for their research when the church has survived, let alone when it has been wiped out. Repeatedly, the difficulty in this research is the lack of sources that survived the particular disaster. Consequently, many things about these events under investigation will remain a mystery unless new sources are discovered.

A few comments on the use of the term "church" are in order. "Church" in this research refers to any indigenous community that self-identifies as Christian, and has some type of ecclesiastical structure (such as leadership, liturgy, and sacraments).[10] What is not being talked about is a foreign presence like a colonial settlement or trading post.

Of course, there are places where the church survived brutal persecution or legal restriction: Tertullian's North Africa experience is one example. Other examples would be the Coptic Church in Egypt, the Russian Orthodox Church under communist rule, or the present-day underground church in China. These and other accounts are success stories of churches that did not die. Nevertheless, not all stories have such happy endings, as the following accounts sadly demonstrate.[11]

WHERE DID THEY DISAPPEAR?

Nubia

South of Aswan following the Nile River there were three sixth-century Nubian Kingdoms (Nobatia in the north, Makuria in the middle, and Alwa in the south). The Christian presence in Nubia (modern-day Sudan) has often been overlooked. However, the attempts in the 1960s to excavate as many sites as possible that were going to be flooded by the damming of the Nile at the Aswan High Dam led to the discovery

---

10. And for this research a "Christian" is anyone who self-identifies as such.

11. For a helpful survey that examines similar phenomena, see Jenkins, *The Lost History of Christianity*. Jenkins's book was not available when this chapter was originally written in 2008.

of artifacts that indicated a vibrant Nubian Christian community that lasted close to a millennium.[12]

Nubia, as Elizabeth Isichei notes, "was one of the few countries in the ancient world that was converted to Christianity without a prior experience of Roman rule; Ethiopia was another."[13] The arrival of Christianity in Nubia was in at least two stages.[14] The first informal stage in the fifth century was through the influence of Christian Egypt. By the early fifth century there were churches and monasteries along the border of Egypt and Nubia, and the influence of Coptic clergy and monks, as well as Christian merchants to Nubia, meant that Nubians had a degree of contact with Christianity. However, there is little evidence of Christianity in the Nile Valley south of Aswan until the sixth century.

The second and more formal stage was through the influence of Christian missionaries in the sixth century. The arrival of missionaries from the Roman Empire coincided with Emperor Justinian's (482/3–565) ambitious *renovatio imperii*, or "restoration of the empire." It was an attempt to reestablish Roman rule throughout the western part of the empire, and to strengthen and expand the empire in the east against threats such as arch-enemy Persia. It was also Roman policy to try to have its neighbors share Roman religion so as to establish bonds of similar beliefs (which would hopefully result in peace).

In the sixth century there were two main factions within eastern Christianity: supporters of the Council of Chalcedon (451) and opponents of the Council (Monophysites). Justinian was of the former, and Empress Theodora the latter (and both sought to see their version planted in Nubia). Egyptian Christianity was predominantly Monophysite,

---

12. For a summary of some of these finds and the scholarship that followed, see Bowers, "Nubian Christianity," 9–12.

13. Isichei, *History of Christianity in Africa*, 31. Welsby argues that the Christian kingdoms of Ethiopia and Nubia did not have much contact with one another, despite their geographical proximity and both being united under the authority of the Alexandrian Patriarchs. The physical barrier of the western and north-western Ethiopian Plateau kept them apart, and the fact that Nubia looked north and south along the Nile Valley while Ethiopia looked east to the Red Sea meant that they had very different spheres of interest. See Welsby, *Medieval Kingdoms of Nubia*, 78.

14. Much of the following material is taken from Kirwan, "Birth of Christian Nubia"; Kirwan, "Introduction"; Kirwan, "Prelude"; Vantini, *Christianity in the Sudan*; Welsby, *Medieval Kingdoms of Nubia*; Grillmeier, *Christ in Christian Tradition*, 263–89; Monneret de Villard, *Storia della Nubia Cristiana*; idem, *La Nubia medioevale*; Cuoq, *Islamisation de la Nubie chrétienne*.

and due to a variety of factors,[15] Nubian Christianity seems to have eventually become predominantly Monophysite.

The Monophysite Syrian church historian John of Ephesus (ca. 507–ca. 586) detailed in his *Ecclesiastical History* the birth of the church in Nubia.[16] His account provides details on the missionary work of Julian (an Egyptian monk) in the years ca. 540–548 in the Northern Kingdom of Nobadia, and the work of Bishop Longinus in the years 569–575 in Nobadia and further south in the Kingdom of Alwa in 579–580.[17] Before leaving for Nubia he had been consecrated the first Bishop of Nubia, and for his work in solidifying the church's presence in Nubia he has been coined the "true founder of the Nubian Church." It appears that by 700 the Christianization of the Nubians had been successful.

The Arab armies advanced into Egypt in 639, and very quickly eliminated Byzantine power. However, unlike their Egyptian co-religionists, the Nubians were able to withstand the onslaught of the Muslim armies. After two failed attempts at conquest (641–42; 652), the Muslims made a permanent treaty called a *Baqt* that recognized the independence of the Nubians and allowed for Nubian culture to flourish.

> Christian Nubia at its height was a land of great cultural vitality. This was reflected not only in its churches and paintings, but also in a new tradition of brightly decorated pottery, characterized by realistic designs from the natural world, an idiom that owes nothing to outside influences, and which has been described as the most distinguished pottery tradition in Africa.[18]

Despite tensions and occasionally conflicts, this situation with the Islamic north remained until the disastrous thirteenth and fourteenth centuries when the Nubian kingdoms collapsed.

The contradictory nature of the evidence means that any conclusions must be tentative, but it appears that a combination of war with

15. After the Arab conquest of Egypt and the concomitant isolation from Constantinople, the closest religious ties for Nubia were with Monophysite Egyptian Christianity.

16. The Nubian sections of his *Ecclesiastical History* are in the opening chapters of Book IV (the first four chapters of Book IV are missing; something lamented by those interested in the early history of the Nubian mission work).

17. John of Ephesus did not mention the conversion of Makouria (most likely converted ca. 569 by Chalcedonian missionaries). Of course, this exclusion is interpreted as evidence of John's anti-Chalcedon bias. See Welsby, *Medieval Kingdoms of Nubia*, 33.

18. Isichei, *History of Christianity in Africa*, 31.

Arabs and Muslims, as well as dynastic intrigues, led to the collapse of Nubian power and the Islamization of Nubia. There are bits of evidence that indicate that some slight Christian presence continued into the fifteenth century and beyond, but by the nineteenth century the once-vibrant Nubian church had disappeared.

North Africa

Christianity arrived relatively early in North Africa. Not much is known about the spread of Christianity in the second century (in fact, less is known about the spread of the church in the second century than in the first), but what is known is that by the end of the second century there was a vibrant and growing Christian community in Carthage and the surrounding area. Tertullian, called by some the Father of Latin Christianity, penned numerous apologetic and theological works that shaped key doctrines such as the Trinity. St. Cyprian of Carthage (d. 258) was an important bishop, theologian, and martyr. St. Augustine of Hippo (354–430) was one of the most important figures in the development of Western theology. These three men are examples of the role that North African Christians played in the life and ministry of the early church. However, despite the encouraging signs of vitality, North African Christianity experienced a significant amount of turmoil.

The Roman persecutions had brought their share of hardship, but the division in the fourth century that occurred after the persecutions ended wreaked havoc within the church. Donatus and his followers were upset with the reinstatement of leaders that had not remained faithful during the persecutions.[19] He and others eventually formed a rival church that claimed to be the true church. A third Christian rival came in the form of Vandal Arianism. The Vandals captured North Africa in the early fifth century, and their form of Christianity was planted in the midst of Donatist and Catholic territory. Not long after the conquest, Donatism and Catholicism faced suppression by the Vandals. A fourth Christian rival came in the wake of Justinian's sixth-century attempt to restore the Western Empire to its former borders and glory. In the wake of the Eastern Roman armies came the eastern form of Christianity. It is difficult to know exactly what impact these four competing Christian communities had on the church's support among the populace, but some

---

19. Frend, *Donatist Church*.

evidence indicates that the geographic spread of the church had condensed by the sixth century to the territory of modern-day Tunisia and the most eastern part of Algeria. Nevertheless, there seems to have been no dangerous regression of the faith.[20] It seems safe to conclude that few, if any, would have foreseen a future with no North African Christianity. Yet that is what happened.

The disappearance of the church can be traced to the conquest of North Africa by the Arab Muslim armies in the seventh century. Arab armies advanced westward from Egypt in 647, and easily defeated the weakened Byzantines in Tunisia. Another thrust in 663 led to further advances westward, and by 698 any final resistance had been crushed and North Africa was under the control of the Arab Muslim invaders. A rebellion by the Berbers in 740 was successful in throwing out most of the Arab invaders, but Islam remained. In the following centuries the once vibrant and dominant church disappeared.[21]

Moravia

The ninth-century history of Christianity in Moravia is complicated by the political intrigues between secular powers that vied for control of central Europe as well as by the competition between Rome and Constantinople over the spread of the faith in central Europe.[22] The arrival of Christianity in Moravia in the mid-late ninth century is often connected to the request in 863 of the Moravian Prince Rastislav to Byzantine Emperor Michael III in Constantinople for Christian teachers. Two brothers, Cyril (827–869) and Methodius (826–885), were quickly sent northward.[23] It appears that Christianity was already pres-

---

20. Schoen, "Death of the Church," 8.

21. Mark Handley argues that the church's disappearance in North Africa was not as rapid as usually assumed. He argues that the decline of the church took place over the course of centuries, and that the church remained a "vibrant, internationally connected and well documented religion" into the eleventh century (Handley, "Disputing the End of African Christianity"). Whether or not the demise was rapid or gradual, the reality was that the church eventually disappeared. See also Leclercq, *L'Afrique chrétienne*, chap. 9.

22. For a detailed account of the political and military struggles for this region, see Bowlus, *Franks, Moravians, and Magyars*.

23. One can read accounts of their lives composed relatively soon after their deaths: *Life of Cyril* (ca. 882) and *Life of Methodius* (ca. 886).

ent in Moravia,²⁴ and what Rastislav sought was the instruction and organization of such disciples (as well as a positive relationship with Byzantium against western threats).²⁵ One of the significant accomplishments of their mission work was to translate the liturgy into the vernacular (something that caused great consternation among German clergy). One author notes that the conversion of the Moravians under the Byzantine missionaries "opened the way to a bright future for the Slavs and for the West."²⁶ But that was not to be.

The sudden end of the nascent church was due primarily to waves of invading Magyars that started in 902. The church was "stamped into the ground by the hoofs of Magyar horses"²⁷ after defeat on the battlefield between the years 905 and 908. The *Chronicle of the Slavs* (ca. 1172) describes the impact on the church in this way:

> At that time churches were burned, crosses mutilated and held to mockery by the barbarians, priests murdered before their altars, clerics herded together with the populace either to be executed or to be led into captivity. The marks of this fury have endured to our own age.²⁸

Not much has remained by way of information regarding the churches. It does appear that although some Christian presence remained,²⁹ organized Christianity was "obliterated," and the "first chapter in the Christianization of central Europe came to an abrupt end."³⁰

Central Asia

The Church of the East (more commonly referred to as the Nestorian Church)³¹ extended from modern-day Syria northeast to the Asian steppes and east to India, China, and beyond. The Church of the East,

---

24. For a discussion of Christianity in Moravia before Cyril and Methodius, see Curta, "Before Cyril and Methodius." For a complete history of Christianity in Moravia, see Dittrich, *Christianity in Great-Moravia*.

25. Dvornik, *Byzantine Missions among the Slavs*, 105.

26. Dvornik, *Slavs in European History*, 3.

27. Ibid., 4.

28. As quoted in Toth, "Christianization of the Magyars," 35.

29. Dvornik, *Byzantine Missions among the Slavs*, 197.

30. Fletcher, *Barbarian Conversion*, 368. Galuska claims that pagan cult places began to return due to the demise of the church (Galuska, *Great Moravia*, 78).

31. For a discussion of the title "Nestorian," see Baumer, *Church of the East*, 7–8.

under the leadership of the Patriarch of Seleucia-Ctesiphon, covered a vast territory—larger than the territory of the Western Catholic Church at that time.

> The 27 Metropolitan sees oversaw some 200 dioceses, which contained approximately seven to eight million faithful. Thus around the tenth to fourteenth centuries between about 12 per cent and 16 per cent of the estimated fifty to sixty million Christians were Nestorians. Until the start of the fourteenth century, the Church of the East was the most successful missionary Church in the world, and it began to be surpassed only in the sixteenth century through the conversion, often forced, brought about by the Catholic colonial powers.[32]

The Church of the East spread eastwards for a variety of reasons. Politically it belonged to an empire (the Persian) that required a break from any loyalty to Rome (Persia's arch-enemy).[33] They were considered in the West to be heretics for their views regarding the two natures of Christ, and were condemned by the Council of Ephesus (431). This theological controversy led to a split from Byzantine Christianity, and the suppression of Nestorian Christianity in Byzantine territory. Due to these political and theological considerations, the Church of the East could not really move west, and so quite naturally moved east.

The homeland of the Church of the East was Mesopotamia (the land between the Tigris and Euphrates rivers), but the faith spread from there, overcoming the difficulties of geography, climate, and local hostilities. The story of the eastward movement is complicated, and covers hundreds of years, but is a success story nonetheless. The first Christian kingdoms were in the east (before Constantine and the Christianization of the Roman Empire in the west).[34] Zealous Nestorian missionaries

---

32. Ibid., 4–5.

33. In 424 the Church of the East had to declare its juridical independence from the church in the West. See ibid., 2.

34. Consider the following examples. Syrian tradition claims that Edessa was the capital of history's first Christian kingdom, Osrhoene (Moffett, *History of Christianity in Asia*, 2:56–64). While some of the events surrounding the conversion of the King of Armenia and the role of Gregory the Illuminator (the Christian missionary involved in the king's conversion) are a bit sketchy (how much is hagiography?), what is generally accepted is the fact that King Tiridates was converted around 301. After his conversion, and with the encouragement of Gregory, the king built a series of churches throughout Armenia and introduced Christian liturgy to the land. Gregory also encouraged the mass conversion of Armenia. See Gertz, "How Armenia 'Invented' Christendom," 46–47.

had spread Christianity as far east as the Hindu Kush mountains by the start of the third century. The Silk Route to China played an important role in the spreading of the faith. Monks and missionaries travelled the east-west trade routes from Persia and Syria to central Asia and China, and had established churches as far east as China by the seventh century. While much of the attention given to the Nestorians is due to their eastward expansion, it should be noted that the movement also spread southward into the Arabian peninsula. Although the peninsula is now basically devoid of any indigenous Christian presence, before the Islamic conquests three of the largest Arab kingdoms were Christian.[35]

What is remarkable about this growth is that the Nestorians did not have the advantages of being a state church. The church also survived in the face of brutal persecutions, such as the century-long one in the Sassanid Empire (fourth to fifth centuries). As Christoph Baumer notes, the Sassanian persecution was exceptionally brutal:

> The Sassanian persecutions were notable for both the nearly unlimited willingness of the Christians to make sacrifices and the extraordinarily cruel, indeed sadistic, performance of the executions. The confessors of faith were not just beheaded, stoned or crucified, they were murdered in clever ways that caused the greatest amount of pain. For instance, the executioner slit the victim's throat in such a way that he could tear out his tongue through the gaping wound. Others ripped the skin off of the face down to the neck or subjected them to the torture of the 'iron combs.'[36]

The rise of Islam presented even more problems for the churches, despite the tolerance that was supposed to be (and often was) granted to Christians due to their being "people of the book." The Christian communities in Arabia were displaced, persecuted, and many eventually (some forcefully) converted to Islam. By the eighth century Christianity in the peninsula had been wiped out.[37]

However, the most destructive blows to the Nestorian churches occurred during the Mongol invasions of the thirteenth and fourteenth centuries. The initial invasions in the thirteenth century by Genghis

---

35. Moffett, *History of Christianity in Asia*, 1: chap. 14. See also Gillman and Klimkeit, *Christians in Asia before 1500*, chap 5.

36. Baumer, *Church of the East*, 71.

37. Gillman and Klimkeit, *Christians in Asia before 1500*, chap. 5.

Khan (ca. 1162–1227) and others were devastating, and while the Muslims were particularly hard hit by the Mongol invaders in this century, the Christian communities also suffered from the appalling damage caused by the invasions.[38]

Despite the damage caused by the Mongol invasions, the church eventually benefited from the *pax Mongolica*.[39] Mongol rule allowed for unprecedented travel, freed Christians from oppressive Muslim rule, and tolerated Christianity (at one time it even looked like the Mongols would convert *en masse* to Christianity).

In the fourteenth century a series of catastrophes occurred. One reason for the demise of the church was the plague that "haunted Central Asia in 1337–1339."[40] Another reason for the collapse of Christianity (for the plague hit all religions with equal fury) was the spread of an "intolerant Islam" that brutally repressed the church.[41] It seemed that the Mongol invaders of the thirteenth century would be victorious over the Muslims (which they were at first), and be allies with the crusaders (which they never became—mainly due to the crusaders' failure to seize the opportunity). After the defeat of the Mongols by the Muslims at the Battle of Ayn Jalut (1260), the Mongols slowly but eventually sided with Islam.[42] The ruler Tamerlane (ruled 1370–1405), or Timor the Great, of Turkish descent, "dealt the deathblow to the ravaged Church of the East."[43] Tamerlane's conquests were exceptionally brutal, and he destroyed churches and synagogues everywhere he conquered; he also enslaved and massacred Christians by the thousands. It should be noted that Muslims suffered equally or worse under Tamerlane's reign, and because of his ruthlessness to his supposed fellow-Muslim believers, one historian states that he "was one of the worst enemies to whom Islamic

---

38. Browne, *Eclipse of Christianity in Asia*, 147.
39. Moffett, *History of Christianity in Asia*, 1: chaps. 18–20.
40. Gillman and Klimkeit, *Christians in Asia before 1500*, 234.
41. Ibid., 234–36.
42. The decades in the early 1300s increasingly became more dangerous for Christians. Mob attacks, church burnings, massacres, martyrdoms and the like occurred throughout Central Asia in these years. See Saunders, "Decline and Fall of Christianity in Medieval Asia."
43. Baumer, *Church of the East*, 233. See also Moffett, *History of Christianity in Asia*, 1:484–85. Saunders is not convinced that Tamerlane should take most of the blame. He notes, as do others, that more Muslims than Christians suffered under his rule. See Saunders, "Decline and Fall of Christianity in Medieval Asia," 102.

civilization ever fell a victim."[44] After Tamerlane, Islam reigned supreme in Central Asia. And after the decline of the Mongols a few decades later, if there were any Christians left in Central Asia, "no one noticed them."[45] The church had disappeared. As for the remnant left in Mesopotamia, more brutal blows would come in the twentieth century.

China

While the arrival of Christianity in China is a part of the history of the Church of the East (and could have been included in the previous section), the following is a specific focus on Christianity in China. Before the nineteenth-century arrival of Protestant missionaries, Christianity had been introduced to China three times: in the seventh century, the thirteenth century, and the sixteenth century. The first two times it was eliminated, and the third time it remained (to this day). The following brief comments focus on the arrival and downfall of the first two attempts.[46]

Christianity arrived in China in 635 (during the Tang Dynasty) through the work of the Nestorian Bishop Alopen. In the following decades Nestorian Christianity was favored by the court, more missionaries arrived, numerous churches were built and monasteries established, and many converts made. The successful spread of the faith continued throughout the eight century. The Tang Dynasty's policy was religious toleration; however, when Wu Tsung came to the throne in 840 the Taoists came to control the court. The Taoists resented the growth of Christianity and Buddhism, and began the persecution of both religions. In 982 a Nestorian monk was sent to China to report on the church. A few years later his report was "Christianity is extinct in China; the native Christians have perished in one way or another; the church which they had has been destroyed and there is only one Christian left in the land."[47]

Despite the demise of Christianity in China, Nestorianism continued to gain strength in Central Asia among the Turks. The Nestorian Church also experienced a remarkable recovery under the Mongols.

---

44. Gillman and Klimkeit, *Christians in Asia before 1500*, 485.

45. Moffett, *History of Christianity in Asia*, 1:488.

46. For further reading, see Latourette, *History of Christian Missions in China*; Moule, *Christians in China*; Cary-Elwes, *China and the Cross*; Deeg, "'Brilliant Teaching"; Standaert, *Handbook of Christianity*.

47. As quoted in Keung, "Nestorianism in China," 120.

As noted above, in the early thirteenth century the Mongols rapidly expanded throughout the Muslim and Nestorian world, and by the middle of the century had conquered most of China. The Nestorian Church in China benefited from the rule of the Mongols. Under their rule Christianity was tolerated, a number of Mongols professed Christianity, and Nestorian priests played an important role in the imperial court of the Mongols. By the middle of the thirteenth century Western Catholic Franciscan missionaries had also arrived in China, and had been successful in planting Catholic churches. The collapse of the Mongol empire in the fourteenth century meant that Christianity's days were numbered. The church had been identified with the Mongols, and was seen by the Chinese as a foreign religion. When the Chinese threw off the Mongols, they also rejected Christianity. Were they killed off? Samuel Moffett writes that the church most likely did not die of persecution, but suffered as a result of the war: "It is just as likely that Nestorians and foreigners were killed indiscriminately in the pursuit of the Mongols, and that without foreign support a church that had become dependent upon it withered away. And because its withering was so undramatic, China lost even the memory of its passing."[48]

Turkey (Asia Minor)

If Jerusalem and the Holy Land was the birthplace of Christianity, Asia Minor (modern day Turkey) was the "Bible belt."[49] The New Testament provides a glimpse of the promising first-century growth of Christianity in Asia Minor, and in subsequent generations Asia Minor became one of the regions most densely populated by Christians in the Roman Empire.

After the collapse of the Western Roman Empire in the late fifth century, the Eastern Empire continued for another thousand years with its capital city in Constantinople. This Byzantine Empire (what we call it today—they continued to call themselves Romans) was officially a Christian Empire, with the emperor and patriarch in Constantinople

---

48. Moffett, *History of Christianity in Asia*, 1:475.

49. "After Palestine, Turkey was certainly the fatherland—or the cradle, as it is sometimes called—of Christianity. It was there that St Paul was born and preached; it was there, at Antioch, that the apostle Peter established his first chair; it was there that the Roman emperor, after his conversion to Christianity, shifted his capital and convoked the founding councils of Christian dogma: Constantinople, Nicaea, Chalcedon, Ephesus" (Kerkhofs, "Church in Turkey," 2).

overseeing an eastern Christendom. The Byzantines were successful in repulsing Muslim invaders from the seventh century onwards, and were seen to be (and in many respects were) the defenders of Christendom, for if Constantinople had fallen, Europe would have been filled with mosques instead of churches.

If someone had suggested in the tenth century that the Church of Hagia Sophia (the seat of the Patriarch of Constantinople) would someday become a mosque, and that Asia Minor would be almost completely Muslim, he or she would have been dismissed as a lunatic. But that is what happened. By the late fifteenth century the church in Asia Minor had declined from four hundred bishoprics to three, church buildings by the hundreds had been turned into mosques (even Hagia Sophia had been converted into a mosque), and over 90 percent of Asia Minor was Muslim.[50] Today around 98 percent of Turkey's seventy million people are Muslim.

The beginning of the end happened in 1071 with the disastrous (for the Byzantines) Battle of Manzikert. Within a few years of their victory, Seljuk Turks had advanced all the way to Nicaea, a short march from Constantinople. But this was just the beginning. The disappearance of Christianity in Asia Minor occurred over centuries in at least three stages: first, the Muslim/Turkish conquests (which waxed and waned from the eleventh to the sixteenth centuries);[51] second, the early twentieth-century genocide of Christians in Eastern Turkey; and third, the Turco-Greek Exchange of Populations that arose from the Treaty of Lausanne (1923). By the end of the 1920s, what had been the heartland of the faith had been transformed into a wasteland of the faith. Tourists still go to see churches in Asia Minor, but the churches they see are derelict buildings of by-gone glory.

Japan

Ikuo Higashibaba notes that there are two periods of "Kirishitan" history: the "Christian Century" (1549–1639) and the underground period

---

50. Vryonis, "Experience of Christians," 195–96; Ménage, "Islamization of Anatolia," 52.

51. Vryonis divides this process of Islamization into four stages: eleventh to late twelfth centuries, thirteenth century, late thirteenth century to mid-fifteenth century, and mid-fifteenth to sixteenth century. See Vryonis, "Experience of Christians," 196.

(1640–1873).[52] Christianity arrived in Japan in the sixteenth century through the Jesuits. Unlike those contacting lesser developed societies, where missionary work was closely linked with colonialism, the missionaries in Japan had to deal with a civilization that was highly advanced, powerful, and far from centers of European power.[53] As a result, new methods of spreading Christianity had to be found.

The famous Jesuit missionary Francis Xavier (1506–1552) and two companions arrived in Kagoshima in 1549. The instability of Japan at that time aided the missionary enterprise. Japan was very divided, with an impotent emperor. The lack of central authority meant that there was no single authority to suppress them, that they could flee from one region that was unfriendly to one that was receptive, and that local leaders who sought to gain from Portuguese trade invited missionaries to their region with the hope of good will (and the trade that would come with it).[54] The general decline of Buddhism and the zeal of the missionaries were also factors that aided the church's growth.[55] Throughout much of Christian history the mission strategy was to target the rulers with the expectation that the subjects would then, *en masse*, be baptized. This strategy was followed in Japan with willing *daimyo*, and was quite successful. The occasionally zealous Christian *daimyo* who burned down Buddhist temples and expelled monks was one allegedly positive spinoff of this top down approach to missions.

Although Xavier stayed less than three years, the mission work that he began, and innovative leaders such as Alessandro Valignano (1539–1606) continued, was extremely successful. The inevitable barriers of language and culture were slowly worked on through a process of ac-

---

52. The Japanese "kirishitan" developed from a transliteration of the Portuguese *Christao*. See Higashibaba, "Historiographical Issues," 29.

53. Cooper, "Mission Interrupted," 393.

54. Ibid., 394–95.

55. Henry Drummond argues that the middle of the sixteenth century was an ideal time for missionaries to arrive. He writes, "This period of Japanese history particularly welcomed a new religious faith. Buddhism had not acquired the sociological power that it later had in Japanese society of the Edo period. Knowledge of Confucianism was limited to but a few scholars, and Shinto had by no means kept pace with the developing cultural sophistication of the nation. No recognizable political power as yet unified the land, and the many *daimyo* were continual rivals to expand the wealth and power of their separate fiefs, and if possible, to extend them at their neighbor's expense" (Drummond, *History of Christianity in Japan*). See also Fujita, *Japan's Encounter with Christianity*, 248–57; Cooper, "Mission Interrupted," 396.

culturation and missionary adaptation to Japanese culture. The building of institutes for the training of indigenous priests, the translation and publication of texts (a printing press was eventually brought to Japan), the development of a catechism (such as the *Dochirina Kirishitan*), the adoption of Japanese dress and manners, the building of Christian churches, and the inclusion of a feast day on 1 January (the most important date in the Japanese calendar) all contributed to the growth of a distinctly Japanese church.[56] Despite adversity, the Jesuits claimed 750,000 converts by 1606 (and increasing by about five to six thousand per year).[57] It seemed as if Christianity had become a genuine segment of Japanese religion.[58] The future looked bright for the fledgling church, but in the early seventeenth century tragedy struck. Toyotomi Hideyoshi (1536–1598) began a policy of persecution that would culminate in the disappearance of the church.

WHY DID THEY DISAPPEAR?

There have been many attempts to identify internal reasons why these churches did not (could not?) survive. A lack of unity is one recurring factor that some point to as a reason why the churches did not survive adversity. For instance, the divisions between Donatists and Catholics in North Africa,[59] Nestorians and Catholics in China,[60] or Jesuits and Franciscans in Japan,[61] have all been seen to be critical weaknesses that crippled the churches in their attempts to survive adversity. A lack of a vernacular translation of the Bible has been seen by some to be the

---

56. For a helpful summary of this process of adaptation to Japanese culture, see Fujita, *Japan's Encounter with Christianity*, chap. 3; Higashibaba, "Historiographical Issues," 34–48.

57. Boxer, *Christian Century*, 187. Boxer argues that another perhaps more accurate account records 300,000 converts. Either way, the number is impressive. As Boxer notes, "the total population of the empire at that time is roughly estimated at about twenty million, but it would be difficult, if not impossible, to find another highly civilized pagan country where Christianity had made such a mark, not merely in numbers but in influence." See ibid., 320–21. Kentaro agrees with the above-mentioned numbers of converts, but claims that there were only twelve million Japanese at the time. See Kentaro, "Roman Catholic Mission," 7.

58. See Higashibaba, "Historiographical Issues," 32.

59. Frend, *Donatist Church*, 335.

60. Saunders, "Decline and Fall of Christianity in Medieval Asia," 102.

61. Boxer, *Christian Century*, 154–63, 247.

reason for the demise of the church in North Africa[62] or in Central Asia.[63] Closely related to the lack of vernacular Bible is the claim that the church remained a foreign body and did not become identified with the people; the church in Mongol China is often considered to be an example of this weakness.[64] It is claimed that theological errors and syncretism within Nestorian missionary attempts undermined the church's ability to stand.[65] Finally, meddling in politics (making political blunders) in Japan has been identified as a cause of government animosity towards the church.[66]

There are difficulties in trying to apportion such blame for these tragedies. One is the difficulty of identifying cause and effect in historical events, especially when there is a paucity of sources for analysis. Another is trying to identify the internal reasons for the disappearance of these churches when apportioning blame is usually shaped by one's confessional perspective.[67] A third factor is the theological assumption that a true and pure church could never be wiped out.

The large-scale eradication of the church also raises difficult theological questions. What happened to God's providential care for his people? Why would God allow such devastation to occur? What about sacred spaces; does God not care that holy places are lost? Is Christendom God's way (or at least a legitimate means) of protecting the church? Does the victory of Islam over Christianity vindicate the claims of Mohammed?[68]

The following does not directly address these many questions. What follows, however, is a summary of the external events that directly contributed to the downfall of the churches. Referring to the decimation of the church in the Middle East, Philip Jenkins writes, "these experi-

62. Cooksey, *Land of the Vanished Church*, 102–4.

63. Saunders, "Decline and Fall of Christianity in Medieval Asia," 101.

64. Moffett, *History of Christianity in Asia*, 1:475; Browne, *Eclipse of Christianity in Asia*, 99.

65. Moffett, *History of Christianity in Asia*, 1:305–13.

66. Boxer, *Christian Century*, 141.

67. In a recent discussion I had regarding the elimination of the church in Japan, a Protestant individual said, "But the Jesuits were Catholics." The point was that the church in Japan was not really a church, and so it was not surprising that they were wiped out.

68. Remember that some converted to Islam because they believed this very thing. See Ménage, "Islamization of Anatolia," 64.

ences remind us of the sad historical lesson that persecution can indeed be very effective, if carried out with enough ruthlessness. Perhaps one cannot kill an idea, but it is not that difficult to massacre or convert everyone who holds or expresses it."[69] His observation also applies to the experiences of the churches in Nubia, North Africa, Moravia, Central Asia, China, Turkey, and Japan; they simply could not survive the brutality and dislocation of their particular hardships, for the waves of invaders, forced migrations, persecution, and (especially) genocides were simply too much to handle.

As one would expect, the eradication of Christian communities was due to a complex series of factors unique to the particular community, time, and place. What follows, then, is a survey of these factors. While they are listed separately, it is obvious that many are interrelated.

Military Conquest/Defeat

What many of these churches faced in common was the successful invasion of a non-Christian people. In North Africa the seventh-century invasion of the Arab armies put an end to any Byzantine or Christian control of the region. The Nubians had been successful in withstanding the southward advance of Islam in the seventh century, but in the disastrous thirteenth and fourteenth centuries Nubian power declined while Muslim power grew. Eventually Nubian independence was eradicated. The relatively new church in Moravia saw its gains wiped out when the Magyars swept out of the east wreaking destruction on whomever they found. The Byzantines saw their centuries-old empire lose half of its territory after the Battle of Manzikert (1071), and then over the next three centuries experienced the gradual erosion of their control of Asia Minor and eventual loss of their capital in 1453 to the Ottomans.[70] The

---

69. Jenkins, *Next Christendom*, 170.

70. It should be noted that the Byzantines also lost territory to the Latin West, and even lost Constantinople to the West for a while in the thirteenth century. Western Christian attacks significantly weakened the Byzantines and contributed to the overall demise of the Byzantines and the success of the Turks. It should also be noted that after the fall of Constantinople, the Patriarch of Constantinople continued to play an important part in the life of the Orthodox throughout the Ottoman Empire. The Eastern church's spiritual and civil capacity was useful for the Sultan and this institution was exploited as a means of administering the empire. See Papadopoullos, *Studies and Documents*, 1–26.

Churches of the East were devastated by the atrocities and wanton destruction of Tamerlane.

In all these cases the military defeat did not in and of itself lead to the destruction of the church. However, the defeats on the battlefield led to conditions that made it possible. In the above-mentioned cases, the church had a privileged position and the protection of the state. The end of that protection led to the destruction and loss of church properties, as well as the isolation of church communities from their base of support.[71] It also made it possible for migrations of new, non-Christian peoples, along with the displacement, persecution, and even genocide of Christian communities.

For instance, in his reflections on the collapse of the Church of the East, Christoph Baumer notes that the genocide and persecution of the church was due to a hostile religion (Islam) and state, and a church unable to protect itself from such threats. He writes:

> In his *Refutation of Christianity*, he [Muslim theologian Ali at-Tabaria, a former Christian] wrote that no religion without a concept of holy war could survive. He referred to the triumph of Islam, which had succeeded and greatly weakened Christianity everywhere, that no one met it with armed force. A passing glance at history shows that, in confrontation with an aggressive religion equipped with military means, only a religion supported by another armed power can maintain itself over the long term. Regions that once had predominantly Christian populations were either radically cleansed of Christians—as happened, for instance, in Anatolia and North Africa—or the Christians came to constitute only a small minority, as in Iran, Iraq, Syria, and Egypt. In contrast, in Christian Europe, it was military operations that either stopped Islam or repulsed it—as, for example, at the Battle of Tours and Poitiers in 732, the *Reconquista* of Spain in the fifteenth century, and at both sieges of Vienna in 1529 and 1638.[72]

---

71. Consider the following examples. The advance of the Turks isolated local churches from the support, assistance, and leadership provided by Constantinople. See Ménage, "Islamization of Anatolia," 63. The success of Islam in Egypt meant that Nubian contact with the patriarch in the north was limited, and the church suffered as a result. See Welsby, *Medieval Kingdoms of Nubia*, 256; Vantini, *Christianity in the Sudan*, 190. Some claim that the church in North Africa died because it was cut off from the larger Christian community. See Schoen, "Death of the Church," 14–15.

72. Baumer, *Church of the East*, 267.

For Baumer, it is clear that the outcome on the battlefield led to conditions that adversely affected the church and its long-term viability.[73] The following sections will outline some of these conditions that afflicted various Christian communities throughout the centuries.

Persecution

One important factor in the collapse of the church in various places at particular times was persecution. As Tertullian noted, sometimes persecution contributes to the growth of the church. However, sometimes persecution leads to its demise. The following few examples will suffice to illustrate this sad reality.

Central Asia

The Church of the East has experienced more persecution than any Western church. Not only did it have to bear a century-long persecution at the hands of the Persian government, it also had to face centuries of persecution under the rule of Muslims. That is not to say that Christians were always persecuted by Muslims. As "people of the book" Christians and Jews were supposed to receive freedom from persecution, and in many places and during various periods they did.[74] This is also not to say that the Church of the East did not experience some benefits from the conquest of Islam.[75] However, as the following lengthy statement by Samuel Moffett indicates, the Church of the East had to live with unimaginable treatment by both Persians and then Muslims:

---

73. As a counterpoint, Moffett argues that depending on the state for protection is precarious, for when the state declines the fortunes of the church decline with it. Regarding the church in China, he writes "If any conclusion at all can be drawn from these various attempts to explain the cause of the collapse of the Chinese church in T'ang dynasty China, it should probably be that the decisive factor was neither religious persecution, nor theological compromise, nor even its foreignness, but rather the fall of an imperial house on which the church had too long relied for its patronage and protection. Dependence on government is a dangerous and uncertain foundation for Christian survival" (Moffett, *History of Christianity in Asia*, 1:313).

74. This freedom to worship came with many—often humiliating—restrictions, and a second-class status as a *dhimmi*.

75. For instance, Baumer notes that Nestorians gained from the Arab conquest, for it allowed them to enter Arab territory that had once been Byzantine (previously they would have been persecuted by the Byzantines for being heretics). See Baumer, *Church of the East*, 151–52.

A third reason, which many believe was the single most important cause of the failure of Christianity in Asia, if failure it was, was Persia's persecution of Christians in the fourth century, which surpassed in number of martyrs and in intensity of religious hatred anything suffered in the West under three hundred years of pagan Roman emperors. Muslim persecution after the conquest in the seventh century was less intense than many have supposed, but nothing in western history, with its centuries of almost unchallenged Christian command of a continent's culture, can compare with the paralyzing effect of Islam's complete dominance of the Middle Eastern heart and center of the Church of the East throughout those same centuries . . . Sharp persecution breaks off only the tips of the branches; it produces martyrs and the tree still grows. Never-ending social and political repression, on the other hand, starves the roots; it stifles evangelism and the church declines. Such was the history of the church in Asia under Islam until, at the beginning of the fifteenth century, Tamerlane swept the continent with the persecution to end all persecutions, the wholesale massacres that gave him the name of "the exterminator" and gave Asian Christianity what appeared to be its final, fatal blow.[76]

CHINA

As noted above, Nestorian Christianity arrived in China in the seventh century, and over the decades grew under the tolerant rule of the Tang Dynasty. However, Wu Tsung's rule (840–846) led to the persecution of Buddhists (the main target of the persecution), as well as Manichaeans and Christians. The reasons for the persecution seem to be more political than religious. Moffett argues that it was due to a "rising tide of xenophobia and sectarian religious strife that grew in direct proportion to the weakening of national unity under a succession of ineffectual emperors."[77] Keung claims that it was due to the Taoist control of the court and their desire to persecute the Buddhists (of whom they were quite jealous).[78] Kenneth Ch'en states that the root of the persecution of Buddhists was economic: the Buddhist monks did not pay taxes, and

---

76. Moffett, *History of Christianity in Asia*, 1:504.
77. Ibid., 1:303.
78. Keung, "Nestorianism in China," 119.

so there was an attempt to discourage monastic life.⁷⁹ Regardless of the cause(s), the end result for the church was persecution.

The attack on "foreign religions" intensified in 845 when a government decree stated that all foreigners had to leave China, and as a result more than three thousand Zoroastrians and Christians had to flee. Moffett declares that the church never recovered from this exodus:

> If Buddhism, powerful as it was under the T'ang dynasty . . . never completely recovered from that nationwide persecution, how much more crippling must have been its effect on the small, scattered groups of Christians in the empire? It took more than four hundred years for Buddhism to regain under the Mongol dynasty something of the numerical strength it had enjoyed under the reign of the T'ang. Even a belated edict of toleration issued by the new emperor, Hsiuan-tsung (847–859), was probably not enough to save the Nestorians from virtual extinction.⁸⁰

As the T'ang dynasty crumbled, the suffering continued. For instance, in the fall of Canton (878) it was reported that 120,000 Muslims, Jews, Christians, and Zoroastrians were slaughtered.

Under the thirteenth-century *pax Mongolica* Christianity in China experienced a return and renaissance (by this time Catholic missions were also a part of the church in China).⁸¹ Christians were favored by the state, were placed in important positions in government and the Royal Court, and the hope for some was a united effort with the crusaders against the mutual enemy Islam. However, with the breakup of the Mongol empire in the following century, and the conversion of an increasing number of Mongols to Islam, the churches' fortunes were shattered as persecutions began. The identification of the Chinese church with foreigners only exacerbated the situation,⁸² as did the eventual

---

79. Kenneth Ch'en, "The Economic Background of the Hui-Ch'ang Suppression of Buddhism," *HJAS* 19 (1956) 67–105, as cited in Standaert, *Handbook of Christianity*, 1:33.

80. Moffett, *History of Christianity in Asia*, 1:304.

81. For a detailed description of the sources (written and archeological) available for a study of Christianity in China during this period, see Standaert, *Handbook of Christianity*, 1:43–111.

82. Standaert and others note how the church at this time seemed to be comprised primarily of foreigners. However, it is difficult to decipher just how much Christianity had penetrated into Chinese culture and had become indigenized. See Standaert, *Handbook of Christianity*, 1:97–98; Saunders, "Decline and Fall of Christianity in Medieval Asia," 101.

loss of communications with church leaders and resources in the west.[83] Tamerlane's destructive empire-building was the final act that ended the church's Chinese presence for a second time.

JAPAN

The persecution instituted by Hideyoshi was a shock for the church. Through ruthless conquest and intrigue Hideyoshi unified much of Japan under his rule by 1590.[84] Why he began to persecute the church after showing no animosity to the church for much of his reign is still not completely clear, but Buddhist agitation and a fear of the political intentions of the Jesuits were most likely a part of it.[85] In 1587 he issued an edict that called for the expulsion of all missionaries. Fortunately for the church, Hideyoshi did not vigorously enforce the edict, and only a few Jesuits actually left the country. The remainder stayed and continued to help the church, although numerous Jesuits, Franciscans, and Japanese Christians were martyred for the faith. After Hideyoshi's death, Ieyasu Tokugawa (1542–1616) managed to gain supreme power. His policy towards Christians was eventually harsher: the goal was the expulsion of all missionaries and the complete eradication of Christianity (as well as the complete isolation of Japan from outside influences). The following years 1614–1638 were marked by brutal torture and the execution of thousands.[86] The willingness of thousands to undergo suffering and even martyrdom for the faith gives evidence of a faith that had taken root in the people.

---

83. "It is this closing of the roads across Asia, far more than any Muslim *revanche*, which led to the isolation and atrophy of the distant and scattered Christian communities of Turkestan and the Far East . . . it is clear that courageous attempts were made by the Latin missionaries to get through to China until the obstacles became quite insurmountable. The last successful breakthrough appears to have been that of John of Marignolli in 1341–53; thereafter the curtain falls." See Saunders, "Decline and Fall of Christianity in Medieval Asia," 104.

84. Much of the following account is taken from Fujita, *Japan's Encounter with Christianity*, chaps. 4–5; Boxer, *Christian Century*, chap. 4; Moffett, *History of Christianity in Asia*, 2: chap. 4; Kentaro, "Roman Catholic Mission," 9–17.

85. For a summary of the possible reasons for the persecution of the church, see Fujita, *Japan's Encounter with Christianity*, 257–73; Boxer, *Christian Century*, chap. 4; Moffett, *History of Christianity in Asia*, 2:80–93.

86. For a detailed description of the gruesome methods, see Boxer, *Christian Century*, 347–54.

Tokugawa's and his successors' anti-Christian policy was successful. In 1640 the "Office for Investigation of Christians" was established for the hunting down of any remaining Christians (it was closed in 1792). The church had to go underground, with no outside contact for the next two hundred years: any remaining Christians became *Sempuku Kirishitan* (hidden Christians).[87] The visible church was gone, but in tiny isolated pockets these hidden Christians tried to pass the faith on to the next generation. Nevertheless, the remarkably successful Japanese church that had seemed so promising was in ashes, and the public witness of the church was wiped out.[88]

Migrations

Another important factor to consider when identifying the reasons for the disappearance of Christianity in certain places is the migration of non-Christian people into land previously dominated by Christians, or the evacuation or displacement of Christians from land where they once had a significant presence. In either case, the rapid or gradual demographic shift led to an increasingly marginalized church that became powerless and vulnerable to the whims of hostile religious and political powers.

North Africa

Ulrich Schoen contends that the "greatest part of the history of North West Africa and its church is not known to us . . . we have to depend on conjecture."[89] That being the case, there is evidence for the arrival of Arab settlers after the conquest of North Africa, as well as the departure of Christians for Christian lands such as Sicily, Spain, or elsewhere.[90] While understandable, the departure of those who were able to flee weakened the church and contributed to a changing demographic that ultimately

---

87. Drummond, *History of Christianity in Japan*, 109–17. For helpful articles on these hidden Christians, see volume two of Turnbull, ed., *Japan's Hidden Christians*; Kentaro, "Kature Kirishitan Tradition."

88. Gordon D. Laman argues that the impact of the persecution and suppression of Christianity effectively immunized the Japanese against Christianity—and thus mission work today struggles in Japan. See Laman, "Our Nagasaki Legacy."

89. Schoen, "Death of the Church," 4.

90. Holme, *Extinction*, 225; Christides, *Byzantine Libya*, 64–65.

shifted power to Muslims, and made conversion to Islam more and more appealing.[91]

Nubia

Vantini claims that the decline of the church in Nubia was due, in part, to the influx of Arab nomads:

> Ibn Khaldun mentions as one of the most important causes of decline in Nubia the coming of the Arab nomads and their intermarrying with Nubian families. Children born of Arab-Nubian parents came into possession of all the landed property and various rights which in the Nubian system were inherited matrilineally.[92]

Bowers echoes this position when he claims that Nubia was under significant pressure from unprecedented numbers of Muslim immigrants that overwhelmed the border defenses and eventually marginalized the indigenous Nubians.[93] While not the only reason for the decline of the church in Nubia, migrations of Muslims certainly played a part.

Moravia

At the end of the ninth and the first half of the tenth century the Magyars were considered to be the "scourge of Europe."[94] They were described as the "breeds of Satan" or "bloodthirsty, man-eating monsters from Scythia" that left a trail of devastation in their wake. The extent of their conquest was impressive from a military point of view, and their successes meant that they could permanently settle in the territory of modern-day Hungary.

The Magyar were mistakenly referred to as "Huns" or "Turks" from the eastern steppe, but they were neither. There is a great deal of consensus today that the Magyar language belonged to the Finno-Ugrian linguistic family. The earliest centuries of this people group are told

---

91. "To a minority, even a formerly privileged one, would it not have become clear that there was little future potential for the community in an environment in which adherence to Islam was the basis of society?" (Savage, *Gateway to Hell*, 96).

92. Vantini, *Christianity in the Sudan*, 207.

93. Bowers, "Nubian Christianity," 16.

94. Unless noted otherwise, the following is taken from Lendvai, *The Hungarians*, chaps. 1–2. For other histories of the Magyars/Hungarians, see Laszlo, *The Magyars*; Fodor, *In Search of a New Homeland*.

in not-too-reliable myths and legends. What is known with certainty is that in the mid-890s the Magyars *en masse* crossed the Carpathians and entered the Danube basin in numbers estimated at around 500,000 (whereas there were probably only 100,000 inhabitants within Moravia at the time). It was this mass movement of people that led to the disruption and disappearance of the church.[95]

TURKEY

The pattern of migrations in Turkey is unique from the previous examples, for not only were there migrations of Turks due to invasions, there was also the migration of people due to the Treaty of Lausanne.

Initial and subsequent invasions and migrations (eleventh to fifteenth centuries)—Vryonis writes that the sources on the Islamization of Asia Minor are of "almost paralytic complexity."[96] Consequently it is difficult to piece together with certainty what happened between the eleventh and the fifteenth centuries when Asia Minor went from being decidedly Christian to decidedly Muslim. The conquest(s) of Asia Minor by the Turks took over 400 years, and Turkish power waxed and waned over this period. What is known is that the arrival of the Turks led to the destruction of Christian towns and villages, the enslavement of Christians, and the eventual displacement of Christians away from the growing settlements of Turks in the Anatolian Plateau.[97] The pressure of the Mongols on the Turks in the thirteenth century led to further westward movement by the Turks as they sought to flee from the Mongols. The Byzantines were too weak to stop this migration, and the Turks

---

95. The church would reappear when the Magyars were converted to Christianity in the coming decades. See Lendvai, *The Hungarians*, chap. 3; Toth, "Christianization of the Magyars."

96. Vryonis, "Experience of Christians," 186. He notes that the difficulties include the bewildering array of languages (Arabic, Persian, Turkish, Georgian, Armenian, Syriac, Greek, Latin, German, French, Serbian, Bulgarian, and Russian), the lack of a set of sources that follows the events from beginning to end, and the disappearance of sources. The fact that the available sources tend to focus solely on Constantinople and not eastern Anatolia only compounds the problem.

97. Vryonis, "Experience of Christians," 201. That overall trajectory being the case, there were also periods of peace, cooperation, and good relations between Muslims and Christians. For instance, see Masters, *Christians and Jews in the Ottoman Arab World*; Braude and Lewis, eds., *Christians and Jews in the Ottoman Empire*; Faroqhi, *Subjects of the Sultan*; Frazee, *Catholics and Sultans*.

advanced even further westward to the fertile valleys and coastline.[98] In 1453 Constantinople fell to Ottoman Turks, and the Byzantine Empire was no more. It should be noted that Christians were not as displaced by the Ottoman conquest in the Balkans, in part because most Turks settled in Asia Minor, and the rapid conquest of the Balkans allowed for a more stable Ottoman rule that was not as disruptive for the church.[99]

Treaty of Lausanne (1923)—The remaining Christians in Turkey faced another major migration in the early twentieth century. The breakup of the Ottoman Empire in the nineteenth century, the Ottoman defeat at the end of the First World War, and the Turkish defeat of the Greeks in 1919–1922,[100] led to the signing of a treaty to bring about a resolution to the longstanding issue of minorities in Turkey and Greece.[101] The Treaty of Lausanne (1923) mandated the compulsory exchange of minorities in Greece and Turkey, and this exchange is considered to be "the first organized transfer of large ethno-religious groups by means of which minorities were forcibly uprooted under the aegis of international law to contribute, in turn, to the reconstruction of ethnically 'pure' homogenous states."[102] Onur Yildirim shows how this treaty set a precedent for decades of population exchanges.[103] Not surprisingly, the contemporary sensitivity to genocide, refugees, and ethnic cleansing has led to renewed scholarly interest in the treaty.[104]

---

98. Ménage, "Islamization of Anatolia," 54–59.

99. Vryonis, "Experience of Christians," 201. While the focus of this study is on Asia Minor, it should be noted that this pattern was followed to a lesser degree in the Balkans. For instance, Lopasic writes: "A very important factor contributing towards Islamization was the depopulation of large areas of Bosnia and Herzegovina due to war and the flight of the Christian population to both Croatia and Hungary." See Lopasic, "Islamization of the Balkans."

100. For a summary of the Greek invasion of Turkey after the First World War, see Smith, *Ionian Vision*.

101. Even before the Treaty there had been hundreds of thousands of refugees from the Balkans Wars and the First World War. For instance, 400,000 to 600,000 Muslims had been displaced by the contraction of the Ottoman Empire due to its losses in the decades leading up to the First World War (defacto deIslamization of parts of the Balkans). See Yildirim, *Diplomacy and Displacement*, 89.

102. Ibid., 10.

103. Ibid., 9–14.

104. See ibid., 1–28. See also Hirschon, ed., *Crossing the Aegean*; Clark, *Twice a Stranger*. For an example of a history written just after the exchange, see Ladas, *Exchange of Minorities*.

The life of refugees is never easy, but to exchange 900,000 Greeks and 250,000 Muslims in a matter of months and in the face of hostilities made for a nightmare for both Muslims and Christians.[105] It should be noted that the Treaty allowed the Greek population in Istanbul to remain (including the Orthodox Patriarch). However, for a variety of reasons, over the decades Greeks have emigrated from the city, leaving only a handful of Greek Orthodox. In Greece this entire process has been called the "Asia Minor Catastrophe" or something similar. Not only did it deliver the final death blow to the church's presence,[106] but it "derailed the entire course of Greek history by ending the hopes for a Greater Greece" in Asia Minor.[107]

Genocide

As defined by the United Nations, genocide is the intent in whole or in part to destroy a national, ethnical, racial, or religious group.[108] Despite Turkish opposition, a growing number of governments in the West now recognize that what happened to the Armenians in Turkey was genocide. The devastation experienced by the Church of the East in Syria and Iraq could be placed in the same category.

This section could have been placed in the above one on migrations, but the extent and degree of wanton violence associated with the disaster among the Armenians and other Christians in Turkey, Syria, Iraq, and

---

105. The total figures are disputed, but Yildirim argues that between 1921 and 1929 there were 577,000 Muslim refugees, and by 1928 1,221,000 Greek refugees. In 1928, one quarter of Greece's population of 6,200,000 were refugees. See Yildirim, *Diplomacy and Displacement*, 90–92.

106. Not surprisingly the Greeks and the Turks have very different perspectives on the events. The following quotation on the ultimate effect of the Treaty is from the Orthodox perspective: "In retrospect, we can see that the cruel solution used to stabilize and homogenize the populations of Greece and Turkey succeeded in de-Christianizing Turkey but left Greece with a substantial Muslim minority. An exchange which was supposed to have protected the international rights of the Ecumenical Patriarchate has, to a great extent, led instead to its captivity and the decimation of its Orthodox Christian population and its minorities. A Turkish nation that is now 99.9 percent Muslim and in desperate economic straits could have shown national maturity by protecting and safeguarding the center of international religion but has instead been consciously and calculatingly bent upon destroying it" (Rexine, "Ecumenical Patriarchate," 172).

107. Yildirim, *Diplomacy and Displacement*, 17.

108. Office of the High Commissioner for Human Rights. *Convention on the Prevention and Punishment of the Crime of Genocide.* http://www.unhchr.ch/html/menu3/b/p_genoci.htm.

Iran warrants a separate section. David Guant's summary and analysis is a sober description of the massacres of Christians in eastern Turkey and further east and south into modern day Syria, Iraq, and Iran during the First World War.[109] His account deals with the Christian communities that had managed to survive the advances of Islam; communities such as the Syriac Orthodox, the Assyrian Church, the Chaldean Church, the Syriac Catholic Church, Armenian Apostolic Church, and Armenian Catholic Church (as well a small number of Protestant missionaries and converts).[110]

In the early years of the First World War[111] the Ottoman government sought to eliminate these historic Christian communities in what Assyrian, Chaldean, and Syriac groups call *Sayfo*—the "year of the sword." Gaunt's description of the events provides a powerful witness to the nightmare:

> The degree of extermination and the brutality of the massacres indicate extreme pent-up hatred on the popular level. Christians, the so-called *gawur* infidels, were being killed in almost all sorts of situations. They were collected at the local town hall, walking in the streets, fleeing on the roads, at harvest, in the villages, in the caves and tunnels, in the caravanserais, in the prisons, under torture, on river rafts, on road repair gangs, on the way to be put to trial. There was no specific and technological way of carrying out the murders like the Nazi's extermination camps. A common feature was that those killed were unarmed, tied up, or otherwise defenseless. All possible methods of killing were used: shooting, stabbing, stoning, crushing, throat cutting, throwing off of roofs, drowning, decapitation. Witnesses talk of seeing collections of ears and noses, of brigands boasting of their collection of female body parts. The perpetrators not only killed but humiliated the victims . . . In Derike, the Syriac Catholic priest Ibrahim Qrom had his beard torn off and was then forced to crawl on all fours with a tormentor in his back while others kicked him, stabbed him, and finally cut him to pieces. Virtually every deportation caravan and village massacre was accompanied by serial mass rape of the women. Young girls were abducted as sex slaves and

---

109. Unless noted otherwise, the material in this section is taken from Guant, *Massacres, Resistance, Protectors*.

110. Ibid.

111. The most intense period was late 1914 to late 1915, although killings continued after these dates.

children as household servants . . . The homes of Christians were broken into, plundered, furniture smashed, windows and doors removed, set on fire.[112]

This genocide of ancient Christian communities led to many being wiped out completely, or displaced with far fewer members. The total number of deaths is hard to determine, but Guant estimates 250,000 deaths in massacres or conflict between 1914 and 1919 out of a total population of 560,000.[113]

Of course, the elimination of the Christian Armenian population mainly throughout central and eastern Turkey was even more disastrous in terms of numbers: estimates range from 1,000,000 to 1,500,000 deaths.[114] Some scholars consider the Armenian genocide and that of the Assyrian, Chaldean, and Syriac groups to be a part of the same grand movement by the Turkish government to cleanse its land of Christians. The rationale for the massacres can be partly understood in the context of the decline of Ottoman power, the development of Turkish nationalism, and the need for a modern Turkish nation free from what were perceived to be internal threats. Regardless, the modern-day dechristianization of Turkey certainly can be attributed in no small part to the genocides of these ancient Christian communities.

Conversions

Another rather obvious factor that led to the decline and eventual disappearance of the church was the reality of conversions from Christianity to Islam. In Nubia, North Africa, Turkey, and Central Asia numerous Christians converted to Islam. The reasons for such conversions are many, and complex.

While Christians in Islamic territory were often granted a particular type of freedom of worship, they nevertheless operated at a distinct disadvantage. As Baumer notes: "Since in Islamic states conversion

---

112. Guant, *Massacres, Resistance, Protectors*, 304–5.
113. Ibid., 300–301.
114. Massacres began in the late 1890s, and tapered off until the First World War. They reached their height in 1915, and waxed and waned until the end of the war. For analyses of the Armenian genocides, see Dadrian, *History of the Armenian Genocide*; Balakian, *Burning Tigris*; Bloxham, *Great Game of Genocide*; Lewy, *Armenian Massacres*; Graber, *Caravans to Oblivion*; Somakian, *Empire in Conflict*; Akcam, *From Republic to Republic*; Winter, ed., *America and the Armenian Genocide*.

from Christianity to Islam was desired, while conversion from Islam to Christianity usually brought the death penalty, the Church of the East was always at a disadvantage in the competition with Islam."[115] The reasons for conversion in such a one-sided system were many, and the following summary does not purport to deal with the complexity of such a conversion process.[116] First, avoidance of the extra tax burden that Christians had to bear was one major incentive.[117] Second, social advancement in a system where only Muslims had free range of opportunities was an important consideration. Third, not wanting to move from one's ancestral homeland in a forced migration was another reason for converting.[118] Fourth, there are accounts of Christians wanting to convert for less than ideal reasons. Some converted in order to take advantage of Muslim divorce laws,[119] and there is one account of a French doctor who sought to convert to escape his gambling debts.[120] Fifth, there were those who were genuinely convinced that Islam was the truth—especially when Islam's military victories seemed to prove that God was on the side of Islam.[121] Sixth, the threat of physical harm was a factor. For instance, Christians in Persia under the rule of Alp-Arsalan (1029–1072) had to wear iron collars around their necks if they did not convert.[122] Other threats were more severe: there are numerous accounts of Christians being faced with the choice "convert or die."[123] Faced with those two options, many chose to convert. It should be noted that forced conversions were a problem

---

115. Baumer, *Church of the East*, 267.

116. For an idea of the complexity of this issue, see Deringil, "No Compulsion in Religion."

117. Vaporis, "Defender of the Faith"; Vantini, *Christianity in the Sudan*, 207.

118. Yildirim, *Diplomacy and Displacement*, 107.

119. Braude and Lewis, eds., *Christians and Jews in the Ottoman Empire*, 34–35.

120. "This was the case for a French doctor, Monsieur Merlot, who converted and took the name of Murad Efendi in 1852. Having incurred rather large gambling debts while serving as an Ottoman government doctor in Erzurum in eastern Anatolia, he presented himself in Istanbul, declaring that he had become a Muslim. The Porte was somewhat embarrassed because his creditors, who were French citizens, were applying pressure through the French Embassy. In the end it was decided that Monsieur Merlot be accepted as a Muslim and given another posting, the caveat being that a certain percentage of his salary was to be withheld at source and handed over to the French consulate in Erzurum" (Deringil, "'No Compulsion in Religion,'" 563).

121. Browne, *Eclipse of Christianity in Asia*, 183–85.

122. Waterfield, *Christians in Persia*, 39.

123. Vantini, *Christianity in the Sudan*, 176; Ménage, "Islamization of Anatolia," 65.

for Muslim authorities at times (for technically they were not supposed to be allowed—and oftentimes conversions were not desired because they decreased tax revenues for the Muslim authorities). One particular problem that the church had to face with forced conversions was that of "crypto-Christians"; those who said that they were Muslims (usually for reasons of economic hardship or physical threat), but secretly kept their Christian faith.[124] This practice was discouraged by the church, but it had to be dealt with nonetheless.

CONCLUSION

The point of this survey is quite simple; it is to look at the recent statements regarding the inevitable benefits of persecution and the feelings of glee surrounding the collapse of Christendom in light of the church's history. After surveying the experiences of the churches in Nubia, North Africa, Moravia, Central Asia, China, Turkey, and Japan it is quite apparent that persecution does not inevitably lead to church growth, and the loss of Christendom may lead to the end of a Christian presence. Of course, there have been other times when churches have survived brutal repression, and have even grown in hostile territory. Churches have also been disestablished and survived. Nevertheless, the story of the churches in many places discussed in this survey runs counter to those happy-ending stories.

Persecution may come, and Western Christendom may never recover. The marginalization of the church in society may even be the biblical model for the followers of Jesus. But be warned: persecution and marginalization may mean the church being wiped out (as far-fetched as that may sound). The blood of the martyrs may have been a seed for the church in the Roman Empire, but in other cases the blood of the martyrs was not enough.

❖ ❖ ❖

---

124. Vaporis, "Defender of the Faith."

Postscript: The massacres and migrations continue to this very day. Consider the account by Jenkins:

> In one typical incident in 2000, on the island of Halmahera, 200 Christians were massacred in an hour-long killing spree by Muslim paramilitaries of the so-called Laskar Jihad. Two hundred more Christians were wiped out later that year on the island of Sapurua. By late 2000, half a million Maluka Christians had been expelled, mainly by Jihad fighters, with the unofficial support of Indonesian armed forces. Thousands of Christians were forced to convert to Islam in public ceremonies, some of which included circumcision for both men and women. Hundreds of Christians were killed for refusing to convert. Large numbers of churches were also destroyed, in a successful act of ethnic/religious cleansing that was largely ignored by Western governments and media. These events raised fears that Christianity would be extirpated across much of eastern Indonesia over the next decade or two.[125]

BIBLIOGRAPHY

Akcam, Taner. *From Republic to Republic: Turkish Nationalism and the Armenian Genocide.* London and New York: Zed Books, 2004.

Balakian, Peter. *The Burning Tigris: The Armenian Genocide and America's Response.* New York: HarperCollins, 2003.

Baumer, Christoph. *The Church of the East: An Illustrated History of Assyrian Christianity.* London and New York: I. B. Tauris, 2006.

Bayer, Charles H. *A Resurrected Church: Christianity after the Death of Christendom.* St. Louis: Chalice, 2001.

Bloxham, Donald. *The Great Game of Genocide: Imperialism, Nationalism and the Destruction of the Ottoman Armenians.* Oxford: Oxford University Press, 2005.

Bowers, Paul. "Nubian Christianity: The Neglected Heritage." *East Africa Journal of Evangelical Theology* 4 (1985) 3–23.

Bowlus, Charles R. *Franks, Moravians, and Magyars: The Struggle for the Middle Danube, 788–907.* Philadelphia: University of Pennsylvania Press, 1995.

Boxer, C. R. *The Christian Century in Japan, 1549–1650.* Berkeley: University of California Press, 1974.

Braude, Benjamin, and Bernard Lewis, eds. *Christians and Jews in the Ottoman Empire: The Functioning of a Plural Society.* 2 vols. New York and London: Holmes & Meier, 1982.

Browne, Laurence E. *The Eclipse of Christianity in Asia: From the Time of Muhammad till the Fourteenth Century.* Cambridge: Cambridge University Press, 1933.

Carter, Craig. *Rethinking Christ and Culture: A Post-Christendom Perspective.* Grand Rapids: Brazos, 2006.

---

125. Jenkins, *Next Christendom*, 176.

Cary-Elwes, Columba. *China and the Cross: A Survey of Missionary History.* New York: P. J. Kennedy & Sons, 1956.

Chao, Jonathan. "Witness of a Suffering Church: The Chinese Experience." *Evangelical Review of Theology* 8.1 (1984) 73–89.

Christides, Vassilios. *Byzantine Libya and the March of the Arabs towards the West of North Africa.* Oxford: British Archaeological Reports, 2000.

Clark, Bruce. *Twice a Stranger: The Mass Expulsions that Forged Modern Greece and Turkey.* Cambridge, MA: Harvard University Press, 2006.

Cooksey, J. J. *The Land of the Vanished Church.* London: World Dominion Press, 1926.

Cooper, Michael. "A Mission Interrupted: Japan." In *A Companion to the Reformation World*, edited by R. Po-chia Hsia, 393–407. Oxford: Blackwell, 2004.

Cuoq, Joseph. *Islamisation de la Nubie chrétienne: VIIe–XVIe siècle.* Paris: Librairie Orientaliste Paul Geuthner, 1986.

Curta, Florin. "Before Cyril and Methodius: Christianity and Barbarians beyond the Sixth- and Seventh-Century Danube Frontier." In *East Central and Eastern Europe in the Early Middle Ages*, edited by Florin Curta, 181–208. Ann Arbor: University of Michigan Press, 2005.

Dadrian, Vahakn. *The History of the Armenian Genocide: Ethnic Conflict from the Balkans to Anatolia to the Caucasus.* New York and Oxford: Berghahn, 1995.

Deeg, Max. "The 'Brilliant Teaching': The Rise and Fall of 'Nestorianism' (Jingjiao) in Tang China." *Japanese Religions* 31 (2006) 91–110.

Deringil, Selim. "'There Is No Compulsion in Religion': On Conversion and Apostasy in the Late Ottoman Empire: 1839–1856." *Society for Comparative Study of Society and History* (2000) 547–75.

Dittrich, Zdenek R. *Christianity in Great-Moravia.* Groningen: J. B. Wolters, 1962.

Drummond, Richard Henry. *History of Christianity in Japan.* Grand Rapids: Eerdmans, 1971.

Dvornik, Francis. *Byzantine Missions among the Slavs: SS. Constantine-Cyril and Methodius.* New Brunswick, NJ: Rutgers University Press, 1970.

———. *The Slavs in European History and Civilization.* New Brunswick, NJ: Rutgers University Press, 1962.

Faroqhi, Suraiya. *Subjects of the Sultan: Culture and Daily Life in the Ottoman Empire.* London and New York: I. B. Tauris, 2000.

Fletcher, Richard. *The Barbarian Conversion: From Paganism to Christianity.* Berkeley: University of California Press, 1997.

Fodor, Istvan. *In Search of a New Homeland: The Prehistory of the Hungarian People and the Conquest.* Budapest: Corvina, 1975.

Frazee, Charles A. *Catholics and Sultans: The Church and the Ottoman Empire, 1453–1923.* London: Cambridge University Press, 1983.

Frend, W. H. C. *The Donatist Church: A Movement of Protest in Roman North Africa.* Oxford: Clarendon, 1952.

Frost, Michael. *Exiles: Living Missionally in a Post-Christian Culture.* Peabody, MA: Hendrickson, 2006.

Fujita, Neil S. *Japan's Encounter with Christianity: The Catholic Mission in Pre-Modern Japan.* New York: Paulist, 1991.

Galli, Mark. "Sometimes Persecution Purifies, Unites, and Grows the Church—Sometimes It Doesn't." *Christianity Today* (1997) 16–19.

Galuska, Ludek. *Great Moravia.* Brno, Czechoslovakia: Moravian Museum, 1991.

Gertz, Steven. "How Armenia 'Invented' Christendom." *Christian History* 85 (2005) 46–47.
Gillman, Ian, and Hans-Joachim Klimkeit. *Christians in Asia before 1500.* Ann Arbor: University of Michigan Press, 1999.
Graber, G. S. *Caravans to Oblivion: The Armenian Genocide, 1915.* New York: Wiley, 1996.
Grillmeier, Aloys. *Christ in Christian Tradition.* Vol. 2, *From the Council of Chalcedon (451) to Gregory the Great (590–604).* London: Mowbray; Louisville: Westminster John Knox, 1996.
Guant, David. *Massacres, Resistance, Protectors: Muslim-Christian Relations in Eastern Anatolia during World War 1.* Piscataway, NJ: Gorgias, 2006.
Hall, Douglas J. *The End of Christendom and the Future of Christianity.* Valley Forge, PA: Trinity Press International, 1997.
Handley, Mark. "Disputing the End of African Christianity." In *Vandals, Romans and Berbers: New Perspectives on Late Antique North Africa*, edited by A. H. Merrills, 291–310. Aldershot, England: Ashgate, 2004.
Hauerwas, Stanley, and William H. Willimon. *Resident Aliens: A Provocative Christian Assessment of Culture and Ministry for People Who Know Something Is Wrong.* Nashville: Abingdon, 1989.
Higashibaba, Ikuo. "Historiographical Issues in the Studies of the 'Christian Century' in Japan." *Japanese Religions* 24 (1999) 29–50.
Hirschon, Renee, ed. *Crossing the Aegean: An Appraisal of the 1923 Compulsory Population Exchange between Greece and Turkey.* New York and Oxford: Berghahn, 2003.
Holme, L. R. *The Extinction of the Christian Churches in North Africa.* London: Clay, 1898. Reprinted New York: Burt Franklin, 1969.
Isichei, Elizabeth. *A History of Christianity in Africa: From Antiquity to the Present.* Grand Rapids: Eerdmans, 1995.
Jenkins, Philip. *The Lost History of Christianity: The Thousand-Year Golden Age of the Church in the Middle East, Africa, and Asia—and How It Died.* New York: HarperCollins, 2008.
———. *The Next Christendom: The Coming of Global Christianity.* Oxford: Oxford University Press, 2002.
Kentaro, Miyazaki. "The Kature Kirishitan Tradition." In *Handbook of Christianity in Japan*, edited by Mark R. Mullins, 19–34. Leiden: Brill, 2003.
———. "Roman Catholic Mission in Pre-Modern Japan." In *Handbook of Christianity in Japan*, edited by Mark R. Mullins, 1–18. Leiden: Brill, 2003.
Kerkhofs, Jan. "The Church in Turkey." *Pro Mundi Vita: Dossiers* 13 (1981) 2–19.
Keung, Lee Shiu. "Nestorianism in China." *Ching Feng* 16 (1973) 113–35.
Kirwan, Laurence. "The Birth of Christian Nubia: Some Archaeological Problems." In *Studies on the History of Late Antique and Christian Nubia*, edited by T. Hagg, L. Torok, and D. A. Welsby, 119–34. Variorum Collected Studies Series 748. Farnham, UK: Ashgate, 2002.
———. "Introduction." In *Studies on the History of Late Antique and Christian Nubia*, edited by T. Hagg, L. Torok, and D. A. Welsby, 1–9. Variorum Collected Studies Series 748; Farnham, UK: Ashgate, 2002.

———. "Prelude to Nubian Christianity." In *Studies on the History of Late Antique and Christian Nubia*, edited by T. Hagg, L. Torok, and D. A. Welsby, 121–28. Variorum Collected Studies Series 748; Farnham, UK: Ashgate, 2002.

Ladas, Stephen P. *The Exchange of Minorities: Bulgaria, Greece and Turkey*. New York: Macmillan, 1932.

Laman, Gordon D. "Our Nagasaki Legacy: An Examination of the Period of Persecution of Christianity and Its Impact on Subsequent Christian Mission in Japan." *Reformed Review* 37 (1984) 151–76.

Laszlo, Gyula. *The Magyars: Their Life and Civilisation*. Budapest: Corvina, 1996.

Latourette, K. S. *A History of Christian Missions in China*. New York: Macmillan, 1929.

Leclercq, H. *L'Afrique Chrétienne*. 2 vols. Paris: Librairie Victor Lecoffre, 1904.

Lendvai, Paul. *The Hungarians: A Thousand Years of Victory in Defeat*. Princeton: Princeton University Press, 2003.

Lewy, Guenter. *The Armenian Massacres in Ottoman Turkey*. Salt Lake City: University of Utah Press, 2005.

Lopasic, Alexander. "Islamization of the Balkans with Special Reference to Bosnia." *Journal of Islamic Studies* 5.2 (1994) 163–86.

MacArthur, John. "How to Handle Persecution: How to Turn Persecution into Production," taken from http://www.biblebb.com/files/MAC/sg1758.htm.

Masters, Bruce. *Christians and Jews in the Ottoman Arab World: The Roots of Sectarianism*. Cambridge: Cambridge University Press, 2001.

Ménage, V. L. "The Islamization of Anatolia." In *Conversion to Islam*, edited by Nehemia Levtzion, 52–67. New York and London: Holmes & Meier, 1979.

Moffett, Samuel Hugh. *A History of Christianity in Asia*. Vol. 1, *Beginnings to 1500*. San Francisco: Harper, 1992.

———. *A History of Christianity in Asia*. Vol. 2, *1500 to 1900*. Maryknoll: Orbis, 2004.

Monneret de Villard, Ugo. *La Nubia medioevale*. Cairo: Imprimerie de L'Institut Français, 1957.

———. *Storia della Nubia Cristiana*. Rome: Pontifical Institute of Oriental Studies, 1938.

Moule, A. C. *Christians in China before the Year 1550*. London: SPCK, 1930.

Murray, Stuart. *Post-Christendom*. Milton Keynes, UK: Paternoster, 2004.

Papadopoullos, Theodore H. *Studies and Documents Relating to the History of the Greek Church and People under Turkish Domination*. Aldershot: Variorum, 1952.

Rexine, John E. "The Ecumenical Patriarchate and the Compulsory Exchange of Populations between Greece and Turkey, 1923–1930." In *Orthodox Theology and Diakonia: Trends and Prospects*, edited by Demetrios J. Constantelos, 155–73. Brookline, MA: Holy Cross Orthodox Press, 1981.

Saunders, J. J. "The Decline and Fall of Christianity in Medieval Asia." *Journal of Religious History* 5 (1968) 93–104.

Savage, Elizabeth. *Gateway to Hell, a Gateway to Paradise: The North African Response to the Arab Conquest*. Princeton: Darwin, 1997.

Schoen, Ulrich. "The Death of the Church." *Theological Review* 2 (1979) 3–20.

Smith, Michael Llewellyn. *Ionian Vision: Greece in Asia Minor 1919–1922*. London: Allen Lane, 1973.

Somakian, Manoug Joseph. *Empire in Conflict: Armenia and the Great Powers, 1895–1920*. London and New York: I. B. Tauris, 1995.

Standaert, Nicolas. *Handbook of Christianity in China*. Vol. 1, *635–1800*. Leiden: Brill, 2001.

Toth, William. "The Christianization of the Magyars." *Church History* 11 (1942) 33–54.

Turnbull, Stephen, ed. *Japan's Hidden Christians, 1549–1999*. Vol. 2, *Secret Christianity in Japan, 1640–1999*. Tokyo: Japan Library, 2000.

Vantini, Giovanni. *Christianity in the Sudan*. Bologna: EMI, 1981.

Vaporis, N. Michael. "A Defender of the Faith: Nektarios Terpos, a Case Study." In *Orthodox Theology and Diakonia: Trends and Prospects*, edited by Demetrios J. Constantelos, 145–54. Brookline, MA: Holy Cross Orthodox Press, 1981.

Vryonis, Speros. "The Experience of Christians under Seljuk and Ottoman Domination, Eleventh to Sixteenth Century." In *Conversion and Continuity: Indigenous Christian Communities in Islamic Lands Eighth to Eighteenth Centuries*, edited by Michael Gervers and Ramzi Jibran Bikhazi, 185–216. Toronto: Pontifical Institute of Mediaeval Studies, 1990.

Waterfield, Robin E. *Christians in Persia: Assyrians, Armenians, Roman Catholics, and Protestants*. London: George Allen & Unwin, 1973.

Welsby, Derek A. *The Medieval Kingdoms of Nubia: Pagans, Christians and Muslims along the Middle Nile*. London: British Museum Press, 2002.

Winter, Jay, ed. *America and the Armenian Genocide of 1915*. Cambridge: Cambridge University Press, 2003.

Yildirim, Onur. *Diplomacy and Displacement: Reconsidering the Turco-Greek Exchange of Populations, 1922–1934*. New York and London: Routledge, 2006.

5

The Local Church

Postmodern Possibilities

LEE BEACH

INTRODUCTION

THE LOCAL CHURCH IS the inevitable outcome of the universal church. The church universal requires the particular expression that only the local church can provide. Only through local expression of the church is the church's nature, character, and mission expressed.

The word *ekklēsia* (church, congregation) occurs 114 times in the New Testament. The vast majority of these references are clearly to a local assembly (e.g., 1 Cor 1:2; 2 Cor 1:1). While the word "church" can mean larger manifestations in the epistles, such as regional networks of churches (e.g., 1 Cor 16:19), the thrust of any teaching directed to the church is intended to bring meaning to and inform the practice of local congregations.[1] From a New Testament and theological perspective, the church in any practical way does not exist outside of its local expression in a particular context.[2]

In many ways in Western society today the local church is under fire. At worst, critics on the outside vilify it as a cultural drag hindering the progress of human ethics and advancement. At best, it is ignored as

---

1. Branson, "Ecclesiology and Leadership," 103–4. Also, Siegwalt, "Local Church."

2. Branson, "Ecclesiology and Leadership," 104. See also, Volf, *After Our Likeness*, 138.

irrelevant. From its own adherents, increasing numbers also question the local church's relevance to their lives. Declining attendance and the drive to try many new ecclesiological initiatives demonstrate the disenchantment many feel with their local bodies. This may be explained as the result of a culture marked by individualism and guided by a consumer mentality. These realities cause some to be dissatisfied with almost every institution in the traditional culture, which makes the work of the church more difficult than ever.

On the other hand some of the apathy and dissatisfaction that the church is confronted with may be of its own making. Part of the cultural passivity directed at the local church in the West is the result of its inability to adapt to the changes that denote our time. Perhaps local churches, in their sluggishness to adapt to shifting realities in the culture and, at times, their outright refusal to do so, are reaping what they have sown. A disregard for change and lack of an adaptive strategy have left many local congregations mired in the fallout of a post-Christian culture shift and immobilized by the prospects of having to minister the gospel in the new landscape that lies before them.

Yet it would seem that in our current postmodern milieu there is a very real opportunity for a local church renaissance. In fact, it would seem that local churches are uniquely positioned to connect with those around them who have dismissed the church, and perhaps even the gospel, as meaningless, as well as those who feel disconnected from their traditional religious experience in their local church. The potential of the local church in postmodern times comes precisely because of its local nature. It is this locality that places the church in a setting where its renaissance as a community within the community holds great potential. This possibility capitalizes on two realities that describe the postmodern ocean on which local churches in the West find themselves floating.

The first of these realities is the postmodern experience of dislocation. Postmodernism is intrinsically a cultural ethos prone to leaving people feeling homeless. At its heart it is a culture that rejects any stabilizing narrative or normative ethic that offers a sense of foundation. Robin Usher and Richard Edwards write:

> Postmodernity, then, describes a world where people have to make their way without fixed referents and traditional anchoring

points. It is a world of rapid change, of bewildering instability, where knowledge is constantly changing and meaning floats.[3]

The fluidity of postmodern thought gives birth to a culture that is also fluid and can leave people feeling adrift. Kevin Vanhoozer points out that in a culture of disposable ideas and shifting fancies, a key metaphor becomes that of the "nomad."[4] A nomad is one who passes through, who does not dwell or make a home. The culture of postmodernity is given to such an experience. "In a postmodern world we are all homeless," write Richard Middleton and Brian Walsh in their book, *Truth is Stranger Than It Used to Be*. Stripped of our modernist myths we are left as "homeless nomads in a postmodern desert."[5]

This analysis alludes to the fact that postmodernism is ultimately a reaction to modernism and thus is a deconstructive movement rather than a constructive one. Postmodernism is a tearing down of former beliefs and patterns of life. It produces not a new "order" of things, but rather a new "disorder." Walsh and Keesmaat infer that the postmodern ethos that questions former assumptions, entertains multiple possibilities, and posits few conclusions is a culture of fragmentation. They write, "When one is accustomed to toying with a multiplicity of perspectives, identities, and worldviews it is not surprising that life starts to feel fragmented."[6] This murky blend is a concoction that produces a fragmented culture and potentially a fragmented self. Such fragmentation can be an isolating experience. In postmodernism the self can slip into a form of isolation that is the result of a loss of connection with stabilizing community.[7] This reality calls for places of stabilization and meaningful connection, a place like the local church when the local church is functioning as it has been designed by God to do.

The second reality that offers hope for a local church renaissance is the postmodern mistrust of the universal, or "meta" truths that were espoused by modernist ideology. Postmodernism is perhaps most often defined by the words of Jean-Francois Lyotard when he stated, "Simplifying in the extreme, I define postmodernity as incredulity to-

3. Usher and Edwards, *Postmodernism and Education*, 7, as cited in Walsh and Keesmaat, *Colossians Remixed*, 23.
4. Vanhoozer, "Condition of Postmodernity," 14–15.
5. Middleton and Walsh, *Truth Is Stranger*, 155.
6. Walsh and Keesmaat, *Colossians Remixed*, 25.
7. Gallagher, *Clashing Symbols*, 92.

ward all metanarratives."[8] This mistrust of any overarching narrative that coheres human existence into its story pushes postmodern people to trust only in that which is personally known to them. Relationship becomes the primary conduit for "truth," as trust is only granted in its fullness to those who are known and whose life gives credence to the words that they speak. Grand narratives espoused by those who are unknown are received with suspicion by people who are steeped in a postmodern mentality. Detached from personal relationship, metanarratives lack the credibility that personal knowledge of the proclaimant offers. In the same way institutions are treated with suspicion.[9] They are perceived as having a life and goals that do not necessarily serve the good of the individual person or local community. The institution is largely self-serving and is guided by a metanarrative that is inadequate for giving guidance to the realities of everyday life. Thus, the universality of institutions is perceived as creating distance and impersonality. Institutions are unconnected to the individual. They lack relational credibility. This mistrust in the "universal" signals a move back to the local. For those enmeshed in postmodern culture, the universal must give way to the local as the best vehicle for conveying trustworthy information. As Stanley Grenz has observed:

> There are no longer any common standards to which people can appeal in their effort to measure, judge or value ideas, opinions or lifestyle choices. Gone as well are allegiances to a common source of authority and a commonly regarded and respected wielder of power. As the center dissolves, our society is increasingly becoming a conglomerate of societies.[10]

Grenz's discerning of a society of societies reflects the shift to localization that is taking place within our culture. It is a localization that is rooted in the primacy of relationship and signals a return to resources neglected by the triumph of modernity. Old anchors like community (and spirituality) become important components of postmodern life as they are authentically experienced in local relationships.[11]

8. Lyotard, *Postmodern Condition*, xxiv.
9. This theme is explored in many places including Beaudoin, *Virtual Faith*; see especially 51–72.
10. Grenz, *Primer*, 19–20.
11. Gallagher, *Clashing Symbols*, 95. The word "local" requires redefinition, for local is no longer necessarily just defined by geography. I would submit that in a cyber age

These two cultural contours provide generative possibilities for the local church because the local church is intrinsically a relationally rooted entity. Its identity as a relational group of people comes from its very nature as an extension of the relationally of God.

THE RELATIONAL GOD AND THE RELATIONAL CHURCH

The story of Scripture reflects God's intention to restore the broken relationship between him and humanity and transform the world into a restored creation. The transforming intention of God is rooted in the original relationship between himself and humanity.

This relational intention of God is clearly seen in creation as he creates man and woman "in his own image" (Gen 1:27), and is further developed in Gen 2:7 when God breathes his very life into the nostrils of the man, thus imbuing the original human with his own breath. It is seen in Genesis 3, subsequent to the original couple's sin, when God is depicted as intimately present with humanity walking in the garden where his people dwell, calling out to the couple for fellowship. With the relationship ruptured, the story develops with a focus on God continuing to seek relationship with those he has created. With the call of Abram, God establishes a people that will be a blessing to "all nations," and will demonstrate the life and call of God to all of humanity.

The unfolding story leads to Israel, subsequent to their deliverance from Egypt, being explicitly reconstituted as a covenant community who will demonstrate the life and reality of Yahweh to the world (Exod 3:7–8, 20). In Jesus and the incarnation God most explicitly demonstrates his desire to be known by humanity and live in a restored relationship. The church carries on as a place where God's very presence dwells in the world (1 Cor 3:16; Eph 2:22). While this is certainly a truncated overview of the biblical narrative, it is not hard to perceive from Scripture that relationship permeates the divine-human experience and that God's goal is redemption of a fallen humanity and the ultimate restoration of that relationship.

The relational nature of God, as it is applied in his relationship with humanity, is of course rooted in God's very own nature. As Father, Son,

---

locality is increasingly a relational term. "Local" relationships may take place in a cyber community whose members reside great distances apart. A "local" church may in fact be an on-line community. However, even in this case relationship is the key to trust and ministry.

and Spirit, God's very nature is relationship. In its essence the conception of the Christian God as Father, Son, and Spirit offers the idea that God is in community, a legitimate community of three persons, together in relationship. Thus, as he chooses a people in whom to dwell, this people becomes an extension of his relational nature. The church is a community that participates in the divine life in its life together. This is foundational to our humanity and the idea of the church. Because God is in community, he created us to be in community. Much of this community was lost as humanity fell into sin. Thus, God's salvation includes restoring people to the communal ideal God had in mind at creation, restoring community with God and with others. Israel and the church are an expression of the communal nature of God. God is in relation with himself as Father, Son, and Spirit, but this relationality also extends to his interaction with his creation. This is foundational to the church, as the church depicts in its fellowship and also through its mission the concept of the divine relationality. This empowers the local church, as it is situated as an entity, both in relationship with God and with its local community, to be a place where people can experience the divine life, a place where the nomadic reality of postmodern culture is provided its ultimate home in community with God and where the mistrust of the detached metanarrative is answered by the local story of a local congregation on a pilgrimage together. Such is the postmodern potential of the local church, to be a true alternate community, a community of the living God. As Bryan Stone writes in his book *Evangelism after Christendom*:

> To construe the message of the gospel in such a way as to hide or diminish the unique social creation of the Spirit that the first Christians called *ecclesia* is to miss the point of what God is up to in history—the calling forth and establishment of a people. The most evangelistic thing the church can do, therefore, is to be the church, not merely in public but as a new and alternative public; not merely in society but as a new and distinct society, a new and unprecedented social existence.[12]

---

12. Stone, *Evangelism*, 15–16.

TRINITARIAN REFLECTION AS A RESOURCE FOR THE LOCAL CHURCH

If local churches are to constitute such a community perhaps there is no more suggestive resource than further reflection on Trinitarian life. This is a rich reservoir that can enable God's life to be formed most powerfully in local congregations. The relational existence of God and his hospitality as the God who shares life with his creation provides generative possibilities for local congregations.

The ecclesiological possibilities of Trinitarian reflection have created a burgeoning conversation. As a contribution to this, here we will consider the formative actions of Father, Son, and Spirit on the local church by reflecting on key defining activities in the life of each member of the Godhead: the Father as initiator of mission, the Son as incarnation of the divine life, and the Spirit as the creative inspiration for contextualized ministry.[13]

Father: The Initiator of Mission

> "It is not the church of God that has a mission in the world, but the God of mission who has a church in the world."
>
> —Tim Dearborn[14]

The call of Abram to establish a people who would be a blessing to all the nations of the world reflects God's missional nature. The relentlessness of God's mission is explicit in the Bible. Israel is constituted as a people who will demonstrate God's relational intention to the nations around them. This mission will not be thwarted, even when his chosen people find themselves in exile, no longer autonomous or in control of their land or destiny; the missional purposes of God will continue through them (Isa 43:9–10; 55:3–5).

The call of Israel to bear witness to the salvation of YHWH continues throughout the nation's history primarily because this call reflects the inner life of the God who called them, the God of relationship, who remains on a mission until relationship with his creation is fully restored.

The ultimate expression of the missional life of God is found in the Father's sending of his Son as a witness to the world. The evangelistic

---

13. I am adapting a formula first introduced to me by Dr. Michael Knowles.
14. Dearborn, *Short-term Missions Workbook*, 125.

significance of Jesus is clearly seen in the Gospels as the authors present him as the one who comes to "proclaim good news to the poor . . . freedom to the captive and recovery of sight for the blind" (Luke 4:18). He comes not for the sake of the righteous but to call "sinners to repentance" (Luke 5:31). He comes "to seek and save the lost" (Luke 19:10). He travels the countryside proclaiming the good news (Mark 1:14, 21, 38). Perhaps most dramatically, the Gospel of John depicts the coming of the Son as epitomizing God's desire to share his life with creation: "Yet to all who received him, to those who believed in his name, he gave the right to become children of God" (John 1:12). The mission of the Father through the life of his Son is to invite people into relationship.

The local church extends the relationality of God through its participation in the mission of God. This participation is characterized by the relationship that a local church has with its community. Just as the missional purpose of God seeks to share his life with people so too the local church seeks to share its life, which is an outflow of its experience of God's life, with those with whom the church (via its members) comes in contact. As Scott Frederickson has written:

> In this way the missional congregation understands the importance of relationship in the being of God, and the congregation can use its own relationship with its context as a way to participate in God's mission for the sake of the world.[15]

As local church ministry is informed by the Trinitarian life of God, mission will inevitably move to the center of the church's own life. This move to mission will inform the church's own sense of being in relationship with its community just as God is in relationship with the world. The Father's model of radical engagement and relational commitment further informs the ministry of the local church. It disallows local churches from remaining insulated from the realities of their community by setting themselves up in their buildings and remaining busy with programs that never touch the community unless someone happens to take the risk of venturing in. The missional initiative of God the Father calls local churches to emulate his relational initiatives in local ways that bring the good news of God to bear in the community in which the church resides. Like ambassadors sent out to represent their home country in another country, those who have established citizenship in the

---

15. Frederickson, "Missional Congregation," 47.

kingdom of God are sent out to share the message of reconciliation with those outside of that kingdom (2 Cor 5:17–18). In so doing the missional intentions of the Father are carried out by his church.

The Son: Incarnation of Divine Life

One of the very few things that New Testament scholars seem to agree on is that the central message that Jesus proclaimed, embodied, and sought to implement was the kingdom (or reign) of God. In this sense Jesus incarnates the divine life of God as both a living reality and a pattern for his followers to emulate. The incarnational life of Jesus is explicitly relational as he connects himself to a community of followers and seeks to form that community into an extension of his incarnational ministry. Just as Jesus comes to demonstrate the divine life, he also comes to inaugurate it in the communal life of his people. At least two implications of incarnation deserve consideration for the life of local churches.

The first is the idea of the church as a "hermeneutic of the gospel."[16] That is, the church is an interpretation of what the gospel truly means. The church is the place where the Trinitarian life of God is incarnated and can be seen by the world. Just as Jesus' incarnation allowed him to say, "Anyone who has seen me has seen the Father" (John 14:9), the church as an incarnation invites a similar kind of scrutiny. This is of course a daunting idea as we survey the imperfections that so often mark the local church. Yet it remains consistent with Jesus' clear intentions to bring to life a community of people who would embody a life that reflects the intentions of God for his created people.

The nature of this kingdom, its incarnational form, is nowhere more clearly seen than in the teaching of the Sermon on the Mount (Matthew 5–7). The sermon offers rules for communal life that are counter-cultural, but constitute a people who are a community of justice (giving to the needy), peace (turning the other cheek, love for enemies), and righteousness (anger is likened to murder, lust is likened to adultery, earthly treasures are of less value than treasures in heaven, seeking righteousness takes priority over all else). They are an embodiment of the nature of God expressed through his Son and in the life of his church. As Mark Lau Branson observes, "The Beatitudes uniquely offer us the gift

---

16. Newbigin, *Gospel in a Pluralist Society*, 222.

of seeing and interpreting reality as God sees and interprets it, and that's the beginning place for the church."[17]

As reflection on the activity of the Trinity shapes the practice of the local church, Jesus' incarnation of the kingdom of God will hone that praxis and push it toward local churches seeking to be reflections of "God's Shalom." That is a place where the presence of God is manifest not in some esoteric way, but in concrete form. Just as Jesus offers a living depiction of God, the church offers a living expression of God's life to the world. The Hebrew term "shalom" expresses this intention as it brings together various elements of who God is and what his kingdom looks like as it finds real, local expression. Shalom is

> a term that weaves together peace and justice in a Spirit created community where human flourishing, blessedness and wholeness is accompanied by the well being of animals and even plant life (Isa 11:1–9).[18]

It is an incarnational expression that points to the living God in tangible ways and continues the incarnation of Christ through the life of the church. Thus, the church presents itself, by God's power, to be a text that the world can read in order to discover God, and it truly becomes the "hermeneutic of the gospel." People are then invited to "enter" in and become participants in God's living kingdom.

Perhaps the most missional thing a local church can do in this present age is take time to meditate on, discuss, and pray through the Sermon on the Mount and ask questions about its implications for the congregation's life corporately and individually. As the church answers those questions it will move more fully into the realization of its incarnational potential.

The second idea that incarnation offers the local church is that of the church as a servant community. This idea is located in an understanding of Jesus' own approach to servanthood as it is rooted in his own experience of Trinitarian relationship and the concept that theologian Gary Simpson calls "perichoretic power."[19]

Jesus taught his disciples that their ways were not like those of the "rulers of the Gentiles" who lord it over those they rule. Instead, leader-

---

17. Branson, "Ecclesiology and Leadership," 99.
18. Stone, *Evangelism*, 70.
19. Simpson, "Reformation," 82.

ship in the kingdom of God is demonstrated by becoming a servant and "slave of all" (Mark 10:42–44; see also 9:35). This kind of approach is a reflection of the incarnational life of Jesus who "came not to be served, but to serve" (Mark 10:45). The apostle Paul seeks to engender this kind of perspective in the church in Philippi when he calls the conflicted church to humility (and servanthood) by recalling Jesus' incarnational example for them to follow (Phil 2:5–11). He reminds the readers of his epistle that Jesus set aside his divine rights and took on "the nature of a servant" in order to fulfill his divine commission. This is what the Philippians are to do in their communal life, practice perichoretic power, just as Jesus did in his work as crucified Saviour. As this kind of practice develops within a church, the church becomes a servant to its community just as Jesus was servant to all.

Simpson's exploration of perichoretic power informs this call on the church to servanthood by mining the inner relationship of the Trinity. The relationship among Father, Son, and Spirit is not based on hierarchical power but rather reciprocal giving and receiving.[20] Such a model of relationship serves as a basis and model for all human relationships. The church incarnates this life as it seeks to live out its "Shalom" with the perspective that it is called to follow Jesus in offering itself as a servant to its community. This life of service is not rooted in conventional Western structures of missional engagement, which are often based on a consumer model of "serving" in an attempt to give good customer service so as to attract people to the church, and its "product," like any other business with a product to sell. Rather it flows from a deep sense of being connected to the life of the God who is in a radically reciprocal relationship as the triune God. As this life spills over into the life of a local church, that church enters its community in a truly servant-like fashion, ready to engage the community in the radical way that Jesus engaged his world, not in order to "sell" their product, but in order to share God's shalom with their local community. In this way, the relational life of God is extended to the local community through the people of God who together reflect the inner perichoresis of their Lord.

As the local church appropriates such a model, it can move into its community in a way that continues to reflect the incarnational life of Christ and his alternative vision for life in this world. This is a life that reflects the servant nature of God and further allows the community to see

20. Ibid., 83.

in the church an interpretation of the gospel that faithfully demonstrates the life of God and invites people to become participants in that life.

The Spirit: Creative Inspiration for Contextualized Ministry

The challenge for every local church is to find appropriate ways to conduct ministry in its context. Contextualization is a primary principle for effective ministry. Churches need to discern how they can minister in, with, and against their contexts so that the message of the gospel can be heard.[21] They minister "in" their context as they take up residence and dwell in a certain place. This residency is foundational to their doing ministry in a place. Jesus took up residence and "dwelled" among humanity in a certain time and place (John 1:14). In this way he ministered "in" a context. Churches minister "with" their context as they learn the ways, rhythms, and particularities of that context and seek to engage them constructively. Again, Jesus' ministry demonstrates his working "with" his context. His teaching references were highly particular, his attending events like a wedding, and eating meals with "sinners" are examples of ministry "with" a culture. At times the church also has to minister "against" a context. In times that call for ministry "against" the context, the church takes on a prophetic role and speaks a word against sin and injustice that corrupts its context and harms those who inhabit that context. In Jesus' ministry an example might be his cleansing of the temple, which entailed both prophetic words and actions designed to demonstrate the corruption and oppression of inappropriate practices within the religious culture of the day.

The challenge for the local church, and increasingly so in these fragmented postmodern times, is to discern how to effectively live in, with, and against its local context. Doing so is essential to its nature and its effectiveness as a servant to the context. This is necessarily Spirit-enabled ministry, and the work of the Spirit is to help the church apply the divine life to its local place.

The very promise of the Spirit alludes to the possibility of effectiveness in local contexts. Jesus' words to his somewhat disoriented disciples just before his ascension indicate that the Spirit would enable localized witness: "but you will receive power when the Holy Spirit comes on you; and you will be my witnesses in Jerusalem, and in all Judea, Samaria and

---

21. Frederickson, "Missional Congregation," 64.

to the ends of the earth" (Acts 1:8). Implied in these words of promise is the idea that the Spirit would provide the resources necessary for effective ministry in drastically different contexts, contexts that perhaps the apostles could not even imagine for themselves or the fledgling church. This promise did lead the early church into all of these contexts, and the Spirit did empower those who found themselves there to do highly creative (and successful) ministry in those disparate contexts. *Certainly this was only an appropriation of Jesus' promise to his disciples that he would be with them always (Matt 28:20).*

The apostle Paul certainly learned to trust the contextualizing leading of the Spirit. Perhaps this was because of the fact that Paul's conversion came through a dramatic, Christ-centered vision that left him blind, and it was only after he was filled with the Spirit through the ministry of Ananias that he regained his sight (Acts 9:17). This experience of the Spirit of Christ enabled Paul to trust the Spirit's work in his subsequent ministry. His theology of the Spirit was that the presence of the Spirit was the presence of the Lord, and when he was present one could trust that liberty and freedom were at hand (2 Cor 5:17). This faith in the Spirit's work enabled Paul to proclaim the gospel with boldness and assurance that his interpretation of the Spirit's work could be trusted as God's direct leading (1 Cor 7:10, 12, 40). As Ray Anderson reminds us:

> Paul's confidence in the Holy Spirit as the Spirit of Christ to provide instruction, guidance and leadership for the emerging churches was bold and uncompromising even though it sometimes led to some degree of confusion and even disorder.[22]

If the intention of the Spirit is to enable the church to share the life of God in its local context, then the apostolic expectation that the Spirit would enable their ministries in every context is the kind of expectation that local churches need to employ in their own contemporary contexts.

In the Spirit's work of helping to creatively enable congregations in the complex enterprise of contextualized ministry it should be the natural belief of the local church that they will receive new insights into the gospel and its application in their community. This was the experience of Peter at Cornelius's house when he saw the Gentiles gathered there receiving the Spirit in the same way that he and the first group of disciples had on the day of Pentecost in the upper room. His experience in

---

22. Anderson, *Emergent Theology*, 73.

this Gentile context broadened and even corrected his understanding of the gospel (Acts 10:1—11:18). Should we expect any less as we allow the Spirit to enable us to share God's life with our own local communities?

As God seeks to extend the invitation of relationship in local contexts he will creatively lead local churches, by his Spirit, into new insights that will enable new acts of contextualization that will further facilitate effective ministry. This is true, in part, because of the natural reciprocity that takes place between a local church and its context. Churches will affect their communities, but communities will also affect the church. As a church engages the people of a community, their lives and stories will affect the way the church understands the practice of its faith and maybe even the interpretation of its faith. New discoveries in both should be expected (again see Peter in Acts 10), and the Spirit who desires to apply the divine life in every context will be present to give guidance to the discerning congregation as they seek to untangle the complexities of ministry in a postmodern context.

This kind of thinking is a matter of course for those who serve in cross-cultural contexts. For missionaries immersed in and ministering to Muslim people, the interplay between their host context and their own faith perspective is ongoing. In order to sensitively adapt Christian worship in an Islamic context, worship services are often held on the Muslim holy day, Friday, instead of the traditional Lord's Day of Sunday. While this may be a relatively simple example, such moves do not come without certain amounts of wrestling through whether Sunday is sacred as a day for Christian worship and whether or not the church would be better served, or would serve better, as a distinct entity and counter-cultural alternative if it were to gather for worship on a day different from the traditional time of worship in the Islamic week. In many such contexts missional leaders have discerned the pleasure of the Spirit in directing them to break with normal Christian convention and worship in a more culturally relevant way. Further, in those contexts an ongoing dialogue takes place about the forms of worship that are appropriate. Can traditional Muslim forms become the forms of Christian worship? Even further, in a Christian context can God be called Allah? These questions are ones that test our trust in the Spirit to lead us in contextualization of the gospel. In Western contexts other issues will challenge our views on doctrine, and we may be forced to broaden, or at times constrict, our understanding of certain beliefs in response to the challenges in our community. One's view of divorce and remarriage may be brought into reconsideration when we are faced with a context in which there are many who are living their lives from within the reality of having been divorced and remarried, maybe even on several occasions. How does the church approach ministry to such people or include them in leadership? This has been a charged issue in the life of the church. The Spirit's role as the one who leads churches in contextualized ministry invites us to seek and trust in his leading so that appropriate responses and applications can be made and people can enter into the life of God through the local congregation in the way that God intends for them.

It may be that the most appropriate way to understand contextualized ministry in this postmodern culture is through the term "bricolage." The term was coined by French anthropologist Claude Lévi-Strauss to describe a rough, improvised assemblage of whatever tools are at hand to solve a problem.[23] Through the interplay of context, congregation, and Spirit, new and effective ways of ministry can be constructed using whatever tools are at hand or what the Spirit supplies.

The Spirit is the ultimate *bricoleur* as he leads the church in assembling the tools, approaches, and language that will enable it to minister creatively and effectively in its context. In following this leading, the church is appropriating the life of the Trinity in its own life and thus is growing as an expression of that Trinitarian life to its local community.

CONCLUSION

Locality is the strength of the church. It is the local nature of the church that allows it to tangibly offer the relational life of God to people in this world. The Trinitarian relationship both informs and empowers this work as it calls into mission, models incarnation, and enables contextualization. If the local church is effectively to take advantage of this powerful resource it will constantly need to be asking two simple and yet challenging questions. The first one defines the present experience of the church: "What is God doing?" This question asks a congregation to discern where God is at work in the mission of the church today. The regular asking and answering of this question is the work that situates a local congregation in its work as an expression of God in Christ. It affirms the presence of God and encourages the church in its ongoing

---

23. This term was introduced to me in Beaudoin, *Virtual Faith*, 149.

attempts to serve its community. As a rule local churches don't ask and answer this question enough. Yet, when we take the time to discern answers to it, we spot the places God is at work and are reminded that we are not alone. Indeed, we come to understand more fully that the Father, Son, and Spirit are graciously choosing to make God manifest through the church, despite its many imperfections. Such discoveries are nourishing to a congregation's faith, and inspirational for its ongoing ministry.

The second question helps define the future: "What does God want to do?"[24] This question asks the congregation to discern where God is moving and how they can join with that movement. This question keeps a congregation moving forward and in step with the formational work of the Spirit. Once again, local churches often don't ask and answer this question enough. This may be because the answer is not always clear and we are given to self doubt when it comes to discerning God's leading effectively. Further, it can cause dissention in a church as people disagree on what the Spirit is saying. Nonetheless, without taking this risk the church misses out on the new innovations that the creative Spirit desires to offer to it. However as we increasingly appropriate the Trinitarian life of God in our midst, our desire to understand his vision and dreams for the church will grow, and the asking and answering of this forward looking question will not be a burden to us. Instead, it will provoke us to trust the Spirit to lead us into a more perfect incarnation of God's mission in our community.

Cultivating an understanding of the relationality of God that calls for a genuine appropriation of Trinitarian life as a defining vision for the church is not an esoteric, theological construction that fails to produce any kind of meaningful practice. Rather, such theology can be preached, taught, and discussed as mission statements are prepared and local church vision is cast. It brings the local church to a place of discovering its true identity as God's people, a people that, by being in relationship with God, brings that life to bear on its relationship with a local community. This can speak a meaningful word to the postmodern nomad desperate for a place to call home, and the postmodern skeptic who rejects universal truth claims but can enter into life in a local community in which the mystical life of Christ and his call to mission is experienced. This is the postmodern possibility that the local church holds in every community.

24. These two questions are offered by Van Gelder, *Ministry*, 59–61.

BIBLIOGRAPHY

Anderson, Ray. *An Emergent Theology for Emerging Churches.* Downers Grove, IL: InterVarsity, 2006.

Beaudoin, Tom. *Virtual Faith: The Irreverent Spiritual Quest of Generation X.* San Francisco: Jossey Bass, 1998.

Branson, Mark Lau. "Ecclesiology and Leadership for the Missional Church." In *The Missional Church in Context,* edited by Craig Van Gelder, 94–126. Grand Rapids: Eerdmans, 2007.

Dearborn, Tim. *Short-term Missions Workbook: From Mission Tourists to Global Citizens.* Downers Grove, IL: InterVarsity, 2003.

Frederickson, Scott. "The Missional Congregation in Context." In *The Missional Church in Context: Helping Congregations Develop Contextual Ministry,* edited by Craig Van Gelder, 44–64. Grand Rapids: Eerdmans, 2007.

Gallagher, Michael P. *Clashing Symbols: An Introduction to Faith and Culture.* London: Darton, Longman & Todd, 1997.

Grenz, Stanley J. *A Primer on Postmodernism.* Grand Rapids: Eerdmans, 1996.

Lyotard, Jean-Fancois. *The Postmodern Condition: A Report on Knowledge, Theory and History of Literature,* translated by Geoff Bennington and Brian Massumi. Minneapolis: University of Minnesota Press, 1984.

Middleton, Richard, and Brian Walsh. *Truth Is Stranger Than It Used to Be.* Downers Grove, IL: InterVarsity, 1995.

Newbigin, Leslie. *The Gospel in a Pluralist Society.* Grand Rapids: Eerdmans, 1989.

Siegwalt, Gerard. "Local Church." In *Encyclopedia of Christian Theology,* edited by Jean-Yves LaCoste, 2:940–41. 3 vols. New York: Routledge, 2005.

Simpson, Gary. "A Reformation is a Terrible Thing to Waste." In *The Missional Church in Context,* edited by Craig Van Gelder, 65–93. Grand Rapids: Eerdmans, 2007.

Stone, Bryan. *Evangelism after Christendom: The Theology and Practice of Christian Witness.* Grand Rapids: Brazos, 2007.

Usher, Robin, and Richard Edwards. *Postmodernism and Education: Different Voices, Different Worlds.* New York: Routledge, 1994.

Van Gelder, Craig. *The Ministry of the Missional Church: A Community Led by the Spirit.* Grand Rapids: Baker, 2007.

Vanhoozer, Kevin. "Theology and the Condition of Postmodernity: A Report on Knowledge (of God)." In *The Cambridge Companion to Postmodern Theology,* edited by Kevin Vanhoozer, 3–25. Cambridge: Cambridge University Press, 2003.

Volf, Miroslav. *After Our Likeness: The Church as the Image of the Trinity.* Grand Rapids: Eerdmans, 1997.

Walsh, Brian J., and Sylvia C. Keesmaat. *Colossians Remixed: Subverting the Empire.* Downers Grove, IL: InterVarsity, 2004.

6

Adapting the House Church Model

Bruxy Cavey *and* Wendy Carrington-Phillips

INTRODUCTION

IN THE 2000 YEARS since Jesus walked the earth, his church has presented itself in many forms, from small home-based meetings to central assemblies, from high liturgy in ornate cathedrals to the communal lifestyle of many Anabaptists. Within each of these models, there is a range of styles of worshipping God in community. In today's world, there are almost as many variations of Christian worship as there are branches and denominations within Christianity.

So what is "church"? The Greek word ἐκκλησία (*ekklēsia*) can be rendered "assembly, gathering, congregation, church,"[1] and was originally used in a political sense to refer to city assemblies.[2] It is a gathering of people with a purpose. In the New Testament sense, it generally denotes the fellowship of believers that developed after the death and resurrection of Christ, such that where Christ-followers purposefully

---

1. "The term ἐκκλησία was in common use for several hundred years before the Christian era and was used to refer to an assembly of persons constituted by well-defined membership" (Louw and Nida, *Greek-English Lexicon*, 11.32). According to BDAG, "the term ἐκκλησία apparently became popular among Christians in Greek-speaking areas for chiefly two reasons: to affirm continuity with Israel through use of a term found in Gk. translations of the Hebrew Scriptures, and to allay any suspicion, esp. in political circles, that Christians were a disorderly group" (BDAG, 303).

2. Coenen, "Church, Synagogue," 291.

gathered, there was ἐκκλησία. While ἐκκλησία refers on a few occasions to the collective body of all believers (e.g., Acts 9:31; 1 Cor 12:28; Eph 5:23; Col 1:18), it more often denotes smaller groups of Christ-followers who met in individual homes.[3]

In recent years, there has been a revival of the house church format for doing church. Small groups of believers are meeting in living rooms each week instead of, or in addition to, a larger congregational gathering. Many of these groups see themselves as following the example of the New Testament body of believers who worshipped and experienced life together in gatherings that adopted a kinship ethos. In his study conducted across the United States in 2005–2006, American evangelical researcher George Barna reported that "in a typical week roughly 20 million adults attend a house church gathering,"[4] and he expected that number "to double in the coming decade, and a growing proportion of house church attenders to adopt the house church as their primary faith community."[5] This paper will examine variations in the house church paradigm of ἐκκλησία, including the structure modeled in the New Testament, the contemporary house church movement, as well as the home church model as adapted by The Meeting House,[6] and demonstrate that worshipping in a house church format is a valid expression of ἐκκλησία.

BIBLICAL INSPIRATION FOR THE HOUSE CHURCH MODEL

Followers of Jesus strive to become more Christ-like by following his teachings and example as recorded in the Bible. While the word ἐκκλησία is used only three times in the Gospels,[7] there is still much to

---

3. These groups would be defined by their geographical location, such as the churches in Jerusalem (Acts 11:22), Corinth (1 Cor 1:2), Laodicea (Col 4:16), and Thessalonica (1 Thess 1:1).

4. Barna Group, "House Church Involvement," lines 19–20. This figure is "based on interviews with more than five thousand randomly selected adults" across the United States by the Barna Group.

5. Ibid., lines 40–41.

6. The Meeting House is a multi-site, home-church-based community of over five thousand people centered in Oakville, Ontario. It is part of the Anabaptist denomination Brethren in Christ. While The Meeting House holds weekly congregational worship services on Sunday mornings, it considers the smaller gatherings in home churches to be "real church."

7. Once in Matt 16:18, referring to the rock on which Jesus will build his church, and twice in Matt 18:17 in a discussion of church discipline. In total, ἐκκλησία appears

learn from Jesus about his vision for the church. Some of the key aspects of community that Jesus conveys are love, relationship, service, prayer, and teaching. Of these, love is foundational as it undergirds all facets of community. In the Synoptic Gospels, when an expert in the Law asked which of the commandments was the greatest, Jesus replied, "Love the Lord your God with all your heart and with all your soul and with all your mind" (Matt 22:37). Jesus added a second element: "Love your neighbor as yourself" (Matt 22:39).[8] Similarly, in John 13:34–35, Jesus told his disciples, "A new command I give you: Love one another. As I have loved you, so you must love one another. By this everyone will know that you are my disciples, if you love one another." Jesus went beyond this directive to advocate loving one's friends, but also one's adversaries: "Love your enemies, do good to those who hate you" (Luke 6:27).[9] Jesus demonstrated this sacrificial love throughout his ministry as he healed the sick (e.g., Matt 14:14; Mark 10:46–52), fed those who were hungry (e.g., Mark 8:2; Luke 9:10–17), and sacrificed his rest to minister to others (e.g., Mark 6:31–34). He redefined "neighbor" by telling a parable that demonstrated responding to the need of an enemy (Luke 10:29–37). In addition, he modeled humility in love through foot-washing[10] as he called his followers to do the same, saying, "I have set you an example that you should do as I have done for you" (John 13:4–15). All these expressions of love came to a climax in Jesus' sacrifice at the cross. This love ethic of Jesus stands firmly as the primary goal in a Christian community. The other expressions of community grow out of love.

Jesus also modeled an ongoing relationship with God, meaningful fellowship among believers, and a gracious inclusion of those who were outcasts in their culture. These relationships occurred as Jesus connected with people through the routines of everyday life. He spoke with his disciples as they walked from Bethany to Jerusalem (Matt 21:18–22), he

---

114 times in the New Testament (Zdero, *Global House Church*, 18). Robert and Julia Banks suggest the inspiration for the community that evolved into ἐκκλησία goes back to Gen 1:26 and the communal nature of God (Banks and Banks, *Church Comes Home*, 24–25). God also gave community to the human he had just created (Gen 1:28). The authors then give a very brief overview of the contexts of worship communities in the Old Testament (25–26).

8. Cf. Mark 12:29–31; Luke 10:27.

9. Cf. Matt 5:44.

10. Foot-washing was a job done by slaves. It was unthinkable that a renowned teacher such as Jesus would perform such a menial task for his followers.

dined with tax collectors (Matt 9:10; Mark 2:15; Luke 5:29) and religious leaders (Luke 7:36; 14:1), and he conversed with a woman drawing water at a well (John 4:7–26). It was through relationships that he reached people with God's message of love and that his close followers grew in understanding. Jesus redefined family as he pointed to his disciples and said, "Here are my mother and my brothers. For whoever does the will of my Father in heaven is my brother and sister and mother" (Matt 12:49–50). The early church embraced this fictive kinship model and those who were ostracized by their families because of their faith were welcomed into this new kinship group. This new model family bound together in Christ "provide[d] a powerful resource for the transformation of the individual believer and the formation of vital and nurturing communities of believers."[11]

Out of loving relationships come compassion and the desire to serve those inside and outside the community of faith: the sick, the poor, and the oppressed. Jesus was known for his compassion, often manifested through miracles, healing Jews and Gentiles alike (e.g., Luke 8:41–46; Matt 15:21–28), driving out demons (e.g., Luke 8:26–37), and teaching and then feeding thousands of seekers (e.g., Mark 6:34–44). He even rebuked his disciples for trying to send away people who were bringing their children to be blessed (Mark 10:13–16). Caring for one another was a hallmark of the early church and may even have contributed to the rise of Christianity.[12]

Jesus spent regular and often extended time in prayer, both alone and in the company of his disciples (e.g., Luke 6:12; John 17). He taught his followers how to pray (Matt 6:5–15), including the difficult and radical command to pray for one's enemies (Matt 5:44). Jesus spent the night in prayer before selecting his twelve apostles (Luke 6:12–16). In his longest prayer, just hours before his crucifixion (John 17), Jesus prayed for his disciples and all believers, and that the Father would be glorified

---

11. DeSilva, *Honor, Patronage, Kinship and Purity*, 237.

12. Rodney Stark contrasts the reactions of pagans and Christians during the plagues that took place in the Mediterranean in the middle of the first and second centuries CE. Because of their beliefs, the Christians stayed and cared for one another and often for their pagan neighbors as well (many of whom subsequently converted). Pagans, on the other hand, fled and were less likely to recover since they received no care. This resulted in a greater percentage of Christians in the population at the end of these epidemics. As well, Christianity became more attractive to pagans by their example (Stark, *Rise of Christianity*, 73–94).

through him. Prayer undergirded his ministry and modeled his love for the Father and his dependence on him.

Finally, Jesus spent much of his time teaching. He privately answered the questions of individuals (e.g., John 3:1–21; 4:7–26) and he taught crowds publicly (e.g., Luke 9:11; 14:25–35). But his priority was mentoring his disciples in order to foster their growth and understanding and to equip them to carry on his work. John spends four chapters (John 13–16) on the teaching that Jesus gave his disciples before his arrest and crucifixion, and although his Sermon on the Mount was accessible to the crowds, his teaching was specifically addressed to his disciples (Matt 5:1–2). Because of the time he lovingly spent preparing them for the mission that lay ahead, and through the power of the Holy Spirit after his departure, his church grew from a small band of followers to a movement that shaped history.

Continuing from the Gospels into Acts, Luke shows how the early believers took these lessons of Jesus and applied the principles of love, relationship, service, prayer, and teaching to the budding Christian community in the first years of the church after the resurrection of Christ. In Acts 2:46, Luke relates that every day the Jewish Christians who initially embraced Jesus as the Messiah "continued to meet together in the temple courts." In Acts 17:2–3, Luke says that "as was his custom" Paul entered the synagogue on the Sabbath to teach about Jesus. Throughout Acts, there are numerous references to Paul teaching in the synagogues on his travels, including those at Thessalonica (Acts 17:1–20), Berea (Acts 17:10), Corinth (Acts 18:1–4), and Pisidian Antioch (Acts 13:14–41). It was in these large gatherings on the Sabbath that Paul preached the gospel until the time came that Christians and Jews parted ways and persecution broke out. While it was a valuable vehicle for reaching large numbers with the message of Jesus, public preaching on the Sabbath was not where or how the early believers primarily experienced church.

After referring to the early believers assembling in the temple courts, Luke goes on to describe them in Acts 2:46 as gathering κατ' οἶκον (*kat' oikon*), meaning "from house to house."[13] κατά here is used in the distributive sense, meaning that there was not just one home where the entire church gathered, but that the believers met "in their various houses."[14] Brad Blue suggests four reasons why these meetings

---

13. BDAG, 512. BDAG considers the NRSV translation, "at home," to be less likely.
14. Barrett, *Acts*, 170.

took place in homes: homes were an easy and readily available choice; they were inconspicuous, which minimized the threat of persecution;[15] such meetings followed the pattern of Jews meeting in house synagogues; and houses had facilities for preparing meals and sharing the Lord's Supper.[16] The home church meeting "was the method the apostles used to make disciples of the thousands of converts they made during the first decades of the New Testament."[17] It was in these homes that the new believers experienced life together. Their vital, growing bond with one another was an outgrowth of their newfound relationship with God and it flourished in these small, informal settings.

In Acts 2:42, Luke lists four components of communal worship that constituted these meetings: "They devoted themselves to the apostles' teaching and to fellowship, to the breaking of bread and to prayer."[18] The apostles instructed the new believers in the teachings of Jesus and the significance of his death and resurrection as they prepared them to apply the love ethic of Jesus inside and outside their community. With the newness of the faith, it was a learning church and the apostles recognized that understanding as well as service to one another could be best accomplished in small, committed groups.

Fellowship, or κοινωνία (*koinōnia*), was an integral part of their daily lives. Robert and Julia Banks point out in *The Church Comes Home* that "Christian community is the shape the gospel takes when translated into relational terms."[19] The Greek word κοινωνία "was often used of the type of mutuality that takes place in marriage."[20] The new believers enacted the love ethic of Jesus daily as they cared for one another, sharing time and resources. The unity that this practice produced strength-

---

15. While widespread persecution occurred later in church history, there was some persecution early on as evidenced by Saul of Tarsus (Acts 8:1–3; 9:1–2).

16. At this point in time, "most synagogues were single rooms in houses" (Blue, "Architecture," 92–93). As Jews converted to Christianity, these rooms may then have been used for Christian gatherings.

17. Huston, "Biblical Basis," par 22.

18. One view is that these four elements comprise a "primitive liturgical sequence" (Peterson, "Worship," 389). Another is that, based on vv. 44–47, Luke may be presenting a variety of activities that the disciples shared together in various places at different times and not describing a standard for church meetings.

19. Banks and Banks, *Church Comes Home*, 42.

20. Bock, *Acts*, 150.

ened them and helped to prepare them for the intense persecution that lay ahead.

There is some discussion as to whether "the breaking of bread" in Acts 2:42 refers to the Lord's Supper alone or the sharing of meals that may or may not have included the Lord's Supper. John R. W. Stott believes that the use of the article in *"the* breaking of bread" τῇ κλάσει τοῦ ἄρτου (*tē klasei tou artou*) indicates that the Lord's Supper was part of the meal and an element of their worship.[21] Using the term "breaking bread" to refer to the Lord's Supper as a ceremony separate from the common meal was not done until the second century.[22] Indeed, Luke does say that the believers "broke bread in their homes and ate together with glad and sincere hearts" (Acts 2:46), linking the two activities. "Breaking bread" was a Jewish phrase referring to the ritual opening of a meal that consisted of the host giving thanks, breaking and distributing the bread, and thus initiating the meal.[23] This ritual took on special significance with the words of Jesus at the Last Supper and this distinctive understanding likely accompanied the common custom at the commencement of their meals.

While it was common in Greek culture for special interest groups to share meals regularly,[24] it was striking that the followers of Christ met *daily* for meals in various homes (κατ' οἶκον, Acts 2:46). Verse 47 adds that they "ate together with glad and sincere hearts." Meeting in homes was comfortable, intimate, and convenient for sharing meals, as the culinary necessities were at hand. It is likely that there was teaching followed by discussions at the meals. As in most cultures, their table fellowship was a time of sharing and conversation—a way to build relationships. Indeed, there is "something about the character of a meal that binds people together in a unique way."[25] Beyond that, W. L. Willis suggests that "within the history of the early church, a shared table is a sign of the shared faith," so much so that "this shared meal experientially embodies the church."[26]

---

21. Stott, *Acts*, 84–85.
22. Blue, "Love Feast," 579.
23. Blue, "Jewish Worship," 488.
24. Keener, *Bible Background Commentary*, 330.
25. Banks and Banks, *Church Comes Home*, 118.
26. Willis, "Banquets," 146.

The fourth element that Acts 2:42 refers to as part of the home church meeting was prayer. "Prayer, by far, was the most common form of expression to God in New Testament era churches."[27] Bock points out how Luke emphasizes prayer as being a part of a community life that "seeks God's direction and is dependent upon God because God's family of people do [sic] not work by feelings or intuition but by actively submitting themselves to the Lord's direction."[28] The prayers, which may have consisted of set Judaic prayers,[29] prayers petitioning God for his guidance and protection, and prayers of thanksgiving, formed part of their corporate worship.

Luke also relates in Acts 2:44–45, "All the believers were together and had everything in common. They sold property and possessions to give to anyone who had need." This radical sharing of resources, which is reinforced in Acts 4:32–35, is not an indictment against personal ownership (Acts 2:46 says they met in private homes), but simply a way the early believers met the material requirements of the community. Possessions were sold as necessary to help the disadvantaged, demonstrating the priority they placed on love and generosity over material goods. The needs of the community may have arisen as a consequence of being rejected by, and thus isolated from, the unbelieving rest of society, which resulted in economic hardship.[30] This mutual sharing of material goods was not required, but was a voluntary expression of their loving care for one another. They were replicating in their community God's care for them as revealed through Christ.

Acts 2:46–47 tells of the joy in the community and the effect of the believers on those around them: "They broke bread in their homes and ate together with glad and sincere hearts, praising God and enjoying the favor of all the people. And the Lord added to their number daily those who were being saved."[31] These small groups of believers, who met κατ'

---

27. Zdero, *Global House Church*, 27. Zdero says that prayer is mentioned "about ninety times from Acts to Revelation."

28. Bock, *Acts*, 151.

29. Marshall, *Acts*, 83.

30. Peterson, "Worship," 391.

31. Wagner points out that one reason for the rapid growth "would have been the relatively low threshold for devout Jews to decide to cross over and follow Jesus as their Messiah. They still worshiped on the Sabbath in the Temple, they kept the law and they maintained their existing social and family ties" (Wagner, *Spreading the Fire*, 103).

οἶκον in thanksgiving, and who extended love and care to those around them, were a powerful witness to their neighbors and their lifestyle contributed to the rapid growth of the church.[32]

House churches continued to be the consistent venue for ἐκκλησίαι as Christianity spread throughout the Roman Empire. This arrangement was caused more by necessity than choice as "there was no community real-estate in the first two centuries."[33] Paul makes numerous references to believers meeting in homes, including the house churches of Priscilla and Aquila (Rom 16:3–5; 1 Cor 16:19), Nympha (Col 4:15), and Philemon (Philm 2).[34] These house churches would have understood their identity as smaller groups belonging to a larger citywide network, such as the church of Corinth or the church at Ephesus.

Paul also adds other aspects of the house church experience to those listed by Luke in Acts. In 1 Corinthians 12–14, Paul lists some of the gifts that the Spirit distributes to various believers for the purpose of building up the community in worship, including prophecy, speaking in tongues, healing, distinguishing between spirits, and miraculous works. As in the Gospels, it is the love ethic that undergirds them all. Paul sums up the nature of a house church gathering in 1 Cor 14:26: "When you come together, *each of you* [emphasis added] has a hymn or a word of instruction, a revelation, a tongue or an interpretation. Everything must be done so that the church may be built up." From the earliest days, the

---

32. Bock contrasts the strong sense of community and caring for one another in the early church, which allowed it to flourish, with contemporary Western culture's focus on self and individualism. "We are taught to have things our way and that being able to have our individual needs catered to is how to measure the success of an organization" (Bock, *Acts*, 155).

33. Lampe, *Christians at Rome*, 372. Zdero disputes this notion that the church had no choice, saying that meeting in homes reflected "their theology of church as family, living out community life together, and the interactive nature of church meetings" (Zdero, *Global House Church*, 25). Likely, there is some truth in both these ideas. There would not likely have been real estate readily available for a communal building, but also the fictive kinship model of the early church suited a house setting so that a larger centralized gathering in a public building might not have been an option they would have selected. Brad Blue's reasons for a house setting, as stated earlier, probably also contributed to this model of church.

34. Lampe suggests that the size of a house church was determined by the size of the dwelling and, as such, the lower classes had smaller house churches than those of means. This would necessitate more house churches than if there were believers gathered in one larger dwelling, resulting in a more fractured Christian community within the city (Lampe, *Christians at Rome*, 372).

church gathering was participatory, with all members contributing according to their gifts "so that the church may be edified" (1 Cor 14:5). Zdero points out, "Such openness and high levels of participation would have been difficult to facilitate in a large group setting, but they were a natural outcome in the smaller more intimate context of the early house-sized churches."[35] It raises the question of what has been lost through the shift to the spectator model that emerged a few centuries later and remains to this day the default model for church.

The early Christians carried the vision of fictive kinship forward, calling each other brothers and sisters—the house being an appropriate setting for such a gathering. In fact, believers are referred to in this way over one hundred times in the New Testament. In their intergenerational "family" gatherings in their homes, there were no distinctions based on sex, race, social standing, or economic position. They ate together, loved and cared for one another, worshipped together, celebrated life as a family, and faced problems together, all in the name of Jesus, woven together by the love ethic he taught. For the early Christians, this was church.

THE CONTEMPORARY HOUSE CHURCH MODEL

The contemporary house church movement is built on the foundation of the New Testament model of church, which was about people not buildings. The believers were the temple, and where they gathered (generally in homes), there was church. There is no sacred space according to the house church model. The Holy Spirit lives in all believers and therefore it is not necessary to go to a church building to meet with God. This view was the norm until the fourth century when Christianity became the state religion and Constantine began building large, centralized houses of worship. No longer was the intimacy of a small gathering in a living room the norm, but rather the less personal and less interactive assembly of a large group facing in one direction.[36] The contemporary house church movement seeks to restore the intimate, participatory style of the early Christian church. Believers involved in this movement champion house churches as the most, if not only, biblical form of church. Others (such as the authors of this paper) see rich principles in the house church

---

35. Zdero, *Global House Church*, 28.

36. In fact, at this point in Christian history, house churches "were effectively outlawed for fear of heresy and splinter groups" (Zdero, *Global House Church*, 61).

model that may take shape in a variety of ways in different contexts. Robert and Julia Banks say the following: "It is not the re-creation of the first-century church that is the goal. The desire is to recapture the spirit and dynamics of early church life in ways that are appropriate to our own culture."[37]

The Starfish Ontario Network is a Canadian network of house churches whose mission is "to see the Kingdom of God manifest in our region, by linking arms as a relational, intentional, and missional network of house churches, that develop and deploy all believers into maturity in Christ as they impact others."[38] Similarly, the House Church Network, which began in 1992, maintains its own registry of home churches. It defines house churches as "small groups of believers—even as few as 2 or 3—who gather in the name of Jesus Christ."[39] The number of participants is important for the success and effectiveness of a house church. When a group grows to 20 or 30 regular attendees, it should consider birthing a new home church.[40] Bigger is not better in a house church. When a group becomes so large that some members become uncomfortable participating, "the family dynamic and closeness will begin to wane."[41] Starting a new house church not only allows the size to remain conducive to intimacy, but also allows continued room for new members to feel comfortable. This process of splitting to form new house churches should take place every six to eighteen months.[42] According to Zdero, at that point, "it is absolutely crucial that house churches form networks that pray, plan, and play together."[43] He gives five reasons why house churches should not remain independent and isolated entities: it is biblical, as the churches in a particular city or region were linked; there is a human need to be part of a larger, global movement; it can be difficult for an isolated group to meet all the social needs of its mem-

---

37. Banks and Banks, *The Church Comes Home*, 24.
38. Simple Church, Starfish Ontario Network home page.
39. House Church Network, "Frequently Asked Questions," lines 2–3.
40. Fitts, *Church in the House*, 41.
41. Zdero, *Global House Church*, 105.
42. Ibid.
43. Ibid., 106. Churches within a local network might come together once a month for worship and fellowship. They might visit one another's churches and leaders could pray together, share ideas or resources, encourage one another, and keep one another accountable (ibid., 108).

bers (e.g., teenagers looking for friends); a group of house churches can have a bigger impact as they share visions, skills, and resources; and a network of churches can provide accountability and help guard against heresy or cults developing.[44]

In recent decades, many denominational churches have begun mid-week home groups, sometimes called cell groups, small groups, life groups etc., in an attempt to foster more intimate communities of believers. But such groups do not generally fully participate in one another's lives as house churches do. Instead, they meet once a week for a couple of hours with a leader and tend to be "relatively homogeneous rather than a microcosm of the whole church."[45] House churches, on the other hand, tend to meet as church at least once a week, each time for several hours. In addition, they come together to share other activities, including tasks, celebrations, leisure time, and ministry. House church is a long-term committed relationship that models the family dynamic. It is meant to develop into a spiritual family that is fully dedicated to God and to one another in all areas of life.

The contemporary house church phenomenon is a movement that is gaining momentum around the globe. In some areas of the world where freedom of religion is suppressed, house churches are the main venue for Christian gatherings. In China, for instance, there are 80 to 100 million people celebrating their faith in house churches.[46] In the West, house church is catching on as people seek alternatives to the traditional Sunday service in a church building. There are various reasons for this trend away from traditional church, including unpleasant memories of past church experiences and the lack of meaning or relevance of institutional church in this culture. Research by the Barna Group found two types of people turning to house churches. The first are baby boomers who are committed Christians searching for a deeper, more intimate expression of their faith in community. This would include many who were brought up in a traditional church setting. The second group consists of young adults who have no interest in what they consider the outmoded institution of traditional church. They are interested in mat-

---

44. Ibid., 106–7.
45. Banks and Banks, *Church Comes Home*, 106.
46. Zdero, "Starfish Files."

ters of faith and spirituality, but are seeking a more contemporary means of expression.[47]

There are other reasons people are attracted to house churches. First, many people are seeking to be more faithful to Scripture and they perceive house church as a part of that priority. They are examining the teachings and examples they find in the New Testament and striving to apply them to their own situations in life. It is not likely that Luke intended his presentation of the house church in Acts to be prescriptive. After all, Acts is historical, not didactic. The model is backed up in the epistles, however, and appears to be the normative way that Christians assembled for the first few centuries of the church. With people seeking alternative expressions of church, they are looking to Scripture and importing its model of house church as a possible means to effectively live in Christian community.

Second, according to the house church movement, a house church can be an effective tool for evangelism. For some, a home environment can be a less threatening venue to investigate Jesus than a church building where one who is not familiar with church culture can feel like an outsider. Organized religion can have bad connotations for some people while others in this culture have never been inside a church. For such people, walking into an environment as foreign as a church building might be too intimidating to risk. While churches are having difficulty attracting people, the house church can fill the gap as an "unthreatening and comfortable [environment]—the ideal place for the teaching and intimate personal ministry of Jesus Christ."[48]

It is also an ideal model for serving the surrounding community. Members not only provide for each other's needs within the house church, but they also collaborate in serving their community. Whereas in a large church, a minority tends to get involved in service projects, in the house church, following Jesus and the New Testament model of community means everyone gets involved in helping those in need. Serving is simply part of their lifestyle and their worship. When believers serve each other, they serve God, because God is present in all believers through the Holy Spirit (Matt 25:31–46). Worshipping God and fellowship go hand in hand. Because there is no money being paid for

---

47. Barna Group, "House Churches Are More Satisfying," lines 59–63.
48. Huston, "Biblical Basis," lines 119–20.

church staff, for upkeep of a building, or for administration, money can be given directly to those in need as was practiced in the early church.

Fourth, one of the appeals of the house church model for some people is the lack of a centralized church or denomination with its rules, hierarchical leadership, etc. The house church believes in the priesthood of all believers. All are ministers, so that the leadership is shared and the gatherings are subject to the leading of the Holy Spirit, rather than being dictated by structure and liturgy. This leadership model extends to children, who may help choose songs or Bible stories. While there is no official leader, as in any group, some are more gifted than others with respect to different leadership tasks and these individuals tend to rise to the surface in exercising their gifts in the group. Some may be skilled in organizing service projects, others in pastoral care or teaching, and still others may be prayer warriors or musicians. There is no passive audience in a house church. All are participants and bring their gifts to God and one another as 1 Cor 14:26 instructs.

Finally, in a harried world where many do not even know their neighbors, there is a hunger for community. In the smaller house church, close relationships develop as members experience life together, a need that is not easily met in a large congregational setting. In house churches, which meet at least once a week either in one home or rotating homes, the members are able to provide support and accountability for one another. They care for one another in all areas of their lives, helping with household projects, babysitting, care in times of illness, or with any other needs that arise, ministering to one another as necessary.

In these ways, the modern house church functions much like the family model of the early church. Members consider themselves brothers and sisters, united not by biological blood, but by the blood of Christ. They are conforming to the model of family that Jesus put in place when he called his small group of followers his family (Matt 12:48), referred to God as "Abba, Father" (Mark 14:36), and taught his followers to do the same in prayer (Matt 6:5–13). This family as it extended into the early church was a diverse group that made no distinction between men and women, young and old, Gentile and Jew, rich and poor. What they held in common was their love for God and their desire to follow him. Such is the example that the contemporary house church strives to follow as the participants learn to live in community with diverse individuals.[49]

---

49. For those who grew up in dysfunctional families, being adopted into this new

Before starting a house church, it is important, according to Robert and Julia Banks, to take time to explore the idea prayerfully with other interested believers.[50] In order for it to be successful, it is necessary to have a sufficient number of people with a variety of gifts and a firm commitment from at least a core group. They must examine whether it is truly a family model that encompasses all aspects of their Christian life that they are seeking or rather a Bible study or other special interest group. Ultimately, it is a decision that should be led by the Holy Spirit. Once a few believers make a commitment to the church, it is not uncommon for them to develop a covenant and a doctrinal statement to be clear about what they stand for in order to keep themselves on track. As the group matures, a "pastoral center" will emerge consisting of "a few people who show evidence of exerting a presence that enables the group to reach its full potential."[51] While some groups may call them elders or leaders, their purpose is not to lead the group (that would imply that there are followers), but to help the members reach spiritual maturity.

While the strengths of the contemporary house church model are numerous, some Christians express concerns regarding it. The first is the danger of straying from accepted doctrine into heresy without accountability to a denomination. Many of the New Testament Epistles were written to correct doctrinal errors and misunderstandings that had arisen as a result of the isolation of various house churches and the resulting susceptibility to outside influences, ideas, and leaders. The church can be especially vulnerable and susceptible to heresy when a charismatic leader rises up. The church can minimize this risk by regularly reviewing statements of covenant and doctrine, by maintaining a non-hierarchical structure, and by ensuring accountability to the group. In addition, organizations such as the Starfish Ontario Network and House Church Network exist, in part, to provide theology, resources, and discussion forums to help keep house churches on track.

There is also the risk of a house church becoming insular, existing only for its members and becoming stale. Service outside of the group must remain a central feature of a house church. Welcoming new members and birthing new house churches help to keep a group dynamic.

---

family model founded on love and care might be a source of comfort, encouragement, and healing.

50. Banks and Banks, *Church Comes Home*, 109.
51. Ibid., 114.

There is great value in a few house churches gathering together on a regular basis for teaching, social events, or service projects. Many house church networks organize communal events to bring individual house churches together.

A final concern involves the practice of evangelism. While, on one hand, some people within our Western culture naturally resonate with smaller home-based groups, others find them even more intimidating than attending a larger, more traditional church service. Anonymity is impossible in a house church setting. For some spiritual seekers, being immersed into an immediate experience of intimate community is an unacceptable first step. These individuals may be more likely to begin an investigation of Jesus and his teaching in an environment that allows them to simply be part of the "crowd" that listened as Jesus taught his disciples (cf. Matthew 5).

The contemporary house church can be an effective vehicle for living out the teachings of Jesus. It is faithful to the biblical model as a family unit that is conducive to spiritual growth, mutual accountability, growing through relationship in community, support and care for the members, and making a significant impact on the local community through serving. But is there a way to enhance this model, combining the benefits of a larger church congregation with the intimacy of a house church?

ADAPTING THE HOUSE CHURCH MODEL: THE MEETING HOUSE HOME CHURCH

The Meeting House is a home-church-based spiritual community. While purists might not consider its small gatherings as "house churches" because they are affiliated with an institutional church and a denomination, their make-up is similar to those house churches that identify themselves with the contemporary house church movement. The term "cell group" or "small group" would not do justice to the character of the home churches that make up The Meeting House community.

There is nothing magical about a house as a venue for church. The point of a house (or apartment, condo, etc.) is that it is where a family lives; it is where people at different stages of development experience life together, good and bad. It is an intimate and interactive setting where individuals learn, grow, and mature, and a place where members of the household love one another unconditionally, offering and receiving hospitality. These are the key components of any healthy home, which is why The Meeting House chooses to identify its small groups as "home" churches.

Looking at Scripture with a Jesus hermeneutic[52] frees the reader from having to legalistically duplicate New Testament church structure, and allows that person to look instead for the principle behind the specific practice outlined in a particular passage. In this case, the guiding principle for The Meeting House is that church should reflect on some level the reality of a spiritual family, an intimate and interactive community to which *each member* contributes, even if at first it is only by their questions, curiosity, and eagerness to learn and grow (reflecting the principle of 1 Cor 14:26). Church has always been meant to be about relationship, both with God and with fellow believers. It is the view of The Meeting House that a home-based spiritual community continues to be a relevant way to accomplish these goals. While large congregational gatherings serve an important function, The Meeting House believes that one of the most effective ways to grow spiritually and relationally is in small gatherings in a welcoming home.[53]

At The Meeting House, church is conceptualized as a spiritual community where the participants challenge one another to live out their faith in daily life and, in turn, invite others to join them. According to leaders at The Meeting House, real church happens when believers turn their chairs to face one another so they can actualize what Jesus anticipated for his followers: "to give and receive, to teach and understand, to carry others' burdens and receive help with our own, to love and be loved."[54]

Giving and receiving are both essential to becoming more Christlike, since humans have a default setting of self-centeredness. What Jesus modeled was extreme others-centeredness, and he invites his followers

---

52. By "Jesus hermeneutic" (a popular exegetical approach at The Meeting House), the leaders at The Meeting House refer to Jesus' example of helping his first-century audience move beyond the letter of the law to see the spirit, to crack open the hard shell of the precept in order to find the principle within. The precept may be time-bound, culturally conditioned, and situation-specific, but the principle within the precept transcends any one culture, point in history, or specific situation.

53. The Meeting House considers home church so important that its goal is to have one within a ten-minute drive of everyone in the Greater Toronto/Hamilton, Ontario corridor.

54. Banks and Banks, *Church Comes Home*, 84.

to do the same: they are to express radical love and generosity in all situations and circumstances. In an individualistic culture, it is a challenge for many to be able to receive. When believers do not accept help from their brothers and sisters, they shut themselves off from what God wants to give them and deprive others of the opportunity to serve. What better milieu is there than home church for these practices to be exercised and for believers "to develop a quality of common life under God, one in which the attitude, values, priorities and commitments of the kingdom of God become communally visible"?[55] Spiritual growth has little value if it is not put into practice in the form of ministering to brothers and sisters and to others outside the spiritual community. Home church is a way to experience community at a deep level, because it seeks to live out the picture of family that Jesus initiated in the New Testament. It is the model that the early church practiced, which resulted in rapid growth, at both the personal and corporate levels.

The Meeting House takes an "irreligious" approach to all church structure. "Irreligious" means that Christians should not hold any one church style or structure to be sacrosanct, but rather they should apply biblical principles in flexible and culturally relevant ways, while always remaining open to change as needed.[56] This ongoing process of allowing the wineskin to flex and expand[57] leaves The Meeting House open to new perspectives and structural change as needed.

The Meeting House approach to community is not only derived from a biblical model, but it is also an outgrowth of the denominational authority to which it submits and by which it is supported. The Meeting House is part of the Brethren in Christ, a two-hundred-year-old denomination with Anabaptist roots. The Anabaptist movement was founded, in part, as an endeavor to restore "essential elements of church life and practice."[58] Such practices, which are part of The Meeting House's tradition, include believer's baptism, the priesthood of all believers, a life of ministry, sharing and communal living, mission and evangelism, and a "functional approach to structure."[59] Anabaptists believe that there

---

55. Ibid., 108.

56. For further discussion, see Cavey, *End of Religion*.

57. In using this terminology we are borrowing from Christ's analogy in Matt 9:16–17.

58. Banks and Banks, *Church Comes Home*, 54.

59. Ibid.

is "no sacred space," no special building to which a person must go to meet with God, since he is present wherever two or three are gathered (Matt 18:20). In this way, it may be more accurate to declare all space as sacred space. Corporately, the body of Christ has the privilege of being the temple where God dwells.[60]

At The Meeting House, Anabaptist principles are expressed in large part through home churches, which are manifestations of communal living within contemporary culture. The Meeting House strives to have an approach that values family-style relationships in community as was practiced in the early church and later by the Anabaptists. The Brethren in Christ denomination takes its name from that original vision of being brothers and sisters in Christ (e.g., Col 1:2). Thus, it follows that a home setting is an obvious place for brothers and sisters to be in relationship, just as they are in a physical family. Unlike friendships, which are relationships that are often based on conditionality, familial relationships cannot be changed. Within a family, individuals practice loving those who may be radically different from themselves. Thus, home churches are intended to be intergenerational, consist of both men and women, be socio-economically diverse, and comprise people at varying stages of spiritual maturity. This structure provides the foundation of authentic community, where people are free to be themselves and experience God's love and acceptance.

What does "family" look like at a home church associated with The Meeting House? Simply put, a family is a group of people who walk through life together. If someone needs their house painted or a fence erected, brothers and sisters come to help—the urban version of a barn-raising. They spend time studying Scripture; they help their neighbors, serving those in need in their local community; they have fun together; and they celebrate baptism and the Lord's Supper together.[61] They are accountable to one another, and they support one another through difficult times. They work through disagreements, and they share meals. This family of Christ-followers that has come together is committed to one another and to God and they demonstrate Christ's love through serving, giving, bringing hurting people into a healing family, and mentoring

---

60. For further discussion, see Cavey, *End of Religion*.

61. Baptism and the Lord's Supper are often done within the individual home churches, although they are periodically celebrated at the larger congregational level as well.

disciples of Jesus. Although the home churches at The Meeting House are far from perfect (they are, after all, filled with imperfect people), they do offer a safe place to examine the teachings of Jesus and grapple with how to apply them to daily life. For these objectives to be realized, church cannot be limited to merely one meeting on a particular day of the week. Church is family in the best sense of the word—a spiritual family that transcends meeting times, programmed activities, and social functions. A family remains a family whenever and wherever they are, not just when they are in the same room.

What format do the weekly meetings take? In general, they involve elements similar to those in the worship life of the early church: Bible study, relationship building, the sharing of meals, and praying for one another. Bible study follows up on the teaching from the weekend services by examining relevant passages in the Bible and by considering how they might apply to one's life. Following the same curriculum allows home churches to be small, while at the same time creating the feeling that they are a part of a larger community; a friend or family member in a home church across town or in a different city will be working through the same material, allowing for points of connection and conversation across the wider Meeting House community. While all the home churches discuss the same questions and passages, the meetings can be quite diverse, depending on the personality of the group and the leading of the Holy Spirit. In this setting, learning moves past the academic to the actualized, because the knowledge that has been acquired in a Sunday service is connected to the application of that knowledge to one's personal life. There is little value in learning about the teachings of Jesus if one does not put them into practice. Because The Meeting House believes that the best way to study the Bible is in community with other believers who are also seeking God's truth, Bible study is a top priority in every home church.

Just as the members of the New Testament church recognized the value of their community bonding over a meal, many home churches at The Meeting House choose to share meals on a regular basis. Some home churches have a full meal before every weekly meeting; for others it is more informal, with food available for anyone. At the very least, there are always snacks and refreshments set out as a gathering point. Home churches are encouraged to consider making the Lord's Supper a part of their meal or to celebrate it as a separate event when appropriate.

As prayer was a central part of the gatherings in the early church, so too prayer is an essential aspect of any home church meeting. There is always time devoted to sharing needs and giving thanks for answered prayer, presenting all of this to God in prayerful worship.

The learning, fellowship, and prayer that take place in the group meeting extend into the caregiving that takes place within the home church family. Home churches are the primary environment for living out the teachings of Jesus in mutual accountability, encouragement, and support. Each one brings their own gifts for the edification of the community, and those gifted in caregiving come alongside others to listen, encourage, pray, and provide help for needs that may be spiritual, emotional, or material. Some home churches have a large money jar at each meeting, so members can contribute as they are able. Thus, when a financial need is brought to the group's attention, money is available to address the situation.

This others-centered approach extends to serving outside the home church community. Serving can range from shoveling a neighbor's driveway to volunteering at a local benevolence organization. In Hamilton, Ontario, for instance, The Meeting House home churches partner with ministries such as Micah House, Living Rock, and initiatives organized by True City. In each case, the local compassion goal of The Meeting House is not to start new ministries in its own name, but to provide important volunteer and financial support to those Christian ministries already involved in compassionate outreach.

Any family is healthier and functions more effectively when everyone plays a role. The home church family is no exception. It is important for the spiritual growth of each member that they be relationally connected to the community of believers and have the benefit of the care of that group, as well as participating in care and service themselves. Home church functions best when everyone comes with the attitude of Christ as laid out in Phil 2:1–11—that of a contributor rather than a consumer. According to the Anabaptist ideal, church is not a spectator event run by a few paid professionals. Thus, the clergy-laity distinction is largely dissolved at The Meeting House in many ways.[62]

In addition to such gifts as those listed in 1 Cor 12:27–31 and 14:26, there are ways that all the members can contribute to the home church

---

62. For example, it has done away with special clothing, special titles, and special seats, which Jesus rebukes in Matt 23:5–7 and Luke 20:46.

community. They can bring questions or their own story to share. They can be encouragers or pray regularly for the needs of the group. They may have administrative skills or ideas for service projects or social gatherings. They can contribute food or other kinds of support for leaders, or they can simply bring passion and enthusiasm to the group. There are no passive observers: there is no hiding in a home church setting.

The main area where The Meeting House differs from the contemporary house church movement is that it holds Sunday services for the whole community of home churches within a region as well as anyone else who wishes to attend. These Sunday gatherings are sometimes called "PPPs" (Public Preaching Points), which refers back to the early church where there were public lectures in addition to house church gatherings. In Acts 20:20, Paul says, "You know that I have not hesitated to preach anything that would be helpful to you but have taught you publicly and from house to house." Likewise, Acts 19:9–10 indicates that Paul rented a lecture hall for two years, apparently both for the instruction of disciples and the continued communication of the gospel to others who would come and listen. Those who do not have time for Sunday church and home church are encouraged to prioritize home church and opt out of Sunday services, since home church is where the application aspects of church really happen.[63]

Sunday meetings at The Meeting House serve as a practical tool in three areas in particular. First, they are a central point for all to gather to hear Bible teaching. Home church follows up on the Sunday teaching by digging deeper into the message and by examining Scripture with an emphasis on application, thereby furthering the teaching-learning process. The Sunday teaching, along with the submission of The Meeting House to the Brethren in Christ denomination, helps to address two of the concerns raised by more traditional churches about the house church model—the risks of heresy and isolation.

Second, the Sunday services are opportunities for evangelism. Although the house church movement asserts that evangelism best happens through house churches, the experience at The Meeting House is

---

63. For those who attend only home church or for those who missed the Sunday service, there is always a review of the main points of the Sunday sermon at the beginning of home church. The discussion questions are designed to be accessible whether or not a person attended on Sunday. The sermons are also available for people to listen to during the week as podcasts on iTunes or at www.themeetinghouse.ca.

that most people enter through a Sunday service and, from there, join a home church.[64] Depending on one's personality, many are intimidated by walking into a small group as a first or even second step. Even when first-time attendees walk into a church, they tend to sit at the back, wanting to remain anonymous until they feel comfortable. It is not possible to be anonymous at home church and newcomers know this.

Third, singing is more comfortable for most people in a larger setting with musical support. Many people in contemporary culture are not comfortable with singing a cappella in a small group. Sunday services help people sing together as a communal expression of the Spirit's work in their lives—a repeated New Testament emphasis (e.g., Mark 14:26; Eph 5:19; Col 3:16).

The larger church as an organized and focused force has the power and resources to do what individuals or a small group cannot. While smaller projects are most effectively managed within the home church, more far-reaching endeavors call for the support of the whole community. For instance, The Meeting House, in partnership with the Mennonite Central Committee and the Brethren in Christ, is involved in helping with the HIV/AIDS crisis in the countries of southern Africa. This project needs the resources and support of the whole community to have a significant impact and is something that could not be accomplished at the home church level alone.[65]

A decision to structure a church community as home-church-based has implications for other areas of church life, such as programs and leadership structure. In Western culture, people live with minimal margin in their schedules. For many people it is unlikely that they will add one more commitment to their church life without reducing their commitment somewhere else. For this reason, The Meeting House realizes that part of having a strong home church base means "de-programming" other areas of church community life. The ministry structure is, therefore, one of minimal programming. Gone are the men's groups, women's groups, prayer groups, single mothers' groups, divorce recovery groups, etc. Instead, as much as possible, the various aspects of healthy church

---

64. At present, approximately 60 percent of the adult Sunday population of The Meeting House is affiliated with a home church.

65. Together the members of The Meeting House are endeavoring to raise millions of dollars for compassion work through the Mennonite Central Committee and other organizations, both locally and overseas.

community are rolled into the home church experience. The Meeting House does discipleship, supports single parents, encourages hurting people recovering from destructive divorces, all by means of home church. Diversity in community is celebrated by this model, as opposed to a traditional model that seeks out others who are at a similar age or point of crisis.

The Bible does not provide a definitive organizational structure for the church to follow. The early church had a basic organization with a flexible structure in order to be able to meet the needs of the Christian community as it grew and evolved. In its leadership configuration, The Meeting House shows its Anabaptist roots through the high value it places on servant and shared leadership. It subscribes to the servant leadership model of Luke 22:24–26, where leaders humbly and sacrificially serve others as their brothers and sisters. The role of leaders is not to perform ministry but to serve and equip church members to minister to their highest capacity (Eph 4:11–12). Leaders also work in teams at every level, which prevents a single figure from being at the peak of a power pyramid. No one pastor is in charge of the vision or structure of the church and mutual submission is woven into the fabric of leadership structure at all levels.[66]

This flexibility of structure has served The Meeting House well as the church has expanded over the years from a single church in Oakville, Ontario to a multi-site church in the Greater Toronto Area, the province of Ontario, and beyond,[67] necessitating significant organizational adjustments along the way. For The Meeting House, being both a multi-site and a home church-based spiritual community results in unique issues regarding leadership. In the New Testament, there seems to be some flexibility in how the church uses the titles of overseer, pastor, and elder, and The Meeting House has capitalized on this flexibility. Home church leaders are called "elders" and are challenged to lead with the pastoral wisdom and servant authority of that title. Elders are the individuals who lead the home churches and provide pastoral care and spiritual

---

66. For instance, Bruxy Cavey, the teaching pastor and most prominent "face" of The Meeting House, is himself part of a teaching team. He teaches only 60 percent of the Sundays, and all messages, in planning and review, are subject to fellow pastors and overseers.

67. The sites outside of Oakville hold Sunday services in local movie theatres. Each site has its own lead pastor and music ministry.

leadership to those in a home church. They receive training for their role, as well as ongoing coaching and support from the lead pastors.

Each large region of home churches has its own lead pastor who cares for its needs and provides leadership at Sunday services. Pastors are the group of elders that are paid and give day-to-day leadership to the ministry of the church family. It is the role of pastors to train, develop, and encourage leaders within The Meeting House, including home church leaders (i.e., "elders"). The various regions are represented at the overall board level on the overseers team, where decisions are made for the collective family of churches. "Overseers" are defined as the group of elders elected by the entire church family to oversee all the ministries of The Meeting House. Subsequently, the senior pastoral staff reports to the overseers. Combined, the overseers, pastors, and elders come together as the Shepherding Team and work together to ensure the health of the church. The Meeting House, then, does not view itself as just a collective family of home churches. It is also a single-church extended family with a shared mission, vision, ethos, and teaching.

The benefits of a home-church-based community supplemented by Sunday services are numerous. At the congregational level, there is the joy of coming together in a larger setting for communal worship, including music and biblical teaching; there are additional opportunities to serve on Sundays and meet new people. Sunday services provide a place to invite friends who would not be comfortable with home church as an entrance point into the community. At the home church level, the members grow in a more intimate relationship with God and others. There is care among people who know and love one another; everyone has the opportunity to participate and exercise their gifts, and serving becomes an enjoyable family event. It is a tangible opportunity to experience a piece of God's kingdom on earth.

CONCLUSION

Was the pattern in Acts 2:42–47 intended for all time? Acts illustrates how the early church functioned in that time and place for certain believers; it does not appear to be presented as a normative model for all time, but rather gives incidental details within the larger narrative of the early church.[68] It is possible that Luke envisioned that church would

---

68. Fee and Stuart, *How to Read the Bible*, 121.

always take this form of meeting in homes, but it is not mandated anywhere in the New Testament. It appears the details have been left open for each congregation to adapt according to its own needs in a way that maximizes its service to God, each other, and its community.

There are many styles of ἐκκλησία, and house church will not suit everyone. Barna found that many people who attend a conventional church tend to be spiritually complacent and content to show up on Sunday, simply accepting what is presented to them: "They place the responsibility for their spiritual growth on the shoulders of the church."[69] Attending a house church, on the other hand, can provide a more conducive atmosphere for those desiring to enrich their spiritual development and cultivate a deeper relationship with God.

The Meeting House has found that having church gatherings on Sundays as a complement to home church is an effective way of ensuring sound teaching, in combination with the mentoring and spiritual growth that take place best in a small group. It is the model that The Meeting House has found to best "recapture the spirit and dynamics of early church life in ways that are appropriate to our own culture."[70] However, even though The Meeting House is clear about its own vision and structure, its theology of flexibility allows it to support other church models, whether home church based or traditional. Ultimately, what is of primary importance is not the letter of the law, but the spirit; not how Christians are in community, but simply that they are.

BIBLIOGRAPHY

Banks, Robert, and Julia Banks. *The Church Comes Home*. Peabody, MA: Hendrickson, 1998.

Barna Group. "House Church Involvement Is Growing." No pages. Online: http://www.barna.org/FlexPage.aspxPage=BarnaUpdate&BarnaUpdateID=241.

———. "House Churches Are More Satisfying to Attenders than Are Conventional Churches." No pages. Online: http://www.barna.org/barna-update/article/19-organic-church/112-house-churches-are-more-satisfying-to-attenders-than-are-conventional-churches?g-house+churches+satisfying.

Barrett, C. K. *A Critical and Exegetical Commentary on the Acts of the Apostles*. 2 vols. ICC. London: T. & T. Clark, 2004.

Blue, Bradley B. "Architecture, Early Church." In *Dictionary of the Later New Testament and Its Developments*, edited by Ralph P. Martin and Peter H. Davids, 91–95. Downers Grove, IL: InterVarsity, 1997.

---

69. Barna Group, "House Churches Are More Satisfying," lines 91–92.
70. Banks and Banks, *Church Comes Home*, 24.

———. "Love Feast." In *Dictionary of Paul and His Letters*, edited by Gerald F. Hawthorne and Ralph P Martin, 578–79. Downers Grove, IL: InterVarsity, 1993.
———. "The Influence of Jewish Worship on Luke's Presentation of the Early Church." In *Witness to the Gospel: The Theology of Acts*, edited by I. Howard Marshall and David Peterson, 473–98. Grand Rapids: Eerdmans, 1998.
Bock, Darrell L. *Acts*. BECNT. Grand Rapids: Baker, 2007.
Cavey, Bruxy. *The End of Religion*. Colorado Springs: NavPress, 2007.
Coenen, L. "Church, Synagogue." In *The New International Dictionary of New Testament Theology*, edited by Colin Brown, 1:291–307. 4 vols. Grand Rapids: Zondervan, 1986.
DeSilva, David A. *Honor, Patronage, Kinship and Purity: Unlocking New Testament Culture*. Downers Grove, IL: InterVarsity, 2000.
Fee, Gordon D., and Douglas Stuart. *How to Read the Bible for All Its Worth*. Grand Rapids: Zondervan, 2003.
Fitts, Robert. *The Church in the House: A Return to Simplicity*. Salem, OR: Preparing the Way, 2001.
House Church Network. "Frequently Asked Questions. New Things." No pages. Online: http://housechurch.org/faq.html.
Huston, David A. "The Biblical Basis for Home Groups." No Pages. Online: http://www.gloriouschurch.com/html/Biblical-Basis-Of-Home-Groups.asp.
Keener, Craig. *The IVP Bible Background Commentary: New Testament*. Downers Grove, IL: InterVarsity, 1993.
Lampe, Peter. *Christians at Rome in the First Two Centuries: From Paul to Valentinus*. London: Continuum, 2003.
Lowe, J. P., and Eugene A. Nida. *Greek-English Lexicon of the New Testament: Based on Semantic Domains*. New York: United Bible Societies, 1989.
Marshall, I. Howard. *The Acts of the Apostles: An Introduction and Commentary*. TNTC. Grand Rapids: Eerdmans, 1980.
Peterson, David. "The Worship of the New Community." In *Witness to the Gospel: The Theology of Acts*, edited by I. Howard Marshall and David Peterson, 373–96. Grand Rapids: Eerdmans, 1998.
Simple Church, Starfish Ontario Network home page. No pages. http://www.simplechurch.com/group/starfishontarionetwork.
Stark, Rodney. *The Rise of Christianity*. San Francisco: HarperCollins, 1997.
Stott, John R. W. *The Message of Acts: The Spirit, the Church and the World*. Downers Grove, IL: InterVarsity, 1990.
Wagner, Peter, C. *Spreading the Fire (Acts 1–8)*. Ventura, CA: Regal Books, 1994.
Willis, W. L. "Banquets." In *Dictionary of New Testament Background*, edited by Craig A. Evans and Stanley E. Porter, 143–46. Downers Grove, IL: InterVarsity, 2000.
Zdero, Rad. *The Global House Church Movement*. Pasadena: William Carey Library, 2004.
———. "The 'Bop Bag' House Church Movement." *Starfish Files* (Winter 2008) 9. Online: http://www.scribd.com/doc/28766242/Starfish-Files-House-Church-Magazine-Winter-2008-Rad-Zdero.

7

The Megachurch in Canada
Promising Future or Passing Fad?

Michael Pawelke

INTRODUCTION

Full parking lots, theatre-like auditoriums, crowded lobbies, glossy programs, administrative wings, well-rehearsed music, and well-crafted yet conversational messages are just some of the hallmarks of the megachurch phenomenon. Such churches became increasingly commonplace throughout the latter part of the last century in larger centers of the American West Coast, the Midwest, and the South. However, the United States was not the only environment that witnessed the expansion of this new entity. Today, megachurches are a global reality and five of the ten largest churches in the world are in South Korea.[1] The theme of this study is a reflection on the megachurch in Canada.

While the megachurch movement is most often seen as an American trend, there are numerous and growing examples of larger churches in the Canadian context. While the megachurch has received praise, it has also invited misunderstanding and drawn criticism causing some to speculate on its future viability. My thesis is that the megachurch is a viable contemporary ecclesial model. The megachurch is not a concept contradictory to Scripture, but can fit within the rubric laid out by New

---

1. "O Come All Ye Faithful," first paragraph.

Testament writers. Based on my experiences in a megachurch context and the body of research available in this area, I suggest that pastors will continue to draw devoted followers of Christ, along with spiritual consumers and seekers, to create and sustain ever-expanding large churches in the Canadian context.

ECCLESIOLOGICAL TRENDS IN THE NEW TESTAMENT

Understanding the origin and identity of the church is foundational to this discussion. The New Testament provides a witness to these features. Therefore, I will provide a brief outline of how I read the New Testament witness regarding the church.[2]

First, the church was a unique and distinct community of believers, which came into existence at Pentecost (Acts 2:14–36). This community was an organic entity,[3] although it did employ organization when functioning on a local level. Second, the universal church is made up of all believers in Christ everywhere, both living and dead (Col 1:24; 1 Cor 1:2; Eph 1:22, 23).

The purpose and functions of the church are definitive. The church is to glorify God through the fulfillment of the great commandment and the great commission (1 Cor 10:31; Matt 22:18–19; 28:18–19). Further, God has ordained local expressions of the church as the vehicle for accomplishing his purposes of fellowship, instruction, worship, and witness (Acts 2:43–47). For these purposes, the church has been given some basic operational guidelines. The local church has been given gifted leaders for the administration and oversight of ministries along with the equipping of believers to execute ministry initiatives (Eph 4:11–16). Two leadership offices are spoken of: elder (bishop, overseer) and deacon (1 Tim 3:1–13).[4] While the Scriptures give mention of additional leadership gifts, the elders have the primary responsibility for pastoral leader-

---

2. I have provided Scripture references signifying where I understand this teaching or example to be elucidated.

3. The most frequent metaphor used to describe the church is the "body of Christ." The Apostle Paul uses the Greek term *sōma* (translated as "body") thirty-seven times. Paul employs *sōma* most frequently in a figurative sense of the "body of Christ, the fellowship of believers regarded as an organic spiritual unity in a living relationship to Christ, subject to Him, animated by Him, and having His power operating in it" (Wuest, *Word Studies*, 56).

4. This assumes that "elder" and "overseer" are to be understood as interchangeable in those particular contexts.

ship and education, while the deacons seem to complement the elders in additional areas of ministry need (cf. Acts 6:1–7). New Testament writers propose specific spiritual and character qualifications for these ministry leaders (Acts 20:17, 18; 1 Tim 3:1–13; Titus 1:5–9). Church leaders are to equip believers in the discovery and development of their own unique spiritual gifts. The result is that the church—the body of Christ—matures, honors God, and fulfills its purpose (Eph 4:7–16; 1 Cor 12:1–31; Rom 12:1–8).

Two significant ecclesial rituals stand out: baptism, which may be understood as the immersion of a believer as a symbol of the believer's own resurrection to new life by faith (Rom 6:3–5; Col 2:11, 12; Acts 8:38, 39), and the Lord's Supper, which was instituted by Christ for the commemoration of his atoning death, prompting believers to somber reflection, spiritual evaluation, and worship (1 Cor 11:17–34; 14:26). The objective of this description of New Testament ecclesiology is simply to acknowledge that while Scripture defines significant parameters and functions of the church, it never defines its boundaries or size.

Historically, the book of Acts affirms this freedom by giving us examples of small house assemblies (Acts 5:42) as well as the massive church at Jerusalem, which may have grown to a very large number. Consider the first six chapters of the book of Acts. Acts 1:15 pictures a gathering of 120 believers, worshipping in the anticipation of some unknown event. The Holy Spirit then came upon them in a dramatic way and Peter led the gathering in a bold evangelistic initiative that resulted in 3,000 new followers of Christ (Acts 2:41). Acts 2:42–47 then describes the growth of the early church in a positive light: "the Lord was adding to their numbers those who were being saved" (Acts 2:47). In Acts 4:4 Luke states: "But many of those who had heard the message believed; and the number of men came to be about five thousand." By mentioning only the men, Luke may have been envisioning families, thus suggesting that there were still additional women and children who embraced faith, making the total significantly larger. In Acts 5:14, following the frightening account of the deaths of Ananias and Sapphira, Luke observes: "And all the more believers in the Lord, multitudes of men and women, were constantly added to their number." While the actual size cannot be determined, the first church of Jerusalem quickly became a "megachurch."[5]

THE STATE OF THE MEGACHURCH IN NORTH AMERICA

In this current era, the modern megachurch is typically defined as a church with over 2,000 or more adults in attendance.[6] Canada has 30 churches that technically fit this narrow definition;[7] however, given the Canadian context, where malls are typically smaller and companies are on average smaller, the term megachurch is often ascribed to churches of 1,000 or more. The following chart describes Canada's larger evangelical churches and where they are found:[8]

Statistical Category	West	East	All Canada
Number of churches	2136	2482	4618
Percentage of Churches	46.3%	53.7%	100.0%
Churches over 1,999 attendance	18	12	30
Percentage to region	0.8%	0.5%	0.6%
Churches 1,000 to 1,999 attendance	30	36	66
Percentage to region	1.4%	1.5%	1.4%
Churches 500 to 999 attendance	91	76	167
Percentage to region	4.3%	3.1%	3.6%

---

5. This trend in diversity of church size continues throughout the history of the church. There have been examples of small rural church bodies and more sizable church assembles that often gathered in large cathedrals throughout Europe. There was a particular wave of cathedral construction from the eleventh to the fourteenth century that served larger gatherings of worshipers within the Roman Catholic tradition. With the birth of the Reformation, it was only a matter of time before Protestants also erected sizable edifices in Europe and ultimately North America.

6. Thumma et al., "Megachurches Today 2005," line 2.

7. Brian Bylsma of The Leadership Centre, Willow Creek Canada, Kelowna, British Columbia, in a telephone conversation, April 29, 2008.

8. Ibid.

Churches below 500 attendance	842	978	1820
Percentage to region	39.4%	39.4%	39.4%
Churches of size unknown	1161	1386	2547
Percentage to region	54.4%	55.8%	55.2%

A noteworthy observation is that there are only 96 evangelical churches larger than 1,000 in attendance in Canada. Most of the churches that are over 2,000 or more are found in Western Canada, while a slightly larger number of churches between 1,000 and 1,999 are found in Eastern Canada. Canada does have numerous highly-regarded ministries characterized by their influence, reputation, and size. The historic People's Church in Toronto, Mississauga's Portico, Kelowna's Trinity Baptist Church, Burnaby's Willingdon Mennonite Brethren Church, Winnipeg's Spring's Church, Oakville's Meeting House, Calgary's Center Street Church, and Calgary's recently relocated First Alliance, are just some of the more well-known megachurches on the Canadian horizon. Not only are such churches seeing growth, but the Canadian landscape is seeing the establishment of more large churches each year.[9]

EVALUATING THE MEGACHURCH

Evaluating the megachurch's contribution to the Canadian church is complex and difficult. The question may be likened to evaluating the benefit of Walmart to the Canadian economy. The answer depends greatly on whom you ask. The shopper will offer one observation, the economist will suggest another, while the small independent storeowner will offer still another perspective. Nevertheless, megachurches have been called "big box" churches, often with an intended pejorative connotation. They are often accused of growing on the backs of smaller churches and are characterized as "Christianity light" or entertainment focused.[10] The list of negative opinions is lengthy but often unfounded. Dave Travis of Leadership Network, and Scott Thumma and Warren Bird of the Hartford Institute for Religion Research have identified eleven frequently cited misconceptions and has done substantive, quantifiable

---

9. Ibid.
10. Guinness, *Dining with the Devil*. The entire book is dedicated to this thesis.

research dispelling these myths. These myths and their attending facts are worth acknowledging, although it should be noted that this research is reflective of American realities.

1. *Myth:* All megachurches are alike.

   Fact: They differ in growth rates, size, and the things they emphasize.

2. *Myth:* All megachurches are equally good at being big.

   Fact: Some megachurches clearly understand how to function as a large institution but others flounder noticeably at being big—and some even struggle and decline.

3. *Myth:* There is an over-emphasis of money in all the megachurches.

   Fact: Our data doesn't show this. Rather it is often a low priority, except when engaged in a building or capital campaign. At the same time, most don't shy away from occasional sermons about putting God first in individual financial priorities and preaching on tithing.

4. *Myth:* Megachurches are just spectator worship and are not serious about Christianity.

   Fact: Our data shows that most megachurches demand a lot; they have high spiritual expectations and serious orthodox beliefs and preaching.

5. *Myth:* These large churches only care about themselves and are not seriously involved in outreach and social ministry.

   Fact: Considerable ministry is going on at the megachurches, from solitary outreach to the local communities, joining with other churches in an area to tackle problems, as well as contributing to efforts nationally (say in New Orleans) and internationally (such as ministry to persons with AIDS in Africa).

6. *Myth:* All megachurches are major political players and pawns or powerbrokers to the Republican Party or George Bush.

   Fact: A vast majority of megachurches surveyed said they are not politically active. This parallels survey data on smaller churches; most churches have an internalized separation of church and state. A few megachurches and their pastors are vocally politically active but not most, not even a majority.

7. *Myth:* All megachurches have huge sanctuaries and enormous campuses.

Fact: Megachurches show widespread use of multiple worship services over several days, multiple venues, and even multiple campuses. Mega refers to attendance, not building size.

8. *Myth:* All megachurches are nondenominational.

   Fact: While many megachurches are nondenominational and most often act like it, the vast majority belongs to some denomination.

9. *Myth:* All megachurches are homogeneous congregations with little diversity.

   Fact: A large growing number of megachurches are multi-ethnic and are intentionally so. Likewise, many of them have considerable diversity in terms of class, education levels, income, ages, backgrounds, occupations, and even theological and political styles.

10. *Myth:* Megachurches grow primarily because of great programming.

    Fact: Megachurches grow because excited attendees tell their friends. They may be encouraged and helped to do so by church leadership but it is not what megachurches "do" in terms of evangelistic programs, neighborhood surveys, etc. that make them grow. The survey did not show any significant correlations between the programmatic items and the increased rates of growth in the fastest growing ones.

11. *Myth:* The megachurch phenomenon is over and on the decline because it was just a Baby Boomer phenomenon. Gen Xers and Millennials aren't interested in megachurches.

    Fact: The increased numbers of megachurches we found is shocking, and it seems there are many more on the way. We see no indication of this trend slowing. Others have pointed out that the biggest churches in all denominations are getting bigger over time, since the 70s. Likewise, the idea that youth don't find megachurches appealing could not be further from the truth. While the megachurch phenomenon exploded with the Baby Boom, it was around before them and will be after them. Many of the fastest growing, largest, and newest megachurches are full of people under 35 years old. Not all youth like megachurches, but neither do all Baby Boomers.[11]

---

11. Bird, Thumma, and Travis, "Megachurches Today 2005," 16–17. Thumma and Travis's book further develops the theme (Thumma and Travis, *Beyond Megachurch Myths*). This lengthy quotation is cited with the permission of the authors and the Leadership Network (website www.leadnet.org, featuring many useful articles for church leadership).

While Bird, Thumma, and Travis's research does correct some misconceptions about megachurches and defends their ministry contribution, they do not attempt to build a case for the superiority of the megachurch. Megachurches cannot boast of more effective discipleship or spiritual formation success on the part of their congregants. Willow Creek Community Church has recently published research demonstrating that churches that rely on programs to produce disciples do not realize their intended objective.[12] However, it should also be noted that smaller churches could not boast any higher success rate of producing "Christ-centered disciples."[13] Megachurches were not necessarily more effective at producing "Christ-centered disciples" than were smaller churches, but neither were they any less effective.

Megachurches also face issues and challenges related to the escalating cost of land and the ever-increasing difficulty in obtaining appropriate zoning to build large edifices. These dilemmas are real and require more energy, time, and finances to resolve. The stewardship of this resource drain is also questioned; however, some large churches are finding solutions not only in multiple services, but also in multiple venues.[14] The emergence of the multi-site model has provided growing churches with the opportunity to grow larger more quickly by utilizing multiple meeting spaces, rather than building enormous expensive campuses. This is one of the creative options that larger churches are exploring to maintain their growth, while addressing the ever-increasing costs of land and construction.

Critics of the megachurch movement often compare megachurches with large corporations and their pastors with corporate CEOs.[15] However, there is no identifiable megachurch leader personality type any more than there is a small church leader personality type. I know colleagues of smaller churches who are "type A" drivers, extroverts, assertive, aggressive, and some who are authoritative. These are the qualities that are often attributed to megachurch pastors. I also have friendships and collegial relationships with pastors of larger churches who are intro-

12. Hawkins and Parkinson, *Reveal*, 57.
13. Greg Hawkins, "Reveal Study," lecture given at the International Leaders Gathering, Willow Creek Association, at Willow Creek Community Church. The conference was held from 19 to 23 November, 2007.
14. Surratt et al., *Multi-site Church*.
15. Guinness, *Dining with the Devil*, 71.

verts, academics, artists, and plodders. Jim Collins, in his book *Good to Great*, has demonstrated that the truly "great" qualities of an outstanding leader are personal humility and an enduring professional will.[16] Such qualities are evident in pastors of both smaller churches and larger churches. Vision and visionary leadership also plays a pivotal function in church leadership. There is too large a body of research that highlights the role of vision in organizational growth for this quality to be ignored.[17]

Some Christians simply do not like the megachurch environment. Charges of being too big, too polished, too corporate, or too modern have all been lobbed at the megachurch from numerous sources—including more traditional and academic sources as well as from some within the emerging church.[18] Opinions differ with respect to megachurches. What follows is a recounting of some of my own experiences within a megachurch setting that have colored my perception.

A FIRST-HAND EXPERIENCE IN A MEGACHURCH CONTEXT

My first ministry experience was serving as a Youth Pastor. I served my home church, which had an attendance of approximately 250 to 300 people. This church had an enormous impact on my life, as it was there that I was discipled after coming to faith in Christ. The resulting familial relationship engendered a connection with individuals from all generational demographics. I loved this church and my time there was rich, meaningful, and life-shaping, as I was initiated into local church ministry.

Following this I assumed the role of a church planter. Over a period of eight years the young church grew from 5 to just under 200. Hospitality was a major feature of this group; we saw people come to faith in Christ, warm community was formed, and people were discipled. I loved this church and the familial atmosphere. I knew everyone by name and could pick out who was or was not in attendance on a given Sunday. It was relatively easy to assimilate newcomers into the church and small group infrastructure. However, attracting and keeping fami-

---

16. Collins, *Good to Great*, 20.

17. See, for example, Bennis and Nanus, *Leaders*; Kotter, *Leading Change*; Hybels, *Axiom*.

18. See, for example, Guinness, *Dining with the Devil*.

lies with adolescents came with some difficulty. Parents were concerned for the spiritual health of their teens; thus, a dynamic youth group was a non-negotiable for their church identification. Even with an attendance of 180, such a program was not feasible for us. As the only staff member, despite the church's wonderful elder board and committed volunteers, I found loneliness a tangible concern. The vision of greater numbers anticipated additional staff, dynamic youth ministry, and funding for more up-to-date musical equipment.

A move to Burlington, Ontario, Canada came in 1994 as I assumed the role of Senior Pastor of a healthy church with an attendance of 450 and a staff of five. The past 14 years have featured non-dramatic, but steady growth in that context. The church has added additional worship services, two church plants, a merger with another church, and, most recently, the grafting in of a smaller struggling church plant. The church's database has some 3,500 names now, while weekly worship attendance fluctuates between 1,150 and 1,450 in three services. Twenty-four staff-members are on the payroll. All the benefits of a megachurch are present, including a competent staff, two attractive campuses, multiple, life-stage appropriate ministries, and numerous service opportunities. However, the hurdles that megachurches face are also close by. Considerable movement of people in and out of the church is a present reality, as some individuals trust Christ and join the community, while others leave because they prefer the ministry down the road. It can also be difficult to assimilate the new person who attends on a Sunday morning amidst a larger crowd. Although for the most part newcomers are welcomed, on occasion failure happens, and guests feel the difficulty of connecting to a large body. Even with 70 vibrant small groups, intentionality is required on the part of the new congregant to connect with one of these. Assimilation initiatives can be a significant hurdle for some to overcome.

Today, I perform a few pastoral home visits, engage in a limited number of hospital visits, attend a ridiculous number of meetings, and have been forced to learn advanced leadership and management skill sets in order to navigate the complexities of a large organization. The sometimes lonely days as a pastor of a smaller church are relatively uncommon now. However, I love the church I serve and continue to have meaningful relationships there even if I don't know everyone. I come to work each day and am surrounded by a wonderful team of colleagues.

Together, the staff stimulates and draws out the best in each other. The Senior Pastor role is predominantly that of a managing leader now; pre-marital counseling, marriage counseling, weddings, hospital visitation, family dedications, and baptisms are still a vital part of the job.

Members of small and large churches can feel positively about their churches. Each Sunday thousands of Christians and spiritual explorers in the Canadian context choose to attend a large church. Each Sunday there are hundreds of leaders and pastors who find joy in leading these ministries, are seeking God's presence and power for their ministries, and are pursuing new and creative ways to grow their church communities. Indeed, the larger church has some unique issues, but smaller churches have their own distinct issues too. The question for many church leaders and members may simply be a question of which issues they want to engage.

CONCLUSION

What will be the future of the megachurch in Canada? The prospects are that gifted, visionary pastors will continue to draw devoted followers of Christ, along with spiritual consumers and seekers, to create and sustain ever-expanding large churches in the Canadian context. We continue to witness the trend of an increasing number of larger churches. Finances may prove limiting and city councils may not be in a hurry to release the appropriate permits. Fewer multi-million dollar campus expansions may occur, and the megachurch will continue to wrestle with its unique challenges and issues. However, it appears that there is still a significant future for the megachurch in the Canadian milieu. These churches may take different shapes, as evidenced in the trend towards multi-site ministries. They will also likely reflect increasing characteristics of the emerging generation as the leadership baton is passed and church culture continues to morph. Nevertheless, Canada continues to need more churches.[19] Some people will grow best in a small setting while others grow better in a larger setting. For both kinds of churches there is a need, and a future.

---

19. Moerman, ed., *Discipling Our Nation*. This is the thesis of the entire book.

BIBLIOGRAPHY

Bennis, Warren, and Burt Nanus. *Leaders: The Strategies for Taking Charge.* New York: Harper & Row, 1985.

Bird, Warren, Scott Thumma, and Dave Travis. "Megachurches Today 2005: Summary of Research Findings." 2006. Online: http://leadnet.org/search/results/42ec018dde792c9e4aa89372408d3891/

Collins, Jim. *Good to Great: Why Some Companies Make the Leap . . . and Others Don't.* New York: HarperCollins, 2001.

Guinness, Os. *Dining with the Devil: The Megachurch Movement Flirts with Modernity.* Grand Rapids: Baker, 1993.

Hawkins, Greg, L., and Cally Parkinson. *Reveal: Where Are You?* Chicago: Willow Creek, 2007.

Hybels, Bill. *Axiom: Powerful Leadership Proverbs.* Grand Rapids: Zondervan, 2008.

Kotter, John P. *Leading Change.* Boston: Harvard Business School Press, 1996.

Moerman, Murray, ed. *Discipling Our Nation: Equipping the Canadian Church for Its Mission.* Delta, BC: Church Leadership Library, 2005.

"O Come All Ye Faithful." *The Economist* (3 November 2007). Online: http://www.economist.com/specialreports/displaystory.cfm?story_id=10015239&CFID=25385374.

Surratt, Geoff, et al. *The Multi-site Church Revolution.* Grand Rapids: Zondervan, 2006.

Thumma, Scott, and Dave Travis. *Beyond Megachurch Myths: What We Can Learn from America's Largest Churches.* San Francisco: Jossey-Bass, 2007.

Wuest, Kenneth S. *Wuest's Word Studies: Ephesians and Colossians in the Greek New Testament.* Grand Rapids: Eerdmans, 1953.

8

The Role and Identity of the Church in the Biblical Story

Missional by Its Very Nature

Michael W. Goheen

INTRODUCTION

ECCLESIOLOGY, OR THE DOCTRINE of the church, has become a central issue in theology in the twentieth and twenty-first centuries. Many factors have contributed to this renewed interest in ecclesiology[1] but perhaps none is as important as the new missionary situation in which European and North American churches find themselves. In this new situation the rich resources of the church's missionary tradition, which has grappled with the church's calling in cross-cultural settings, hold much promise for the renewal of ecclesiology.

German theologian Jürgen Moltmann believes that "today one of the strongest impulses towards the renewal of the theological concept of the church comes from the theology of mission."[2] According to Moltmann, Western ecclesiologies were formulated in the context of

---

1. For example, major factors stimulating renewed reflection on the church are the ecumenical movement in the twentieth century, Vatican II, the burgeoning worldwide Pentecostal movement, the emergence of Base Ecclesial Communities in Latin America and African Initiated Churches in Africa.

2. Moltmann, *Church in the Power*, 7.

a Christianized culture. European churches were established churches that lacked a missionary self-understanding because they found their identity as part of a larger complex called the *corpus Christianum* or the Christian West. Today that Christian West is disintegrating, both culturally and geographically, and the Western church finds itself in a new missionary situation.

Consequently, a new context is needed for ecclesiology. Here is where Moltmann sees the importance of missionary theology. The new context is what God is doing in world history, and God's work in history is best described in terms of the *missio Dei*. The church discovers its place and function within this story of the redemptive work of the triune God in the world. The Father sends the Son and the Son sends the church in the power of the Spirit. As Moltmann puts it, "If the church sees itself to be sent in the same framework as the Father's sending of the Son and the Holy Spirit, then it also sees itself in the framework of God's history with the world *and discovers its place and function within this history*."[3] Mission, then, is no longer simply one of the activities of the church; rather it defines the church's existence. "What we have to learn," says Moltmann, "is not that the church 'has' a mission, but the very reverse: that the mission of Christ creates its own church. Mission does not come from the church; it is from mission and in the light of mission that the church has to be understood."[4]

Understanding the calling of the church in the context of God's mission leads not simply to a fresh look at our mission in the world, but to a whole re-evaluation of the nature and ministry of the church and its role in God's redemptive purpose. In fact, the Dutch theologian Hendrikus Berkhof believes that what is needed is nothing less than a whole reformulation of our entire ecclesiology, from the standpoint of mission.[5]

A good start has been made along these lines in the last half century. However, the church in the West is still a long way from thinking of itself as a missional community. What Moltmann says about European churches is equally valid for the churches in North America: "Yet up to now the European churches have found it hard to discover Europe as a

---

3. Ibid., 11. Emphasis mine.
4. Ibid., 10.
5. Berkhof, *Christian Faith*, 410.

missionary field or to see themselves as missionary churches."[6] This essay joins with the work of others in an attempt to push the North American church toward a fuller missional self-understanding.

There remains much room for good exegetical, theological, historical, and contextual work to be done on this topic. Unfortunately, the concept of missional church is often considered to be trendy, the latest theological flavor of the month that remains on the margins of "real theology." While some books on missional church would seem to confirm such a view, this is a mistake. The problem is that mission is viewed as an activity or strategy (maybe marginal or maybe very important) that can be treated after ecclesiology. But the Roman Catholic scholar John Power is correct when he says that mission is not a "fringe activity of a strongly established Church, a pious cause that [may] be attended to when the home fires [are] first brightly burning." He continues by quoting Jesus in John 20:21: "'. . . so am I sending you'—the very word 'send' means mission and so the whole Church is on mission, and cannot be otherwise. . . . Missionary activity is not so much the work of the Church as simply the Church at work."[7] To miss the missional nature of the church is to fundamentally misunderstand what the church is. Emil Brunner is correct when he says that "the church exists by mission as fire exists by burning."[8] Beginning with the New Testament, church and mission belonged together: "Because the church and mission belong together from the beginning, a church without mission or a mission without the church are both contradictions. Such things do exist, but only as pseudostructures."[9] Mission ought to be central to all theological endeavors if they are faithful to Scripture and this certainly includes ecclesiology.

One could treat missional ecclesiology from a number of theological angles—biblical theology, systematic theology, historical theology, and practical theology. Within each of these areas many fruitful approaches are possible. In fact, a variety of perspectives will open up fresh insights into a missional ecclesiology. But in this essay I approach ecclesiology from the standpoint of biblical theology. Wilbert Shenk is right when he says that "the Bible does not offer a definition of the church or

---

6. Moltmann, *Church in the Power*, 8.
7. Power, *Mission Theology*, 41–42.
8. Brunner, *Word and the World*, 108.
9. Braaten, *Flaming Center*, 55.

provide us with a doctrinal basis for understanding it. Instead, the Bible relies on images and narrative to disclose the meaning of the church."[10] While I will only make brief reference to the images of the church, this essay will trace the role and identity of God's people in the narrative of the Bible.

WHAT IS MEANT BY MISSIONAL ECCLESIOLOGY?

The dimensions of a missional ecclesiology will emerge as the role of God's people is traced through the biblical story. But it might be helpful to say up front a few words about what is meant by the adjective "missional" when it is used to describe ecclesiology. A couple of definitions by the British biblical scholar Christopher Wright can clarify the meaning of mission. First, he writes: "Fundamentally, our mission (if it is biblically informed and validated) means our committed participation as God's people, at God's invitation and command, in God's own mission within the history of the world for the redemption of God's creation."[11] Mission is first of all what God is doing for the sake of the world; it is his long-term purpose to renew the creation. The church is missional by its very nature in that it is taken up into this work for the sake of the world. Second, "God's mission involves God's people living in God's way in the sight of the nations."[12] This second definition gives us a sense of how God will employ his people in his mission. He will make them a display people who embody God's original creational intention for human life. He will come and dwell among them and give them his *torah* to direct them to live in the way of the Lord. As such, his people will be an attractive sign before all nations of the goal toward which God is moving—the restoration of the creation and human life from the corruption of sin. So, contrary to widespread definitions of mission, Israel's mission was, in short, "to *be* something, not go somewhere."[13]

Two orientations define the identity and role of God's people: "chosen by God" and "for the sake of the world." The church does not exist for itself. Rather, it exists for the sake of God's mission and for the sake of others toward whom God's mission is directed. The church is like an

10. Shenk, "Foreword," 9.
11. Wright, *Mission of God*, 22–23.
12. Ibid., 470.
13. Wright, "Old Testament Perspectives," 271.

ellipse with two fixed focal points that define its existence. The first fixed focal point is "chosen by God": the church's role and identity can only be understood in terms of being chosen to play a role in God's mission. The second focal point is "for the sake of the world": God's purpose is to bring his salvation to all nations, indeed the whole creation. The church exists as the place where God begins his work of restoration and then as a channel whereby that salvation might flow to all peoples.

DISCONTINUITY AND CONTINUITY OF THE CHURCH WITH OLD TESTAMENT ISRAEL

The Bible tells the true story of the world.[14] To properly understand the church we must enquire into the role and identity of God's people in the story of the Bible. Our starting point is the observation that, on the one hand, with the work of Christ and the coming of the Spirit something new has taken place in history: in the church a new community has emerged in God's plan. Yet, on the other hand, this community called "church" is the continuation of a people who have existed for several thousand years. Paul, in his reflection on the gospel and the Old Testament people of Israel, makes this clear with a vivid image. Those who believe the gospel, Gentiles who are taken up into God's saving work in Christ, are like branches that are grafted onto a tree that has been growing for some time (Rom 11:17–24). They join and become part of an ancient community, and enter into a long story.

Gerhard Lohfink's observation concerning the disciple-community that Jesus formed is helpful to clarify the approach we will take: "After a history of more than a millenium [sic], the people of God could neither be founded nor established, but only *gathered* and *restored*."[15] The church is not something that is founded or established for the first time with Jesus and the Spirit. Ecclesiology may not begin with the New Testament. Rather, it is a covenant community that has been gathered and restored to its original calling. Thus we must first probe the nature of God's people in the Old Testament. Along this line Johannes Blauw rightly notes:

> When we speak about the Church as "the people of God in the world" and enquire into the real nature of this Church, we can-

---

14. Goheen, "Urgency."
15. Lohfink, *Jesus and Community*, 71.

not avoid speaking about the *roots* of the Church which are to be found in the Old Testament idea of Israel as the people of the covenant. So the question of the *missionary* nature of the Church, that is, the real relationship between the people of God and the world, cannot be solved until we have investigated the relation between Israel and the nations of the earth.[16]

Thus, to properly understand the church we must *first* understand the role and identity of God's people in the Old Testament. But *then* we must attend to what is new in this community we call *ekklēsia* or church. What difference has the coming of Jesus and the outpouring of his Spirit had on the community of God's people? What do the images employed by New Testament authors to describe the church divulge about its new identity? That is how we will proceed in this brief essay. What will emerge is that both the continuity and the discontinuity of the church with Israel make clear the missional identity of the people of God.

TWO TEXTS—ONE HERMENEUTICAL LENS FOR READING THE BIBLICAL STORY

There are two texts in the Old Testament that together offer a helpful hermeneutical lens to view the role and identity of God's people in the biblical story. In Gen 12:2–3 God outlines his redemptive plan to Abraham in a promise. God will make Abraham into a great nation, and through that nation bring blessing to all nations. In Exod 19:3–6 God spells out the role this nation will play in bringing blessing to the nations. The remainder of the Old Testament traces a story of how faithful Israel is to their calling.

> "I will make you into a great nation,
> and I will bless you;
> I will make your name great,
> and you will be a blessing.
> I will bless those who bless you,
> and whoever curses you I will curse;
> and all peoples on earth
> will be blessed through you" (Gen 12:2–3 TNIV)

---

16. Blauw, "Mission of the People of God," 91.

This "stupendous utterance"[17] made to Abraham in Genesis 12 is set in the context of the first eleven chapters of Genesis. Indeed, those first chapters pose the problem to which the promise to Abraham is the solution. These chapters are universal in scope: God is the Creator of the heavens and the earth, and is Lord of all the nations. Sin pollutes all cultures of humankind and likewise God's judgment on sin is universal. In reference to Genesis 3–11, Gerhard von Rad speaks of the author's "great hamartiology," his focus on sin, its effects, consequences, and God's judgment.[18] Now in Genesis 12, the biblical story narrows from its universal scope to a particular focus; from all nations God centers his attention on one man and one nation. The bad news of sin, alienation, and curse on all nations is met with a promise of good news: God has chosen one man to bring blessing back to his creation and all peoples.

Paul Williamson speaks correctly of a "twofold purpose" in Gen 12:1–3.[19] Abraham is first of all to be formed into a great nation and be a recipient of God's covenantal blessing. The purpose is so that all nations on earth might be blessed. This final clause "all peoples on earth will be blessed through you" is a "the principal statement of these three verses." It is a "result clause" that indicates that the final goal of God's election and blessing of Abraham is the salvation of the nations.[20] Thus the "*election of [Abraham and] Israel is fundamentally missional, not just soteriological* . . . God's calling and election of Abraham was not merely so that he should be saved . . . It was rather, and more explicitly, that he and his people should be instruments through whom God would gather that multinational multitude that no man or woman can number . . . it is first of all election into mission."[21]

We are not told precisely how Abraham will be a blessing to all nations. That will be given further clarification in Exod 19:3–6. However, already in Gen 18:18–19 we are given a clue. It will happen as Abraham and his family "keep the way of the Lord" and do "what is right and just." Both phrases point to a life that lives in God's way before the nations.

> Then Moses went up to God, and the Lord called to him from the mountain and said, "This is what you are to say to the house

---

17. Wolff, "Kerygma of the Yahwist," 140.
18. von Rad, *Old Testament Theology*, 154.
19. Williamson, "Covenant," 145.
20. Dumbrell, *Covenant and Creation*, 64–65.
21. Wright, *Mission of God*, 263–64.

of Jacob and what you are to tell the house of Israel: 'You yourselves have seen what I did to Egypt, and how I carried you on eagles' wings and brought you to myself. Now if you obey me fully and keep my covenant, then out of all nations you will be my treasured possession. Although the whole earth is mine, you will be for me a kingdom of priests and a holy nation.' These are the words you are to speak to the Israelites." (Exod 19:3–6 TNIV)

The means by which God will bring blessing to the nations is given more detail in Exodus 19. These "programmatic" verses are the "lens through which one may view the entire book of Exodus."[22] This is significant for our subject of ecclesiology because the book of Exodus describes the birth and formation of God's people. It is not a "literary or theological goulash" but rather has a "theological unity" that is reflected in its literary structure.[23] Indeed, the literary structure has profound theological implications for the identity and role of God's people in the biblical story.

The first eighteen chapters narrate the *redemption* of Israel from slavery in Egypt. For many of us, redemption is just one more word in a large biblical catalogue of theological concepts to describe salvation. However, here in Exodus it draws on a familiar cultural and social image. A redeemer was a family member who was responsible to recover family lives or goods that had fallen into bondage.[24] Redemption could involve the liberation of a relative from slavery and restoring them to their original family relationship (cf. Lev 25:47–55). Here, as Redeemer, God acts to free his firstborn son from slavery to Pharaoh to restore him to his rightful place in God's family (Exod 4:22–23). This redemption of a son "contains the essence of the meaning of the entire exodus story."[25] Since Pharaoh was considered to be an incarnation of the Egyptian god Re,[26] and since pagan religion shaped all of the political, social, and economic life of Egypt,[27] this redemption was a profoundly *religious* liberation. Israel was freed to serve the Lord in every area of their lives.

---

22. Fretheim, "Whole Earth is Mine," 229.
23. Durham, *Exodus*, xxi.
24. Proksch, "λύω," 330–35.
25. Magonet, "Rhetoric of God," 65.
26. Curtis, "Man as the Image," 86–96; Middleton, *Liberating Image*, 108–11.
27. Frankfort, *Kingship*.

This perspective is strengthened by the fact that Egypt ruled its subject peoples with covenants. This made the Pharaoh the covenant lord over Israel. God breaks Pharaoh's dominion and establishes his covenant lordship over Israel.

> In the Exodus, the power of the suzerain is broken; the pharaoh, the god-king of Egypt, was defeated and therefore lost his right to be Israel's suzerain lord; the Lord conquered the pharaoh and therefore ruled as King over Israel (Exod 15:18). As their deliverer, God had claimed the right to call for his people's obedient commitment to him in the covenant.[28]

In Exodus 19–24 God establishes a covenant people. Covenants were common instruments employed by the Hittite and Egyptian world empires of Moses' day, so it should not surprise us that God also employs the familiar notion of covenant to bind his people to himself.[29] But what made this such a suitable image? Craigie offers an answer: "Like the other small nations that surrounded her, Israel was to be a vassal state, but not to Egypt or the Hittites; she owed her allegiance to God alone."[30]

But why had God—the Lord of all nations—liberated this one small nation? What role does God have for them to play? The answer is offered in Exod 19:3–6. Here we find the "unique identity of the people of God."[31] And it will be this "special role" that will become a "lens through which Israel is viewed throughout the rest of the Bible."[32] God promised that Abraham would become a great nation that would bring blessing to the whole earth. The book of Exodus shows the formation of that nation, and specifically Exod 19:3–6 tells us how Israel will accomplish that role.

Three terms are used to describe Israel in their identity and role in God's mission: treasured possession, priestly kingdom, and holy nation.

---

28. Craigie, *Deuteronomy*, 83.

29. The remarkable similarity between Old Testament covenants, especially in Exodus 19–24 and Deuteronomy, has been explored thoroughly for the last half decade in biblical scholarship. Cf., for example, Mendenhall, "Ancient Oriental and Biblical Law" and "Covenant Forms in Israelite Tradition." It is much more debatable to suggest, as I intimate here, that the Pharaoh employed a covenant with Israel. Craigie offers evidence that vassal covenants were employed by Egypt to subject foreign labor groups within Egypt. This raises the real possibility that the Pharaoh would have been viewed by Israel as their covenant lord (Craigie, *Deuteronomy*, 23, 79–83).

30. Craigie, *Deuteronomy*, 28.

31. Wells, *God's Holy People*, 34.

32. Durham, *Exodus*, xiii.

We may summarize the significance of these labels in terms of Israel's call to mediate God's salvation to the nations as they lived before the nations a communal life that embodied God's design for human life. As Durham points out, Israel was to "be a display people, a showcase to the world of how being in covenant with Yahweh changes a people."[33] As a holy nation Israel was to be "a societary model for the world," a picture of what God intends for the whole world—human life under God's authority.[34] Karl Barth describes Israel's role with the metaphors of sign, light, and exemplary existence with universal significance for all nations.[35] The universal horizon of God's action in choosing Israel and making them a priestly kingdom and holy nation is seen in the words "because the whole earth is mine" (Gen 12:5).[36] All the nations belong to God and his choice of Israel is to call them back.

Israel was to live out God's creational intentions for human life as a picture of the goal toward which God was moving—the renewal of all of human life. As such, Israel's life would be attractive. To use the later language of Isaiah, Israel was to be a light to the nations (Isa 42:6). Or to use the older language of missiology, Israel's mission was centripetal: their life was to be attractive to draw the nations into covenant with God.

God's people living in God's way before the nations: this is how we have described mission. Thus we are not surprised that immediately upon the heels of this call the *torah* is given to guide Israel in living out their calling as a holy nation. This instruction, which would be significantly expanded in Deuteronomy before Israel entered the land, covered the full spectrum of human life. It pointed back to God's creational intention for human life, now set contextually in this ancient Near Eastern setting. "The people of God in both testaments are called to be a light to the nations. But there can be no light to the nations that is not shining already in transformed lives of a holy people."[37]

33. Ibid., 263.
34. Dumbrell, *Covenant and Creation*, 87.
35. Barth, *Church Dogmatics*, IV.1:56.
36. Dumbrell rightly notes, contrary to the TNIV, that the phrase "because [*ki*] the whole earth is mine" should be understood "not as the assertion of the right to choose but as the *reasons* or *goal* for choice" (Dumbrell, "Prospect," 146). Fretheim translates this "because the whole earth is mine" and notes that this links this text with the missional purpose of God first articulated to Abraham in Gen 12:3 (Fretheim, "Whole Earth is Mine," 237).
37. Wright, *Mission of God*, 358.

The final chapters of Exodus deal with the tabernacle and the story of Israel's rebellion with the golden calf (Exodus 25–40). Together we see that the final brick in the building of God's people in Exodus is God's *presence*: As holy yet merciful and forgiving (Exod 34:6–7), God comes to dwell in their midst. God will now carry out his mission to bring blessing to the nations as he lives among Israel as their divine King. Robert Martin-Achard calls attention to the importance of this for mission: "The evangelisation of the world is not primarily a matter of words or deeds: it is a matter of presence—*the presence of the People of God in the midst of mankind and the presence of God in the midst of His people.* And surely it is not in vain that the Old Testament reminds the Church of this truth."[38]

The book of Exodus renders to us the identity and role of God's people: they are a redeemed people (Exodus 1–18), a covenant people (Exodus 19–24), and a people in whom God dwells (Exodus 25–40). God's work of forming a people finds its focus in the calling to be a priestly kingdom and holy nation before the watching eyes of the surrounding nations (Exod 19:3–6). As Durham says of these verses, "This special role becomes a kind of lens through which Israel is viewed throughout the rest of the Bible. . . . It is this special role, indeed, that weaves the Book of Exodus so completely into the canonical fabric begun with Genesis and ended only with Revelation."[39] Or, as Dumbrell puts it even more strongly, "The history of Israel from this point on is in reality merely a commentary upon the degree of fidelity with which Israel adhered to this Sinai-given vocation."[40]

ON DISPLAY IN THE LAND: MISSION AS THE MEANING OF ISRAEL'S HISTORY

Thus Gen 12:2–3 and Exod 19:3–6 provide a hermeneutical lens through which to read the Old Testament, indeed the entire biblical story. Duane Christensen rightly observes that "'Israel as a light to the nations' is no peripheral theme within the canonical process. The nations are the matrix of Israel's life, the *raison d'être* of her very existence."[41] Christopher

---

38. Martin-Achard, *Light to the Nations*, 79.
39. Durham, *Exodus*, xxiii.
40. Dumbrell, *Covenant and Creation*, 80.
41. Christensen, "Nations," 4:1037.

Wright agrees: "God's mission is what fills the gap between the scattering of the nations in Genesis 11 and the healing of the nations in Rev 22. It is *God's mission in relation to the nations*, arguably more than any other theme, that provides the key that unlocks the biblical grand narrative."[42]

In the Old Testament "the nations" is a theological category:[43] they are viewed from the standpoint of their relation to God and to Israel, God's covenant people. Negatively, the nations are alienated from God and under his judgment. In their idolatry they also pose a threat to Israel. Positively, they belong to God by virtue of creation and are subject to his divine rule over all history. Ultimately, they are the object of God's redemptive activity in Israel.

Israel is placed on the land to shine as a light in the midst of and for the sake of the nations. They are placed at the crossroads of the nations and the navel of the universe[44] as an appealing display of a people visible to the surrounding peoples.[45] From this point on "Israel knew that it lived under constant surveillance of the then contemporary world."[46] Displayed in the land "Israel was visible to the nations." Indeed, the "life of God's people is always directed outward to the watching nations."[47]

However, we note an interesting phenomenon in the remainder of Old Testament history in the way Israel's story is told. Even though God's mission to the nations is "the meaning of Israel's history" yet "during the whole history of Israel this comes to realization little if at all."[48] I will not stop to probe this in detail but for the purpose of this essay the following two observations are important.

The focus of the Old Testament historical narratives is on the work of God in the midst of Israel to form them as a holy nation. There are two sides to this story. The first side is God's work of grace and judgment in their midst according to the covenant. The history of Israel is

---

42. Wright, *Mission of God*, 455. My emphasis.

43. Hedlund, *Mission of the Church*, 67.

44 A number of Jewish and rabbinic texts situate Israel at the center of the world, as the navel of the universe. For example, *Midr. Tanh.*, "Just as the navel lies at the center of Man's body, thus the Land of Israel is the navel of the world . . ." This centrality should be interpreted missionally. God puts Israel in the "center of the world" so that they might be seen by the nations.

45. Wright, *Mission of God*, 467; DeRidder, *Discipling the Nations*, 43–44.

46. Bavinck, *Science of Missions*, 14.

47. Wright, *Mission of God*, 371.

48. Blauw, *Missionary Nature of the Church*, 27; cf. Bauckham, *Bible and Mission*, 30.

prophetic as it is narrated from the standpoint of God's covenant word in Deuteronomy. Israel's faithfulness brings blessing, prosperity, and life. Israel's unfaithfulness brings curse, destruction, and death. The second side is Israel's struggle with the idolatry of the nations that surround them.[49] Israel's mission is to be a holy nation in the midst of the nations. The pagan idolatry of the nations poses a constant threat and temptation to Israel. And, sadly, over and over again the light of Israel's life and worship is overcome by the darkness of this idolatry.

Israel's struggle with idolatry is an important thread in the story but this too must be understood in a missional context. Mission is God's people living in God's way in the sight of the nations. However, those nations are not neutral and passive observers so to speak. In their social and cultural lives they do not serve the Lord but idols. Thus Israel's calling was one of a "missionary encounter"[50] with the idolatrous cultures of the surrounding nations, a confrontation of the pagan gods with the claims of the living God. Israel's life was an alternative shaped by God's *torah* and as such was a light in the midst of pagan darkness. Sadly, Israel's history demonstrated that instead of being a solution to idolatry they often became submerged in it becoming part of the problem.

Even though the narrative of the historical books zooms in on God's work in the midst of Israel and Israel's struggle with idolatry amidst the nations, we must not forget the bigger picture in which this drama is set: God's mission in and through Israel. Israel's history is something like narrowing in and focusing attention on certain details of a painting without forgetting the bigger picture. That bigger picture is God's work in Israel for the sake of the nations. Put another way: God has a universal goal (all nations, whole creation) but uses particular means (Israel). Much of the focus of the historical books is on the particular means. However, the universal goal remains the ultimate horizon and backdrop of God's mission and Israel's history in the historical books. So mission remains the meaning of Israel's history even when it is not the explicit focus of the narratives.

---

49. This is a very important theme for mission. God's people must always embody the good news of God's renewing work in the midst of peoples who live out of other idolatrous worldviews and serve other gods. If God's people are faithful there will always be a "missionary encounter" between the story of God's coming kingdom and the stories of these cultures.

50. This is the language of Lesslie Newbigin (e.g., *Foolishness to the Greeks*, 1).

A second observation is important: it is primarily in the Psalms and the prophetic books that the universal horizon of Israel's election and existence is unmistakably expressed. Israel's role and calling in the midst of the nations was constantly nourished by their liturgy. W. Creighton Marlowe calls the psalms the "music of missions."[51] The title of an essay by Mark Boda captures what I am saying: "Declare His Glory among the Nations: The Psalter as a Missional Collection."[52] George Peters counts over 175 universal references to the nations of the world in the book of Psalms, and says that "the Psalter is one of the greatest missionary books in the world, though seldom seen from that point of view."[53] It is hard to listen to Psalm 67 without a strong sense that Israel is blessed *so that* they might bring blessing to the nations.

> May God be gracious to us and bless us
> and make his face shine on us—
> *so that* your ways may be known on earth,
> your salvation among all nations.
> May all the peoples praise you, God;
> may all the peoples praise you. . . .
> May God bless us still,
> *so that* all the ends of the earth will fear him. (Ps 67:1–3, 7 TNIV)

This is far from an isolated reference. The psalms are rife with Israel's orientation to the nations: there are exhortations to Israel to sing of God's mighty deeds among the nations (Ps 9:11; 18:49; 96:2–3; 105:1); the psalmists lead Israel in responding to the exhortations with a personal commitment to sing among the nations (Ps 18:49; 57:9; 108:3); there are numerous summons to the nations to praise God (Ps 47:1; 66:8; 67:3; 96:7, 10; 100:1; 117:1); there are promises of a future in which the nations will join Israel in praise of the Lord (Ps 22:27; 66:4; 86:9).

The prophetic message regarding Israel's future also reveals a universal horizon and Israel's missional calling within it. As Israel fails in their missional calling, and their history slides increasingly downhill into rebellion, the prophets emerge on the scene. While their first message to Israel is to repent, they turn their attention to the future. Even if Israel fails, God will not fail in his mission to bring salvation to

---

51. Marlowe, "Music of Missions."
52. Boda, "Declare His Glory."
53. Peters, *Biblical Theology of Missions*, 116. See also Kaiser, *Mission in the Old Testament*, 29–38; Wright, *Mission of God*, 474–84; Legrand, *Unity and Plurality*, 15–18.

the nations. He will usher in a worldwide kingdom through a Messiah and by the Spirit. At that time he will regather and restore Israel (Ezek 36:24–27). *Then* the nations will know the Lord (Ezek 36:22–23). *Then* restored, regathered, and purified, Israel will fulfill their calling and be a light to the nations. There will be a "pilgrimage of the nations" to Jerusalem. Joachim Jeremias describes this eschatological pilgrimage of the Gentiles described by the prophets in terms of five features. First, God will reveal himself to the world (e.g., Isa 40:5). Second, this disclosure is accompanied by his Word, which summons the nations to acknowledge him (e.g., Isa 45:20–22). Third, the nations hear this summons and journey to Jerusalem, the mountain of the Lord (e.g., Isa 2:3; 19:23). Fourth, there the nations see the glory of God and worship him (e.g., Isa 66:18; Zeph 3:9); and finally, they join the people of God in a messianic banquet (Isa 25:6–8). Lohfink observes the role of Israel in all this:

> A decisive element of the prophetic conception of the pilgrimage of the nations to Zion is that the Gentiles, fascinated by the salvation visible in Israel, are driven of their own accord to the people of God. They do not become believers as a result of missionary activity; rather, the fascination emitted by the people of God draws them close. In this connection, the prophetic texts speak mostly of the radiant light which shines forth from Jerusalem.[54]

> See, darkness covers the earth
> and thick darkness is over the peoples,
> But the LORD rises upon you
> and his glory appears over you.
> Nations will come to your light,
> and kings to the brightness of your dawn. (Isa 60:2–3 TNIV)

> This is what the Lord Almighty says: "In those days ten people from all languages and nations will take firm hold of one Jew by the hem of his robe and say, 'Let us go with you, because we have heard that God is with you.'" (Zech 8:23 TNIV)

Thus, the prophets foresee that in the last days God's missional purpose in and through Israel will be fulfilled. The gathering of the nations to a regathered and purified Israel will be an eschatological event when the Messiah and the Spirit bring about the kingdom. Both the constant

---

54. Lohfink, *Jesus and Community*, 19.

refrain in the psalms and the vision of the prophets show that this is the way Israel understood their history. In fact, as Lohfink points out in his discussion of the pilgrimage of the nations in the prophets, this is the way that Jesus himself understood Israel's calling: "The conception of the pilgrimage of the nations demonstrates that Jesus saw the role of Israel in the universal horizon of Isaiah. Israel was not chosen for its own sake, but *as a sign of universal salvation* for all nations."[55]

GOD'S PEOPLE IN THE OLD TESTAMENT: ELEMENTS OF CONTINUITY

At this point, before proceeding with the conclusion of this story, it would be good for our purpose of sketching an ecclesiology to pause and summarize what we have learned about the people of God from our brief narrative. Again, the reason for this, as we shall see, is that there is a fundamental continuity between the people of God in the Old Testament and the people of God in the New Testament. We can note the following:

- Israel was a *chosen* people. Out of all the peoples on the earth God chose Abraham and Israel to be his treasured possession.
- Israel was a *redeemed* people. Israel was liberated from service to Pharaoh and the gods of Egypt to serve the living God with the whole of their lives.
- Israel was a *covenant* people. God bound Israel to himself in a covenant relationship in which God promised to be their God and they were pledged to be his people.
- Israel was to be a *holy* people. From the beginning God called his people to walk in his way, a way of justice and righteousness. God gave his people the *torah* to shape their lives according to his creational purposes. Much of Israel's history was bound up with God's work in their midst in their battle with idolatry.
- Israel was a people that knew God's *presence*. This meant that Israel enjoyed an ongoing relationship with God. It also meant a covenantally faithful response of love, faith, and obedience to their covenant Lord who lived in their midst. Further, Israel was to be a people who responded to God's presence in worship.

55. Ibid., 71.

What is important for the purposes of this paper is to recognize clearly the missional fabric into which each of these themes is woven. Indeed, to wrench any of them from their missional context of the biblical story would be to misunderstand them. Israel was *chosen* so that they might mediate God's salvific blessing to the nations. They were *redeemed* to serve the Lord alone so that their *holy* lives might display before the nations what a nation looks like when God dwells in their midst. Indeed, it would be the *presence* of God and the wisdom of the *torah* that would set Israel apart and make them an attractive model before the watching eyes of the nations (Deut 4:6–8). The *covenants* that God established with Abraham and with Israel at Sinai both had for their goal the salvation of the nations. Thus, Israel's role and identity was missional from the beginning, that is, their life was directed outward toward the nations.

These marks characterize the New Testament church as well. This must be unfolded in the rest of the story but already at this point we can note three things. First, by faith in Christ we are incorporated into the Abrahamic covenant (Gal 3:8–9; Acts 3:25–26). We become part of the people of God shaped by that covenant. Thus, we too are blessed along with Father Abraham but also called like him to be a blessing. Second, Paul's struggle with the relation of the new covenant people of God to Israel is instructive.[56] Especially helpful is his metaphor of ingrafting (Rom 11:17–21). Gentiles are ingrafted into an olive root. They become part of this ancient people and their story. And, finally, precisely the text (Exod 19:3–6) that we noted was probably the most programmatic statement regarding Israel's calling is now applied to the church with its full missional implications:

> But you are a chosen people, a royal priesthood, a holy nation, God's special possession, that you may declare the praises of him who called you out of darkness into his wonderful light. Once you were not a people, but now you are the people of God; once you had not received mercy, but now you have received mercy. . . . Live such good lives among the pagans that, though they accuse you of doing wrong, they may see your good deeds and glorify God on the day he visits us. (1 Pet 2:9–10, 12 TNIV)

Yet continuity is not the only word; there is discontinuity as well. God's people are transformed by the coming of the kingdom in Jesus and

---

56. Cf. Ibid., 80–81.

his Spirit. And when we take up this next chapter in the story we see that the missional character of God's people is intensified.

JESUS, THE KINGDOM, AND THE PEOPLE OF GOD

When Jesus steps onto the public stage of history, he announces that the end-time kingdom has arrived (Mark 1:15). His announcement is nothing less than this: God is breaking into history and is now acting in the Messiah by the power of the Spirit to restore all of creation and all of human life to again live under the rule of God. God is becoming king again! The last days foreseen by the prophets have arrived.

The kingdom has already arrived in Jesus by the Spirit; but it has not yet fully come. It is in this intervening period between the advent of the kingdom and its final completion that gathering can take place. In the parable of the great banquet the "delay" between the announcement that the banquet is ready and its full enjoyment is taken up with gathering. Referring to this parable and others, Bavinck comments that "[A]ccording to the above parables such work consists particularly in going out into the highways and byways to invite all to the marriage feast of the king. One may say thus that the interim is preoccupied with the command of missions, and it is the command of missions that gives the interim meaning."[57]

The prophets had made clear in a variety of ways and in many places that with the dawning of the kingdom the Gentiles would be gathered in to the people of God.

> In the last days
> the mountain of the LORD's temple will be established
> as the highest of the mountains;
> it will be exalted above the hills,
> and all nations will stream to it.
> Many peoples will come and say,
> "Come, let us go to the mountain of the LORD,
> to the house of the God of Jacob.
> He will teach us his ways,
> so that we may walk in his paths." (Isa 2:2–3 TNIV)

Jesus affirmed this prophetic perspective throughout his ministry: "I say to you that many will come from the east and the west, and will

---

57. Bavinck, *Science of Missions*, 32.

take their places at the feast with Abraham, Isaac and Jacob in the kingdom of heaven" (Matt 8:11 TNIV). Yet, while affirming this ingathering of the nations, he limited his own mission and that of his disciples to the Jews: "I was sent only to the lost sheep of Israel" (Matt 15:24; cf. Matt 10:5–6). How are we to explain the seeming contradiction between Jesus' universal scope of all nations and his particular focus on Israel?

Jeremias has taken up this problem.[58] His conclusion is that Jesus fulfilled the message of the prophets. The pattern of God's plan must be observed. Since God had chosen Israel to be a light to the nations, and they had failed, then God's plan for the last days was first to regather and restore Israel, and then to draw the Gentiles into his covenant family. Jeremias says: "we have to do with two successive events, first the call to Israel, and subsequently the redemptive incorporation of the Gentiles into the kingdom of God."[59] Jeremias further concludes that there were two prior conditions that had to be fulfilled before God's call could go out to the Gentiles: the announcement and invitation of the good news of the kingdom to Israel, and Jesus' vicarious death on the cross.[60]

The first condition was to prepare Israel to carry out their role to draw the nations. For that to happen Israel must be regathered and renewed so that they might live in obedience to God's *torah* and shine as a light to the nations. Ezekiel offers a glimpse of both of these features—gathering and purifying—in God's eschatological future. Israel has failed in their mission and profaned the Lord's name among the nations (Ezek 37:16–21). However, God says to Israel that he will act so that the nations will know that he is the Lord when he is "proved holy *through you* before their eyes" (Ezek 37:22–23). Thus God will act to complete his mission through Israel:

> For I will take you out of the nations; I will gather you from all the countries and bring you back into your own land. I will sprinkle clean water on you, and you will be clean; I will cleanse you from all your impurities and from all your idols. I will give you a new heart and put a new spirit in you; I will remove from you your heart of stone and give you a heart of flesh. And I will

---

58. Jeremias, *Jesus' Promise*.

59. Ibid., 71.

60. Ibid., 71–73. Blauw speaks in a similar vein. Two events must happen before the nations are gathered: (1) the salvation of the kingdom must first be offered to Israel and (2) the blood of the true Passover lamb must be shed (Blauw, *Missionary Nature of the Church*, 71).

put my Spirit in you and move you to follow my decrees and be careful to keep my laws. (Ezek 36:24–27)

Jesus' task, then, is in keeping with "the historic context of revelation" that begins with the conversion of the Jews.[61] In keeping with Ezekiel's imagery of a shepherd gathering his lost sheep (Ezek 34:23–34), Jesus begins to assemble the lost sheep and tribes of Israel, forming them into a little flock to whom he will give the kingdom (Luke 12:32). Against this background, when Jesus appoints his twelve this must be seen as a *"symbolic prophetic action"*[62] of the beginning of the new Israel (Mark 3:13–19). N. T. Wright comments:

> The very existence of the twelve speaks, of course, of the reconstitution of Israel; Israel had not had twelve visible tribes since the Assyrian invasion of 734 BC, and for Jesus to give twelve followers a place of prominence, let alone to make comments about them sitting on thrones judging the twelve tribes, indicates pretty clearly that he was thinking in terms of the eschatological restoration of Israel.[63]

This renewed Israel begins to take part in Jesus' mission of gathering the lost sheep of Israel (Mark 3:14; Matthew 10). Jesus applies to this renewed Israel Old Testament images that portray Israel's mission. Especially significant are Jesus' words in the Sermon on the Mount. Jesus says to the disciples: "You are the light of the world. A city on a hill cannot be hidden. Neither do people light a lamp and put it under a bowl. Instead they put it on its stand, and it gives light to everyone in the house. In the same way, let your light shine before others, that they may see your good deeds and glorify your Father in heaven" (Matt 5:14–16 TNIV). Together, the images of light and city refer to "the eschatological Jerusalem, which the prophets foretell will one day be raised above all mountains and illumine the nations with its light (cf. Isa 2:2–5)."[64] The Torah goes forth from Zion and the disciples' mission can only be effective through their good deeds if they build their lives upon the rock

---

61 Blauw, *Missionary Nature of the Church*, 68; DeRidder, *Discipling the Nations*, 146–55.

62 Lohfink, *Jesus and Community*, 10. Emphasis his.

63. Wright, *Jesus and the Victory of God*, 300.

64. Lohfink, *Jesus and Community*, 65.

foundation of Jesus' teaching (Matt 7:24–27). In the mission of Jesus, Israel is being restored to be a light to the nations.

This gives us the proper perspective on the kingdom mission of Jesus. His gathering and formation of a restored community, the (re)new(ed) Israel is a sign that the kingdom has arrived. Rudolf Schnackenburg rightly says that "the company gathered around Jesus the Messias is just as much a sign of the powerful presence of God's reign as his word and deeds, the forgiveness of sins, his expulsions of devils and the cures."[65]

Before Gentiles can be gathered in to this community three events must take place: Jesus must pour out his blood for many for the forgiveness of sins (Matt 26:28);[66] Jesus must rise from the dead inaugurating the age to come; and Jesus must pour out his Spirit to give this newly gathered Israel the life of the kingdom (Luke 24:49; cf. Ezek 36:26). These central events constitute the hinge of history.[67] With the death of Christ the old age dominated by sin, death, and Satanic power has been defeated and its dominion has come to an end. With the resurrection of Christ the age to come promised by the prophets has arrived. The outpouring of the Spirit gives his people a share in this new creation. By these events regathered Israel is renewed Israel.[68] To employ the language of Ezekiel, Israel has been gathered, cleansed, and given a new heart and Spirit. They are now ready to continue the gathering process that Jesus initiated: first, the rest of the Israelite nation (to the Jew first) and then the Gentiles.

The Gospels end with the commissioning of this new Israel to their task of gathering in the nations. Perhaps Matt 28:18–20 is the best known since it has been at the center of the Western missionary enterprise since the eighteenth century. It has been interpreted primarily as a command to go applied to missionaries, yet it is fundamentally an ecclesiological statement. In it the identity of this new Israel is given. They are a people who are now sent to all nations to continue the gathering process in this

---

65. Schnackenburg, *God's Rule and Kingdom*, 223.

66. See Jeremias, *Eucharistic Words*, 123–25, 148–52, for the meaning of *polloi* (many) as a great multitude from the nations.

67. This image is employed a number of times by Lesslie Newbigin. See, for example, *Open Secret*, 50, and "Hinge of History."

68. This reconstitution of the nucleus of the New Israel in the Twelve also assumes God's severe judgment on Jews who refused be gathered. It now becomes this regathered community, along with those who are added to it, that become the new body employed by God in his missional purposes.

interim period. John 20:21 gives us a similar statement. This nucleus of the new Israel is sent to continue the mission that Jesus has begun: "As the Father has sent me, I am sending you."

THE CHURCH AFTER PENTECOST

The "delay" of God's judgment and the final completion of the number of guests in the banquet of the kingdom continue. The already-not-yet period of the kingdom remains the era in which we live; and, as Newbigin has noted so strongly:

> The meaning of this "overlap of the ages" in which we live, the time between the coming of Christ and His coming again, is that it is the time given for the witness of the apostolic Church to the ends of the earth. The end of all things, which has been revealed in Christ, is—so to say—held back until witness has been borne to the whole world concerning the judgment and salvation revealed in Christ. The implication of a true eschatological perspective will be missionary obedience, and the eschatology which does not issue in such obedience is a false eschatology.[69]

This newly gathered Israel remained at first in Jerusalem; they were a Jewish community that began the gathering of Jews into the newly constituted Israel. Acts 2:42–47 gives us a picture of this community in mission after Pentecost. They are a people committed to four things that will enable them to more and more take hold of the life of the kingdom—the apostles' teaching, fellowship, breaking of bread, and prayer (Acts 2:42). As such they are an attractive community, a light shining in the midst of Jerusalem (Acts 2:43–47). Their lives of compassion, justice, joy, worship, and power emit a radiant light and "the Lord added to their number daily those who were being saved" (Acts 2:47).

However, it would take persecution to send this community beyond Jerusalem. Perhaps they still thought in terms of the prophets' words that the nations would stream to Jerusalem. In any case, persecution drove them far afield, yet still spreading the gospel among the Jews (Acts 8:1, 4; 11:19). But in Antioch a new thing began to take place, and a new kind of community was formed. The good news was preached to the Greeks, and a community was formed made up of both Jews and Gentiles (Acts 11:19–21). While the description of this church mirrors

---

69. Newbigin, *Household of God*, 153.

Jerusalem, a new thing was taking place. The Spirit moved that church to set aside Barnabas and Saul to travel throughout the Roman Empire planting new communities that embodied the light of the gospel in the midst of the nations (Acts 13:1–3). This disturbed the eschatological expectations of the Jewish church in Jerusalem but the concern was settled at a council in Jerusalem when the words of the prophets concerning the gathering of Gentiles were invoked (Acts 15:12–19).

The planting of new communities and the gathering of Jews first and then Gentiles into these communities continues throughout the rest of the story Luke tells in Acts. It ends on a rather abrupt note. The inconclusive ending is a literary strategy of Luke to invite the reader into the story[70]—to repent and believe in Jesus, and to become part of this growing worldwide community called to embody and announce the good news of the kingdom.

THE CHURCH IN THE NEW TESTAMENT: ELEMENTS OF DISCONTINUITY

This brief narrative enables us to approach the question: "What is new about the New Testament church?" The fundamental continuity is clear. The nucleus of the community that Jesus formed is Israel regathered and purified. Gentiles are engrafted into this community. Thus, the New Testament church shares the missional calling of the Old Testament people of God. Nevertheless, with the coming of Jesus and the outpouring of his Spirit something new has emerged in history.

The fundamental difference is *eschatological*. In Jesus and the Spirit, the end-time kingdom, the last days, the age to come, the new creation, resurrection life, has arrived. This means, first of all, that each of the characteristics of Old Testament Israel has been transformed. The church is an elect people but they are chosen in Christ (Eph 1:4). We are a redeemed people but redeemed not by the mighty act of the Exodus but the much mightier act of the cross (1 Pet 1:18–19). We are a holy people but now the Spirit enables us to live in obedience to the *torah* (Rom 8:3–4). The church is a covenant people but are bound to God in the new covenant in Christ's blood (Luke 22:20). We are a people in whom God dwells now with the intimate presence of Christ's Spirit

---

70. Bauckham, *Bible and Mission*, 24; Johnson, *Acts*, 476.

(1 Cor 3:16). Each of these is fulfilled, yet the missional implications of each remains.

The new eschatological era has at least three further significant implications for the people of God after Pentecost. First, God's people now experience the end-time salvation of the kingdom, the resurrection life of the new creation. Since the Spirit has been given, the people of God have been given a foretaste of the renewal of human life and creation that is coming at the end of history. As such they are previews of that future salvation. Various images of the church in the New Testament point to the church as being the new humanity (Eph 2:10–17) that participates in the new creation (2 Cor 5:17) and exhibits the new life of the future in the present (Eph 4:22–24; Col 3:9–11; Rom 6:4–6). The church is the firstfruits of the final harvest of the kingdom of God (Jas 1:18), and the eschatological people of the second Adam (Rom 5:12–21).[71]

The second eschatological implication is concerned with our place in the story. This time is a time of the gathering of Israel and then the nations to the ends of the earth. The gathering of a community to share in the salvation of the kingdom is an eschatological event: "And this gospel of the kingdom will be preached in the whole world as a testimony to all nations, and then the end will come" (Matt 24:14). It has been well emphasized above that the already-not-yet era of the kingdom is a time characterized by mission, specifically the gathering of all nations into the kingdom community. On the one hand, the centripetal movement that characterized Israel remains. The church is to be an attractive community that embodies the end-time salvation. Yet there is a new centrifugal element. The people of God are now sent to live among the nations.

Closely connected to this, the *form* of the new covenant people of God is new. God's people are now a non-geographical and non-ethnic community that lives in the midst of all nations. God's people now live as a light in the midst of all the peoples of the earth. This creates a much more difficult prospect for the mission of God's people than in the Old Testament. In the Old Testament, Israel lived as a nation with their own story, their own culture, their own social institutions, all shaped by God's word. The nations around them posed an external threat that was, sadly, too often taken into the bosom of their culture. However, the church must live as members and participants of the cultures that are formed by a different story. A missionary encounter in which God's people live

---

71. Minear, *Images of the Church*, 105–35; Driver, *Images of the Church*, 83–123.

in an alternative way or counter to the idolatrous ways of their culture is a much more difficult and complex calling. The church now lives in constant tension as it embodies the life of the kingdom in the midst of nations where idolatry reigns.[72]

Each of these characteristics intensifies the missional nature of the people of God. The end has been revealed and accomplished by Jesus, and thus the church in the power of the Spirit is empowered to make God known in ways Old Testament Israel could not. The already-not-yet era of the kingdom is distinguished precisely by the gathering of all peoples to Christ. The non-geographical and non-ethnic form of God's people renders them suitable precisely for this task. The church is missional by its very nature; its identity and role in God's mission is to make known God's salvation. As Newbigin puts it, "'As the Father has sent me, so I send you' defines the very being of the Church as mission. In this sense everything that the Church is and does can be and should be part of mission."[73]

The images of the church in the New Testament further explicate the continuity and discontinuity between the church and Israel.[74] Most of the images of the church employed in the New Testament are either borrowed from the Old Testament or indicate the newness of what has come in Christ and by the Spirit. All these images, then, to use Driver's term, are "images of the church in mission."[75] Similarly, Newbigin is correct in his observation concerning these ecclesial images: "Without mission, the Church simply falls to the ground. We must say bluntly that

---

72. John Driver develops this theme in his book showing that this kind of missionary encounter was essential to the New Testament church as seen in the images it employs for its own self-understanding. The church is a "contrast-society set in the midst of the nations as a sign of God's saving purpose for all peoples" (*Images of the Church*, 33).

73. Newbigin, "Bishop," 242.

74. The classic work on this subject is Minear, *Images of the Church*. There, he discusses 96 New Testament images. For a summary of those 96 images see *Images of the Church*, 268–69.

75. "*The church, by the very nature of its calling, must be in mission.* According to Minear, the church is the human community that experiences and communicates the saving intention of God. Often this vital sense of identity, inspired by the biblical images, is missing; then the church's vision dries up, its missional activity is deformed, and it falls short of following God's saving purpose for all creation" (Driver, *Images of the Church*, 12).

when the Church ceases to be a mission, then she ceases to have any right to the titles by which she is adorned in the New Testament."[76]

CONCLUSION

Archbishop William Temple is often quoted as saying that "the church is the only society that exists for the benefit of those who are not its members." Indeed, the church's mission to the world defines the role they play in the biblical story. We might try to capture what has been said in one phrase—new Israel. The church is the continuation of *Israel* and their mission to be a light to the nations. They are chosen, redeemed, bound in covenant, instructed in the way of life, and indwelt by God to live an exemplary existence before the watching eyes of the world, and to make known in life, word, and deed the good news that God is renewing the creation. But the church is the *new* Israel: in Christ and the Spirit God has broken into history and powers of the future age are flowing into history. The church is that people who have begun to taste of that resurrection life, and in this era are charged with the task of making it known in communities set in every nation of the world. It is this mission that defines the church's very existence.

BIBLIOGRAPHY

Barth, Karl. *Church Dogmatics*. Vol. 4. *The Doctrine of Reconciliation*. Edited by G. W. Bromiley and T. F. Torrance. 4 vols. Edinburgh: T. & T. Clark, 1961.

Bauckham, Richard. *Bible and Mission: Christian Witness in a Postmodern World*. Grand Rapids: Baker, 2003.

Bavinck, J. H. *An Introduction to the Science of Missions*. Translated by David Hugh Freeman. Phillipsburg, NJ: Presbyterian and Reformed, 1979.

Berkhof, Hendrikus. *Christian Faith: An Introduction to the Study of Faith*. Translated by Sierd Woudstra. Grand Rapids: Eerdmans, 1976.

Blauw, Johannes. "The Mission of the People of God." In *The Missionary Church in East and West*, edited by Charles C. West and David M. Paton, 91–100. London: SCM, 1959.

———. *Missionary Nature of the Church: A Survey of the Biblical Theology of Mission*. New York: McGraw-Hill, 1962.

Boda, Mark. "'Declare His Glory among the Nations': The Psalter as a Missional Collection." In *Christian Mission: Old Testament Foundations and New Testament Developments*, edited by Stanley E. Porter and Cynthia Long Westfall, 13–41. MNTS. Eugene, OR: Wipf & Stock, 2010.

Braaten, Carl E. *The Flaming Center: A Theology of the Christian Mission*. Philadelphia: Fortress, 1977.

---

76. Newbigin, *Household of God*, 163.

Brunner, Emil. *The Word and the World*. London: SCM, 1931.
Christensen, Duane L. "Nations." In *ABD*, edited by David Noel Freedman et al., 4:1037–49. 6 vols. New York: Doubleday: 1992.
Craigie, Peter C. *The Book of Deuteronomy*. NICOT. Grand Rapids: Eerdmans, 1976.
Curtis, Edward Mason. "Man as the Image of God in Genesis in the Light of Ancient Near Eastern Parallels." PhD diss., University of Pennsylvania, 1984.
DeRidder, Richard R. *Discipling the Nations*. Grand Rapids: Baker, 1971.
Driver, John. *Images of the Church in Mission*. Scottsdale, PA: Herald, 1997.
Dumbrell, William J. *Covenant and Creation: A Theology of Old Testament Covenants*. Nashville: Nelson, 1984.
―――. "The Prospect of the Unconditionality of the Sinaitic Covenant." In *Israel's Apostasy and Restoration: Essays in Honor of Roland K. Harrison*, edited by A. Gileadi, 141–55. Grand Rapids: Baker, 1988.
Durham, John I. *Exodus*. WBC 3. Waco, TX: Word, 1987.
Frankfort, Henri. *Kingship and the Gods: A Study of Ancient Near Eastern Religion as the Integration of Society and Nature*. Chicago: University of Chicago Press, 1948.
Fretheim, Terence E. "'Because the Whole Earth Is Mine': Theme and Narrative in Exodus." *Int* 50 (1996) 229–39.
Goheen, Michael W. "The Urgency of Reading the Bible as One Story." *ThTo* 64 (2008) 469–83.
Hedlund, Roger E. *The Mission of the Church in the World: A Biblical Theology*. Grand Rapids: Baker, 1991.
Jeremias, Joachim. *The Eucharistic Words of Jesus*. Translated by Arnold Ehrhardt. Philadelphia: Fortress, 1977.
―――. *Jesus' Promise to the Nations*. Translated by S. H. Hooke. London: SCM, 1958.
Johnson, Luke. *The Acts of the Apostles*. Collegeville, MN: Liturgical, 1992.
Kaiser, Walter C. *Mission in the Old Testament: Israel as a Light to the Nations*. Grand Rapids: Baker, 2000.
Legrand, Lucien. *Unity and Plurality: Mission in the Bible*. Translated by Robert R. Barr. Maryknoll, NY: Orbis, 1990.
Lohfink, Gerhard. *Jesus and Community: The Social Dimension of the Christian Faith*. Translated by John P. Galvin. Philadelphia: Fortress, 1984.
Magonet, Jonathan. "The Rhetoric of God: Exodus 6.2–8." *JSOT* 27 (1983) 56–67.
Marlowe, W. Creighton. "Music of Missions: Themes of Cross-Cultural Outreach in the Psalms." *Miss* 26 (1998) 445–56.
Martin-Achard, Robert. *A Light to the Nations: A Study of the Old Testament Conception of Israel's Mission to the World*. Translated by John Penney Smith. Edinburgh: Oliver & Boyd, 1962.
Mendenhall, George E. "Ancient Oriental and Biblical Law." *BA* 17 (1954) 26–46.
―――. "Covenant Forms in Israelite Tradition." *BA* 17 (1954) 50–76.
Middleton, J. Richard. *The Liberating Image: The Imago Dei in Genesis 1*. Grand Rapids: Brazos, 2005.
Minear, Paul S. *Images of the Church in the New Testament*. Philadelphia: Westminster, 1960.
Moltmann, Jürgen. *The Church in the Power of the Spirit: A Contribution to Messianic Ecclesiology*. Translated by Margaret Kohl. Minneapolis: Fortress, 1977.
Newbigin, Lesslie. "The Bishop and the Ministry of Mission." In *Today's Church and Today's World*, edited by J. Howe, 242–47. London: CIO, 1977.

———. *Foolishness to the Greeks: The Gospel and Western Culture*. Grand Rapids: Eerdmans, 1986.

———. "The Hinge of History." *Lutheran Standard* (1967) 10–11.

———. *Household of God: Lectures on the Nature of the Church*. New York: Friendship, 1954.

———. *The Open Secret: An Introduction to the Theology of Mission*. Rev. ed. Grand Rapids: Eerdmans, 1995.

Peters, George W. *A Biblical Theology of Missions*. Chicago: Moody, 1972.

Power, John. *Mission Theology Today*. Maryknoll, NY: Orbis, 1971.

Proksch, Otto. "λύω." In *Theological Dictionary of the New Testament*, edited by G. Kittel, 4:328–35. 10 vols. Grand Rapids: Eerdmans, 1967.

Schnackenburg, Rudolf. *God's Rule and Kingdom*. Translated by John Murray. New York: Herder & Herder, 1963.

Shenk, Wilbert. "Foreword." In *Images of the Church in Mission*, by John Driver, 8–10. Scottsdale, PA: Herald, 1997.

von Rad, Gerhard. *Old Testament Theology: The Theology of Israel's Historical Traditions*. Old Testament Library. Translated by D. M. G. Stalker. Louisville: Westminster John Knox, 2001.

Wells, Jo Bailey. *God's Holy People: A Theme in Biblical Theology*. Sheffield: Sheffield Academic, 2000.

Williamson, Paul R. "Covenant." In *Dictionary of the Old Testament Pentateuch*, edited by T. Desmond Alexander and David W. Baker, 139–55. Downers Grove, IL: InterVarsity, 2003.

Wolff, Hans Walter. "The Kerygma of the Yahwist." Translated by Wilbur A. Benware. *Int* 20 (1966) 131–58.

Wright, Christopher J. H. *The Mission of God: Unlocking the Bible's Grand Narrative*. Downers Grove: InterVarsity, 2006.

———. "Old Testament Perspectives on Mission." In *Dictionary of Mission Theology: Evangelical Foundations*, edited by John Corrie, 269–73. Downers Grove, IL: InterVarsity, 2007.

Wright, N. T. *Jesus and the Victory of God*. Christian Origins and the Question of God 2. Minneapolis: Fortress, 1996.

9

Reflections on the Church *Then* and *Now*

Steven M. Studebaker

INTRODUCTION

THE ESSAYS INCLUDED IN this volume interact with biblical, historical, and contemporary issues of ecclesiology from both scholarly and practical perspectives. The benefit of this approach is a multi-faceted and multi-disciplinary discussion of ecclesiology. This is significant because biblical and theological scholars and ministry practitioners often operate safely insulated from one another. Specialization within the respective disciplines of academic biblical and theological studies and practical and pastoral theology is important. However, efforts to build bridges between these disciplines so that they might engage in mutually enriching dialogue are equally important. With these considerations in mind, my concluding essay seeks to accomplish three tasks. First, it recaps the salient features of the earlier essays in this volume. Second, it engages in preliminary analysis of certain aspects of the preceding essays. Finally, it endeavors to draw the contributions into critical and constructive interaction. Given the number of essays and limited space available, a thorough investigation of each essay is impossible. Nevertheless, the key contributions of each essay and some of the interrelationships between essays can be probed.[1]

---

1. Please note that the following interaction was originally based on the version of the papers presented at the 2008 Bingham Colloquium at McMaster Divinity College and may not take into account all revisions of the essays submitted for publication.

REFLECTIONS ON THE CHURCH THEN

Knowles: The Least, the Lost, and the Last

Knowles begins by highlighting the problem facing the person who wants to use the Gospels for ecclesiology. The problem is, how do we discern the ways the Gospels inform our understanding of the church? Except on rare occasions, the Gospels do not even refer to the church. The solution Knowles proposes to this apparent impasse is that it seems plausible to take Jesus and the twelve disciples as a normative example of what the Gospels expect the church to be like. In other words, the Gospels can inform ecclesiology because the "continuities" and "contiguities" of the Gospels display the historical and theological characteristics of the first-century church (i.e., the "continuities" and "contiguities" of the Gospels are a window to the *Sitz im Leben* of the early church). Thus, Knowles seeks to characterize the first-century church in terms of the patterns of behavior and thought that the Gospels promote through their stories and teachings of Jesus and his disciples.

Knowles identifies five characteristics of the church that the Gospels share in common. First, the early Christians were known by their association with Jesus; they were followers of Jesus; they performed their activities in the "name" of Christ. Bearing his name meant to do and to face the same range of experiences, both good and bad, as he did. These activities and experiences included prayer, welcoming others, preaching the gospel, casting out demons, and, more negatively, accepting a call to forsake family and friends, to be hated, and to face persecution. Knowles calls this the "christomorphic" nature of the church.

The second important characteristic of the early church was its kinship with Christ and the Father. The early Christians, like Jesus, refer to God as "Abba Father." They also have a sense of familial familiarity, on the one hand, with Jesus, as they would have with their siblings, and, on the other hand, with the Father, as they would have with their parents. Yet, as Knowles reminds us, inclusion in the family of Jesus' Father often leads to exclusion and separation from our blood fathers and their families. As Jesus warned his disciples,

> I have come to set a man against his father, and a daughter against her mother, and a daughter-in-law against her mother-in-law; and one's foes will be members of one's own household. Whoever loves father or mother more than me is not worthy of me; and

whoever loves son or daughter more than me is not worthy of me. (Q 12:52–53; 14:26; Matt 10:33–39)[2]

Even if discipleship rarely took on this radical demand, the bar is nonetheless set high for a familial tie with the heavenly Father that surpasses all other ties.

Third, the issue of the church's boundary markers and its posture of inclusion and exclusion is paradoxical. On the one hand, the boundaries are clear—"Whoever is not with me is against me, and whoever does not gather with me scatters" (Q 11:23; Matt 12:30). On the other hand, the boundaries are less clear—"Whoever is not against us is for us" (Mark 9:40; and similarly Luke 9:50). Moreover, as Knowles points out, the Parable of the Good Samaritan "advocates radical 'compassion' (Luke 10:33), expressed in the form of hospitality towards ethnic rivals and religious enemies."[3] Thus, radical devotion to Christ, which takes concrete form in the imitation of his life, marks the church. However, there is a paradox. The behaviors, especially of those imitating his mercy and forgiveness, serve as the clearest boundary markers of the church. But they do not lead to the exclusion and alienation of others who are not part of the church, but to the inclusion or, at the least, to the invitation of others to become members of the community of Christ.

Fourth, the constituency of the church was "the least, the lost, and the last" of first-century Mediterranean society. According to the Gospels, the focus of Jesus' ministry was the socially marginalized and stigmatized; he was interested in the least and not the most productive, powerful, and influential. He also sought the lost: the sinners, the poor, and the sick. Moreover, membership in the church does not mean the least are now the most, the lost are now the found, and the last are now the first. Rather, Christians remain the least, the lost, and the last. The cross, the most well-known and illustrative symbol of Christian identity, is also its most ironic. Jesus proclaims, "whoever does not take up their cross and follow me is not worthy of me" (Matt 10:38; Luke 14:27). The irony is that what makes one "worthy" to bear his name is what makes one most unworthy and loathsome in the first-century Mediterranean culture. Jesus came to save the least, the lost, and the last; and his follow-

---

2. As in Knowles's paper, "Q 12:52–53," etc., designates putative Q material via Lukan verse numbering.

3. Knowles, "Least, Lost, and Last," 22.

ers become the least, the lost, and the last as they take up their crosses and follow him.

Furthermore, Jesus not only saves those who are considered the least, the lost, and the last in their cultural context, but he calls them to continue to be last in his kingdom. Yet, he does not ask them to do so in a way that replicates the domineering and stultifying hierarchy of their society, but in a way that rejects it. Christians are the "last" primarily because they become humble servants ("slaves") of others and then because they associate with the fringe elements of society. Knowles points out that Jesus' call to be "last" was a drastic inversion of first-century social custom. It is no less drastic today. After all, who wants to be "last" and to be a servant or a "slave"? Certainly we laud such piety when we see it and heartily affirm it in the proper pious contexts, but its scarcity among us belies our confessed interest in such imitation of Christ.

The fifth characteristic of the church is its shared rituals of baptism, footwashing, holy kiss, and Lord's Supper. The rituals of the church perform two important functions in its life. They dramatize the ethos of Jesus' life and teaching and, as people participate in them, they become ways to embody Jesus' life and teachings. Knowles notes that footwashing was an activity reserved for the lowliest slave. The ritual of footwashing may have been, along with baptism, part of the initiation of new Christians into the church. As such, it had meaning for both participants. The church members who washed the feet of new members became the "least" and the "last" by humbling themselves to wash the feet of the least and the last. Moreover, the new members who had their feet washed dramatically displayed their status as the least, the lost, and the last by acknowledging their need for cleansing.

Knowles also points out that public kissing was socially inappropriate in respectable Jewish and Greco-Roman first-century culture. Conversely, it seems to have been practiced more commonly by the lower classes. Perhaps it is a first-century counterpart to "y'all" in a northern USA context today. Although "y'all" is an appropriate part of a greeting across social strata in the southern regions of the United States, in the northern states, and I suspect in Canada too, it instantly invites unflattering appellations, such as "hick," "redneck," and "country bumpkin." Similarly, the holy kiss may have functioned as an intentional way for the early Christians to signal to one another their shared social debasement and identity as one of Christ's least, lost, and last, much the way a southerner saying "how y'all doin'" in a northern social context signals to other southerners present, "I am one of you," at the risk of similar social embarrassment.

Porter: Saints and Sinners

Stanley Porter engages in a description of Pauline ecclesiology. Based on the Pauline Epistles he presents eight characteristics of Paul's vision of the church. According to Porter, the Pauline church is: (1) a confessing community; (2) a faith community; (3) a local and universal community; (4) an egalitarian community; (5) a community that maintains practices of worship—baptism, Lord's Supper, and public worship; (6) a community that is charismatic in its organization; (7) a community that demands ethical behavior; and (8) an evangelistic and eschatological community. Porter's description of the Pauline church invites several areas of comment and correlation with the contemporary church.

First, Porter's presentation of Pauline ecclesiology raises the issue of the exclusive and inclusive nature of the church. As a confessing and thus exclusive community, the church, or better, the people who comprise the church, confess that Jesus is Lord. The confession of Jesus as Lord is a confession by individuals empowered by the Holy Spirit. It entails belief in God; the fact that Jesus is identical with Yahweh of the Old Testament; that he was resurrected from the dead; that he was God incarnate; and that he will preside over the climactic end of world history.

Porter also notes that the Pauline church's identity as a confessing community has an implication for the way we understand the inclusion of unbelievers in the church. Contemporary churches often encourage believers to invite unbelieving friends to attend services and organize events with the specific intention of drawing in unbelievers. Porter's characterization of the Pauline church as a confessing community calls that practice into question. It suggests that for Paul, the church is not a clearinghouse of belief and unbelief, but a community characterized by a decisive, clear, and committed confession that Jesus is Lord and lifestyle consistent with that confession. The confession of Jesus as Lord, therefore, signals the exclusive nature of the church. The church includes all those who confess Jesus as Lord, but none of those who do not.

Yet, the inclusive activity of the church supplements its exclusive posture. Although the church is a community that is exclusive in the sense that it consists of people who confess Jesus as Lord and embrace patterns of life consistent with that confession, the church also has an inclusive mission. The church seeks to draw others into its community of faith through the proclamation of the gospel of Jesus Christ in light of its faith in Christ's return that will consummate the age. Thus, the evangelistic and eschatological character of the church invites the unbeliever to become one who confesses Jesus as Lord and thereby is included in the community of the church.

The challenge for contemporary ministry leaders is to negotiate the programmatic terrain between activities and ministries of the church that are more or less oriented toward those who have confessed Jesus as Lord and activities that seek to invite non-believers to become confessors of Jesus as Lord. In short, which activities have club members and which have non-members in mind? Are ministries that seek to address both groups appropriate from the perspective of Pauline ecclesiology, such as the seeker-service or small groups that seek both to nurture the saints and to attract the sinners?

Second, Pauline ecclesiology relates to the perennial issue of equitable social relations. Porter highlights Paul's egalitarian vision for the church: the church is a community of equals. The church is a group of people bound together on the basis of their common confession of Jesus as Lord and participation in the grace of Christ. Porter specifies, "Within the church, Paul does not see any distinction on the basis of criteria such as race, socio-economic standing, or gender."[4] However, he also warns that Paul's radical vision for equality is primarily ecclesial. Paul was not promoting a broader social agenda for what we might call in our time civil rights. Yet at the same time, Paul's ecclesial egalitarianism does not admit the neat compartmentalization reflected in some contemporary notions of the separation of church and state and private and public spheres of life. For example, Paul expects Philemon to receive Onesimus (who was Philemon's delinquent slave) as a brother in the Lord. Paul's admonition to Philemon is quite countercultural to the inequitable social hierarchy of his day. Thus, without calling for social revolution and agitation, Paul nonetheless expects that Philemon's experience of the grace of Jesus Christ will lead him to extend the principles of ecclesial equality to his broader and non-ecclesial social relations (also, for example, see the household codes of Col 3:18–4:4 and Eph 5:21–6:9 that

---

4. Porter, "Saints and Sinners," 52.

urge believers not to show partiality, in contrast to the social norm of partiality in the first-century Roman world).

The contemporary church should follow Paul's egalitarian ethos. However, the church can find it easy to adopt the same hierarchical schemes for valuing human life and effort as the capitalist and consumer culture of North America. We prize ministry leaders who can achieve maximal growth and community impact, which is the ecclesial version of our culture's fixation on profit and production. Denominations make strategic plans to target middle-class urban and suburban communities for church plants because these communities have the shiny happy people who will have the shiny coins to fund ever increasing visions of denominational expansion and market share. Yet Paul's vision of an egalitarian and impartial church might recommend alternative strategies, perhaps ones in which the church becomes the community of "the least, the lost, and the last" so that it might become the community for "the least, the lost, and the last."

Third, Paul's demand for ethical behavior within the church is as challenging now as it was then. The church is a community of people who have confessed Jesus as Lord and *repented* of their sins, but not a community of people who have confessed Jesus as Lord and *continued* in their sins. The problem arises in the implementation of the expectations of ecclesial holiness. Which sins warrant exclusion from the church, or which sins call for giving someone the right foot rather than the right hand of fellowship? Often, at least in my experience, the church concentrates on trivial sins such as smoking, movie ratings, and certain FM stations. It overlooks severe sins such as gossiping, slander (whoops, we euphemize these activities as sharing "prayer requests"), malice, "discord, jealousy, fits of rage, selfish ambition, dissensions, factions and envy"—if you have not recently witnessed the latter traits, just attend the next board meeting of your church (Eph 5:19–20; Col 3:5–11). The challenge facing church leadership is to discern what sins are so bad that they call for what is in effect the Pauline ban. Where do we draw the line? Should unmarried teenagers and young adults who are occasionally sexually active be allowed to remain in the church and only those who are so on a regular basis be excluded? Should business people who routinely underpay their employees for the sake of personal profit (i.e., greed and selfish ambition) be allowed to remain in the church because their contributions are important for the church's bottom line and next building project? At any rate, one sure sign of being a New Testament church is the need to sort out "sin in the camp."

Westfall: The Church and the Synagogue:
Continuity and Discontinuity

Cynthia Long Westfall details the changing understanding of the relationship of early Jewish Christians with first-century Judaism on the one hand and with Gentile-Christian communities on the other hand. New Testament scholarship has often and anachronistically interpreted the first-century synagogue in terms of the fourth-century rabbinic synagogue. Westfall shows that scholars now believe that the relationship between early Christianity and Judaism was closer than earlier scholars often assumed. The Gentile churches established by Paul and often taken as the normative and dominant model of early Christian ecclesiology were a later development, stemming from Paul's "frontier missions," and distinct from the earlier and well established Jewish Christian church in Jerusalem. Moreover, whereas Paul's mission churches are sometimes characterized as having a tenuous relationship with the Jewish synagogue, the Jeruslaem church and its offshoots retained a strong connection to the Jewish temple, synagogues, and rituals in Jerusalem. Thus, a tension, or at the least differences, existed in primitive Christianity, with varying degrees of continuity and discontinuity vis-à-vis the relationship between Jewish Christianity and Gentile Christianity and their respective relationships to Judaism. Westfall's presentation focuses on Jewish Christianity and she presents the case that the early Jewish Christians not only perceived themselves in a theological sense as standing in continuity with Israel as the people of God, but also saw themselves as standing in a significant level of continuity with the concrete practices and institutions of first-century Judaism.

Westfall's contribution relates most directly to Cavey and Carrington-Phillips's case for the house church. Westfall's argument that the church in Jerusalem was a center of early Christianity and that it was primarily a form of Christianity with close ties to the Jewish community and the Jewish synagogue questions Cavey and Carrington-Phillips's assumption that the house church was the normative model of ecclesiology in the New Testament. For example, Westfall points out that the practice of a sacred meal in the home of Christians was a practice the early Christians adapted from Judaism. The early Christians' unique practices vis-à-vis Judaism, rather than a distinct ecclesiology, necessitated their meeting in homes for the meal rather than in the "*triclinium* (a formal dining room in a Roman building) built into the synagogue."[5] The conflict between the Christians and the synagogue, portrayed for example in Revelation, originated with the Jews and not the Christians. The motivations for the Jewish disassociation from the Christian movement included their theological problem with Christian Christology and political expediency, since the Roman government increasingly associated Christianity with "atheism" and civil rebellion. The early Christians likely did not separate from the synagogue for theological and ecclesiastical reasons, but because they were forced out by the Jewish community. Westfall usefully illustrates the relationship between Jewish Christianity and Judaism in the following way: "The relationship of the Jewish Christians to the synagogues appears to be similar to the behavior of people today in the Charismatic Movement who, by definition, continue to attend their traditional churches and to associate with their denominations after experiencing a sign gift and a paradigm shift."[6]

Furthermore, Westfall's presentation suggests that the Pauline house church, as the exclusive and/or primary corporate form of the church, may be more reflective of Gentile Christian communities, which were only nascent in the first century relative to the established Jewish Christian community in Jerusalem. Indeed, the early Christians' migration toward the practice of the house church and their separation from Jewish religious institutions in the second century was likely more a result of their disestablishment by the Jewish communities than of their implementation of an ideal and "biblical" ecclesiology. In other words, the house church movement of the first century was a response to the cultural exigencies "on the ground"; which is perhaps the heart of biblical ecclesiastical practice.

Her point that the Jewish-Christian churches and the Gentile churches established by Paul reflected significant points of continuity and discontinuity is also important for the church *now*. She suggests that the search for *the* "biblical" or "New Testament" model of the church is misguided precisely because it assumes a uniform ecclesiology and ecclesiastical practice that are absent from the New Testament. Moreover, the diversity of early church practice, composition, and contextualized

---

5. Westfall, "Church and Synagogue," 76.
6. Ibid., 77–78.

forms suggests that contemporary ministry leaders, parishioners, and theologians should not be overly concerned with denominational differences and diverse ministry styles. Indeed, just as the diversity of gifts that enabled the early church to function as a healthy body of Christ was a sign of the Holy Spirit, perhaps the diversity of ministry styles today is similarly a gift of the Holy Spirit that can enable, rather than detract from, the church being the vibrant body of Christ. The way for diversity to enable rather than detract from the vitality of the body of Christ is probably the same today as it was when Paul addressed the potential that diversity has for divisiveness. As long as we confess Jesus as Lord and live a life consistent with that confession (this means letting go of the habit of making *adiaphora* mandates), we should recognize and appreciate that the diverse gifts and expressions within the body of Christ are gifts of the Holy Spirit and that the diversity of gifts and ministry styles is precisely what makes the church healthy in its unique cultural habitats.

Heath: When . . . and Where the Church Was Wiped Out

Gord Heath raises an important caution against the often triumphalist declaration that persecution is good for the church ("the blood of the martyrs is a seed"). Instead, persecution sometimes destroys the church and it is perverse to wish for the suffering of others even if it is for the purpose of church growth. Indeed, to wish for persecution so that the church might grow or be holier is to apply a brutal ecclesiastical utilitarianism. The importance of Heath's essay is that it highlights some of the often neglected histories of the church. Heath charts the unhappy story of the initial flourishing, but eventual decline, of Christianity in the areas of Nubia, North Africa, Moravia, Central Asia, China, Turkey/Asia Minor, and Japan. He identifies military conquest, persecution, migration and population displacement, genocide, and conversions (willing and forced) as factors that led to the decline and extinction of the church in these areas.

There is a good reason why these stories are often ignored. After all, who wants to hear a story in which everyone is slaughtered, dispossessed, and consigned to historical anonymity, especially when those suffering the abuse are your religious kindred? Christians often like stories with happy endings and in which "the good guys win." So we prefer to focus on the stories that portray the church "saving" Western civilization from total disintegration in the wake of the dissolution of the Western

Roman Empire. To be sure, from our standpoint in Western culture now characterized as post-Christendom, the end of our own story looks like it will be far from a happy Hollywood one, but certainly we need not fear galloping horsemen from the Eurasian steppes.

Heath concludes: "the waves of invaders, forced migrations, persecution, and (especially) genocides were simply too much to handle."[7] This suggests a correlation with Knowles's characteristics of the first-century church. Perhaps the churches described by Heath eventually disappeared because they were gospel churches—that is, churches of the least, the lost, and the last—and in the end went the way of the Lord to be crucified. Although this observation will hardly tickle the ears of the heralds of the church growth movement, the defeat of the church in these areas may be indicative of their success in following in the footsteps of the one who was, more than all others, the least, the lost, and the last: the crucified one. Is it possible that when we see the near or full extinction of the Christian church in the areas catalogued by Heath as a failure of the church in some respect, we have implicitly adopted an evaluative creed of power and numerical success more informed by the Western churches' experience (prior to the collapse of Christendom) and of Western capitalist-consumer culture than one informed by the histories of non-Western churches and by the life of Jesus?

Furthermore, to approve of Tertullian's famous quip that the "blood of the martyrs is the seed" of the church from a retrospective vantage point is perhaps too easy and logically suspect. For, had not Constantine endorsed Christianity and given it legal and social sanction, had not the Frankish and Burgundian forces under the leadership of Charles Martel checked the expansion of Muslim forces at the Battle of Tours, who knows whether the blood of the martyrs would have been able to be the fertile seed of Western Christendom?

As Western Christians still living in a culture with the vestiges of Christendom, we are tempted to consider the Nubian or Nestorian churches' history of growth, declension, and demise to be different from our own. But as with most temptations, we should resist. The phenomenon of Christendom that characterized the Western church for centuries in its various locales of continental Europe, Britain, Canada, and the United States is on life support at best, and just had the plug pulled at worst. Moreover, as Philip Jenkins highlights, while the star of Western

---

7. Heath, "Blood of the Martyrs," 114.

Christendom may have fallen, Christianity in the Global South and non-traditional Christian groups in the former domains of Christendom are on the ascent. Perhaps at some point in the future, the history of the church in the West will look more like the history of the church in North Africa and Nubia than like its more recent but fading history of cultural dominance.

Finally, at least two of the factors that Heath outlined as causes of the effective extinction of the Christian church in its earlier areas of presence are at work in the marginalization of Christianity in the West. These are migration and persecution. First, the influx of immigrants to North America promotes various forms of pluralism, including social, ethnic, and religious pluralism. Unchecked pluralism and diversity tend to challenge and alter hegemonic cultures. The ever-increasing presence and representation of religious diversity in Western culture means a corresponding diminution of Christianity's cultural domination. This statement is not an evaluative but a descriptive one. Regardless of whether one perceives Christianity's dislocation from cultural centrality in a negative or positive light, the fact seems incontrovertible.

Second, Heath highlights two forms of persecution. In one form, states, political powers, and religious groups perpetrate physical harm and even death on Christians, destroy their buildings, and confiscate their property. In another form, which is perhaps more destructive than the first, the new dominant cultural powers consistently marginalize the church from social and political influence and thereby rob the church of its ability to expand and play a significant role in society. Although the church in the West has not recently suffered from physical persecution, it does suffer from the less obvious but more insidious and probably more destructive persecution of cultural marginalization. Since the Enlightenment, the church has been more and more pushed out of the centers of social influence and denied access to the levers of cultural power and control. Indeed, vis-à-vis North American culture that is largely post-Christian, the "Red States" in the USA may be analogous to Byzantine Constantinople as the last bastion of the Christian east.

REFLECTIONS ON THE CHURCH NOW

Beach: The Local Church

Lee Beach addresses contemporary issues of ecclesiology from the perspective of the local church in a postmodern context. He presents a case for the church as the community of people who participate in the life and fellowship of the trinitarian God. He maintains that this trinitarian vision of the church can effectively engage and nurture postmodern "nomads." In the following, I highlight and interact with several of the important issues he raises in his essay.

Beach suggests that the focus of ecclesiology is the local church. Outside of its local expression, the "church" is largely an abstraction. Beach suggests that "from a New Testament and theological perspective, the church, in any practical way, does not exist outside of its local expression in a particular context."[8] Although I understand and agree with his point, I also think that it is important to remember that the body of Christ, the church, transcends any one of its local expressions. The theological category that keeps the notion of the universal church from becoming an abstraction vis-à-vis the local church is pneumatology. The Holy Spirit unites all Christians together in one body of Christ in a way that transcends temporal and spatial boundaries. Yet, as Beach helpfully reminds us, the local church is the warp and woof of the concrete manifestation of the body of Christ.

Beach also highlights the tenuous state of the church in North America. Since this colloquium is on the church *then* and *now*, the similarity between Beach's analysis of the problems facing the church and the diagnosis offered by H. Richard Niebuhr over seventy years ago is useful to note. Niebuhr maintained that the church faces two threats: one from outside the church or the non-Christian culture, and one from inside the church or the church's tendency to forsake its calling.[9] Although the specifics of the threats are different (for Niebuhr it was nationalism, capitalism, and anthropocentrism), the essential nature of the problem remains the same. Beach suggests that, on the one hand, the church faces pressure from the post-Christian and at times even anti-Christian culture. On the other hand, the church seems to be buckling under its own inertia and inability to come to grips with its changing cultural location

---

8. Beach, "Local Church," 134.
9. Niebuhr, *Church against the World*.

and the emergence of postmodern culture in early-twenty-first century North America.

However, Beach maintains that the current postmodern condition also offers an opportunity for a "local church renaissance" for two reasons. First, the local church can provide people with the personal anchors that the postmodern culture strips away from them. In place of dislocation, isolation, and fragmentation, the church locates people within a caring and nurturing community. Second, postmoderns distrust impersonal institutions that trade on self-justifying metanarratives that often have little to do with the contextual realities of individual people, families, and communities. The local church, precisely because it is local, coheres with the postmodern shift away from universal to local concerns. The local church can be a community of Christians embodying the grace and love of Christ for the sake of the community in which it exists and not for the sake of a larger religious institution (also known as the denomination). Thus, the church becomes a place where people connect with each other and where the loving relational activities that emanate from it to its surrounding community verify the truth of the gospel.

Beach also draws a parallel between the outward orientation of the local churches' ministries to their communities and the Father's initiative in sending the Son to the world. Just as the trinitarian God goes outside of his eternal fellowship in order to create and invite human persons to join in his loving fellowship, so the church cannot ghettoize, but must reach out to invite others to participate in its loving and redemptive community.

Keeping with a trinitarian vision for the local church, Beach points to the Son's incarnation in Jesus Christ as both a demonstration and inauguration of the church's calling to embody loving fellowship with God and other people. In other words, the church is a "hermeneutic of the gospel," which means the church is to exegete the gospel in terms of its contextual location. In this respect, the church is analogous to the Incarnation. As the Son incarnated the life of God in and through the human nature of Jesus Christ, so the church embodies its union with Christ through its ministries. As Beach clarifies, "as Jesus offers a living depiction of God, the church offers a living expression of God's life to the world."[10]

10. Beach, "Local Church," 143.

Theologians often talk of the scandal of Christ, which is the Christian claim that Jesus Christ is the definitive Savior. They identify this as the key apologetic problem of the church in a postmodern culture. Although it is certainly a challenge, the key apologetic challenge facing the church is the scandal of *the church*; that is, its inability to apply the "hermeneutic of the gospel." Jesus perhaps feared this when he prayed for the church, "that all of them may be one, Father, just as you are in me and I am in you. May they also be in us *so that the world may believe that you have sent me*" (John 17:20–21; emphasis added). In other words, the greatest apologetic problem and promise for the church is to exegete or to embody in an authentic way the loving fellowship with the triune God offered to us in the gospel of Jesus Christ. To be sure, intellectual arguments have their place, but *then* and *now*, the most effective verification of the gospel is its demonstration in the community known for its confession of Jesus as Lord.

Finally, Beach completes the trinitarian ecclesiology by highlighting the role of the Spirit in the local church. On the Day of Pentecost, the Spirit spoke in many tongues and subsequently empowered a series of local ministries in Jerusalem, Judea, Samaria, and finally in diverse communities throughout the Mediterranean. The Spirit who spoke through the many tongues of Pentecost continues to speak in diverse tongues and to inspire a *bricolage* of ministry practices adapted to the unique cultural circumstances of the local church.

Cavey and Carrington-Phillips: The House Church

Bruxy Cavey and Wendy Carrington-Phillips present a vision for the church that seeks to follow the pattern of the church in the New Testament and that characterized the church up to the time of Constantine. They propose that the church described in the New Testament, and prototypically modeled in Jesus' method of discipleship, was a house church ecclesiology. The house church went out of favor in the Constantinian era when large, centralized, impersonal, ritualized, and professionalized worship in cathedrals became the norm. However, they believe that several factors commend a return to the house church model.

First, baby-boomers and younger adults alike desire an authentic spirituality that they sense is unavailable in the traditional church experience. Second, the house church can be an effective tool for evangelizing people who are unlikely to attend a traditional church service. Third, the house church provides a better way to embody the priesthood of all believers; the house church provides for organic and participatory leadership in contrast to the traditional church that focuses leadership in specialists and tends to be a spectator event for most attendees. Fourth, the house church provides an effective and intimate way for Christians to engage in community service. Finally, the house church promises to recapture a more biblical form of the church. I want to dialogue with this last attribute of the house church.

To be a "biblical" and a "New Testament" church is (or at least it should be) the aspiration of every Christian church. Of course, the question is, "What does that mean?" Cavey and Carrington-Phillips recommend the house church movement as the answer to that question. In one sense, the house church may be the "biblical" way of meeting as a local group of believers. This means that historically the earliest Christians met in homes to participate in the corporate dimensions of the Christian faith. In this respect, as the house church seeks to follow "the example of the New Testament body of believers who worshipped and experienced life together"[11] they are being "biblical." However, in this sense of "biblical," one could say the "biblical" mode of travel is by foot, donkey, and ship as these are the ways Jesus and the Apostle Paul traveled. In this sense, "biblical" does not mean a normative and trans-cultural practice.

In another sense, the house church may not be "biblical." We need to ask the important cultural and contextual question, "Why did the early Christians meet in homes?" In other words, is the New Testament house church indicative of an ideal, indeed "biblical," model for local congregations or was it an appropriate response to its first-century cultural location? The early Christians could not meet in synagogues as a group of Christians; they could not build separate Christian places of worship, so they met in what was available to them, homes. In this light, the house church was culturally appropriate, but may be no more normative and trans-cultural than was Jesus' traveling by donkey. In this perspective, to be "biblical" does not mean to reproduce what the early Christians did in the sense of imitating their practice, but in the sense of imitating their appropriate cultural hermeneutics and response. They met in homes because homes were available, or were perhaps the only viable option open to them.

---

11. Cavey and Carrington-Phillips, "House Church," 152.

If the house church is trying to be "biblical" by simply replicating the practice of the New Testament era Christians without considering the cultural reasons for the way they met, then I suggest they are not being "biblical" in the most important sense and thus not doing what the New Testament Christians were doing. The New Testament Christians endeavored to come together on a regular basis (weekly) that made sense given their social context. If the contemporary house church movement believes that home churches better enable the church in twenty-first-century North America to embody the normative ideals and trans-cultural practices of the church within the cultural setting of North America than do the megachurch and traditional church models, then it is being "biblical" and doing what the New Testament Christians did. In short, I wonder if the house church movement has thoroughly applied its "Jesus hermeneutic" to its reading of the home church practice of the New Testament.

Now, clearly Cavey and Carrington-Phillips seek primarily to be "biblical" in this second, and, I argue, more important respect. The problem is that their essay employs both "biblical" strategies to support the rationale for the house church. For example, they state the house church seeks to employ the "Jesus hermeneutic," which "frees the reader from having to legalistically duplicate New Testament church structure, and allows that person to look instead for the principle behind the specific practice outlined in a particular passage."[12] They further suggest that "the Bible does not provide a definitive organizational structure for the church to follow."[13] In respect to the practice presented in Acts, they state "It is not likely that Luke intended his presentation of the house church in Acts to be prescriptive."[14] Yet, in other places, they draw on the early church's practice as paradigmatic for the contemporary church. Explaining the rationale for house churches, they remark that "The contemporary house church movement is built on the foundation of the New Testament model of church, which was about people not buildings."[15] Statements such as "they see themselves as following the example of the New Testament body of believers who worshipped and

---

12. Ibid., 167.
13. Ibid., 174.
14. Ibid., 163.
15. Ibid., 160.

experienced life together,"¹⁶ implies that the house church model is an ideal, trans-cultural, normative, and paradigmatic form for the church.

Let me summarize with two observations. First, in the effort to be "biblical" and to pattern the house church practice on the New Testament "model," the house church can decontextualize the New Testament practice and overlook the cultural circumstances that gave rise to and made the house church sensible in the first century. In this respect, the contemporary house church is not biblical. Second, in the effort to discern and practice effective ways of embodying the New Testament ideals of fellowship, service, evangelism, and so on in an early-twenty-first century North American culture that often militates against the biblical values of fellowship, mutual nurturing, and enrichment, the house church is being biblical. The house church is biblical when it enables believers to embody the corporate dimensions of faith in Christ in a way that is both authentic to the normative values of the church and appropriate to the church's given cultural circumstances.

Pawelke: The Megachurch

Mike Pawelke presents a biblical, historical, and personal case for the viability of the megachurch. He maintains that "gifted, visionary pastors will continue to draw devoted followers of Christ, along with spiritual consumers and seekers, to create and sustain ever-expanding large churches in the Canadian context."¹⁷ His argument has two central elements: (1) some pastors have the leadership skills to develop and lead large churches and, thus, will naturally produce such churches as they deploy their personal leadership skills in the context of church ministry; and (2) megachurches have met and will continue to meet the needs of "spiritual consumers and seekers."

Pawelke is sensitive to the critiques of the megachurch. For example, he protests that, "megachurches have been called 'big box' churches, often with an intended pejorative connotation. They are often accused of growing on the backs of smaller churches and are characterized as 'Christianity light' or entertainment focused."¹⁸ He then characterizes these criticisms as "myths" and offers a number of responses to them.

---

16. Ibid., 152.
17. Pawelke, "Megachurch," 188.
18. Ibid., 182.

Without a doubt, many who characterize the megachurch by the terms mentioned above do so with a pejorative intent. But at the same time, and more positively, these characteristics can be terms of cultural hermeneutics. For example, to refer to the megachurch as the "big box" church relates the phenomenon of the megachurch to broader cultural trends. An obvious correlation exists between the emergence of big-box retailers and megachurches. Indeed, the criticism that the megachurch forces smaller churches to close their doors as religious consumers migrate to the panoply of religious services and products offered by the megachurch parallels the protests heard when Wal-Mart announces plans to build a new location. Wal-Mart is often accused of destroying local and family businesses. One can discuss whether or not this is positive or negative, but to deny that it occurs seems to deny economic as well as ecclesiastical realities.

Moreover, the strongest rationale for the megachurch may be its obvious reflection of cultural trends. The megachurch, by virtue of its imitation of corporate strategies of economies of scale, proliferation of consumer options, and emphasis on packaging, may be an appropriate and effective expression of congregational life in twenty-first-century North American urban and suburban settings. In his oral presentation, Pawelke suggested this point when he said, "Perhaps some of you still attend a megachurch because the services provided by the larger church meet your present needs better than the smaller church was able." I think this statement reflects the reason for the megachurch's popularity (it provides a smorgasbord of religious services to religious consumers) and suggests what many of its detractors see as its problematic characteristic. The megachurch seems to be the religious incarnation of the North American consumer culture and some wonder whether in its effort to be culturally effective it has accommodated too much to and assimilated too much of the culture. I think apologetic strategies for the megachurch would be better served by acknowledging and directly tackling this characterization of the movement rather than by dismissing and avoiding it.

Goheen: The Missional Church

Michael Goheen maintains that the changing cultural location of the church in North America (also known as the disintegration of Christendom) provides an opportunity to reconsider the nature of the church from the perspective of mission. Mission is a meta-term and concept that does not merely define one of the activities of the church, but the very nature of the church. The problem in past missiological thought is that mission has been understood as one among many of the church's activities rather than as a category for understanding the very nature and identity of the church. In contrast to such a perspective, Goheen suggests that the church is the community of people who participate in the mission of the triune God (*missio Dei*); in other words, the church *is* missional. In order to develop the missional nature of the church, Goheen seeks to situate an understanding of the church in the biblical narrative of the mission of God. Thus, ecclesiology needs to attend to the characteristics of the church that bear continuity with the Old Testament people of God and the characteristics that are unique to what the New Testament refers to as the "church."

Goheen draws on two key Old Testament texts. The first is Gen 12:2–3, in which God calls and establishes a covenant with Abraham, not only to save Abraham but through Abraham to redeem the world.[19] The second is Exod 19:3–6, which defines Israel as a priestly kingdom and a holy nation. In continuity with calling and establishing a covenant with Abraham, God redeems the people who will become Israel from Egyptian servitude and thereby breaks the Pharaoh's covenant claim and establishes his own over the Hebrews. But importantly, the redemption of the Hebrews is not only to save them, but to establish them as a holy people who will be a light to the nations. In other words, God redeems the people of Israel so that they can be his vehicle of redeeming the nations. The giving of his *torah* provides the people of Israel with patterns of living that will display to the nations the divine intention for human life. In short, God redeems people so that they can participate in the mission of God.

Bridging to the New Testament church, Goheen draws the connection between Jesus and the Old Testament prophetic tradition concerning the renewal of Israel and the realization of its covenant purpose to be a light to the nations. Jesus reconstitutes the Old Testament people of God through his ministry, the disciples he calls, and the church he establishes in order to bring light and redemption to the nations. Goheen also articulates several ways the New Testament church stands in continuity with the people of Israel as the covenant community of God.

19. Goheen, "Role and Identity of the Church," 195.

Yet Goheen also maintains that the New Testament church is unique vis-à-vis Israel: "The fundamental difference is *eschatological*. In Jesus and the Spirit, the end-time kingdom, the last days, the age to come, the new creation, resurrection life, has arrived."[20] He outlines two implications of the eschatological difference. First, the church participates in the eschatological kingdom; the church has a foretaste of the future everlasting kingdom of God. Second, the church is a gathering community; that is, the church is a community whose embodiment of the mission of God and of God's design for the flourishing of human life should gather people and draw them into the church so that more and more come to participate in the kingdom of God.

I wonder if it would be better to call the unique aspects of the church points of development or fulfillment relative to the Old Testament people of God rather than points of discontinuity. Discontinuity suggests a lack of cohesion between the Old Testament people of God and the New Testament church. However, the unique characteristics of the church seem to be the fulfillment or, at the least, a fuller fulfillment of God's ongoing purpose for his covenant people than that which was experienced by the Old Testament people of God. Perhaps an analogous relationship exists between the people of God in the Old Testament and the New Testament, and the New Testament people of God and the eschatological kingdom of God. For example, the everlasting kingdom will certainly usher in a fuller experience of fellowship with the trinitarian God and the people of God's kingdom than that which is enjoyed by members of the church in this age, and in that sense it will be unique relative to the church's experience prior to the eschaton, but it will be more of a fulfillment than a discontinuity.

Goheen's thesis is one that needs to be heard in the North American church. He states, "Two orientations define the identity and role of God's people: 'chosen by God' and 'for the sake of the world.' The church does not exist for itself. Rather, it exists for the sake of God's mission and for the sake of others toward whom God's mission is directed."[21] Much of the church and its activities have club members in mind. The marginalization of its missional calling is perhaps correspondent with the church's adoption of a consumer ecclesiology. The key questions become: "What do people want?" and "How can we give it to them?" The

20. Ibid., 212.
21. Ibid., 193.

"people" considered in those two questions are not the least, the lost, and the last, but the club members who show up on Sunday morning and who hopefully pay the tithes to fund member activities. Goheen calls the church to remember that it does not exist to purvey religious commodities to religious consumers, but rather to empower the people called and redeemed by the triune God to participate in the triune God's redemptive work in this world.

CONCLUDING QUESTIONS AND REFLECTIONS

Is any one of the megachurch, the home church, or the local church closer than the others to the early church's status as the least, the lost, and the last? What type of church best reflects the status of the early church or, conversely, the contemporary culture's values of prestige, power, production, and consumption? What models of the church and church practices best enable twenty-first-century North American Christians to be the community that confesses Jesus as Lord and to embody the patterns of church life consistent with that confession? What ecclesiastical methods and ministries will help keep the church from being wiped out, not so much to retain and/or to regain the cultural power of Christendom, but to persevere as an authentic community of Christ? What patterns of organization and practice can help the church to fulfill its calling to participate in the mission of the triune God to redeem this world? Perhaps *now*, as *then*, the answer lies in a *bricolage* of approaches as long as they are inspired by the *Bricoleur*: the Holy Spirit who inspires diverse ministry practices appropriate to the diverse cultural habitats of the church in twenty-first-century North America.

BIBLIOGRAPHY

Niebuhr, H. Richard. *The Church against the World*. Chicago: Willett, Clark & Co., 1935.

Ancient Sources Index

OLD TESTAMENT

Genesis

1:26	153
1:27	138
1:28	153
2:7	138
3–11	196
3	138
11	201
12	196
12:1–3	196
12:2–3	195, 200, 237
12:3	199
12:5	199
12:7	32
15:3–5	32
15:13	32
15:18	32
17:9	32
18:18–19	196
26:24	32
26:3–4	32
28:3–4	32
35:12	32

Exodus

1–18	200
3:7–8	138
4:22–23	197
19–24	198, 200
19	197
19:3–6	195, 197, 198, 200, 206, 237
25–40	200
32:13	32
33:1	32
34:6–7	200

Leviticus

11:44–45	23
19:2	23
20:26	23
21:8	23
25:47–55	197

Numbers

6:1–21	74
6:9–12	75
6:13–20	74
23:10	32

Deuteronomy

1:8	32
4:6–8	206
21:20	27
34:4	32

Joshua

24:3	32

2 Samuel

5:2	19

1 Chronicles
11:2	19

2 Chronicles
20:7	32

Psalms
9:11	203
18:49	203
22:24	32
22:27	203
47:1	203
57:9	203
66:4	203
66:8	203
67	203
67:1–3	203
67:3	203
67:7	203
77:20	19
78:52	19
79:13	19
80:1	19
89:9	203
95:7	19
96:2–3	203
96:7	203
96:10	203
100:1	203
100:3	19
105:1	203
105:6	32
108:3	203
117:1	203

Isaiah
2:2–5	209
2:2–3	207
2:3	204
9:1–2	28
11:1–9	143
19:23	204
25:6–8	204
28:16	64
40:5	204
41:8	32
42:1–4	28
42:6	199
43:9–10	140
45:19	32
45:20–22	204
55:3–5	140
56:7	80
60:2–3	204
65:9	32
66:18	204

Jeremiah
23:1–4	19
31:10	19
33:26	32

Ezekiel
20:5	32
34:2–10	19
34:23–34	209
36:22–23	204
36:24–27	204, 209
36:26	210
37:16–21	208
37:22–23	208

Joel
2:32	64

Micah
2:12	19

Zephaniah
3:8	204

Zechariah

8:23	204
9:9 [LXX]	25
13:7	19

APOCRYPHA

4 Ezra

8:16	32

3 Maccabees

6:3	32
6:4	32

4 Maccabees

18:1	32

Psalms of Solomon

9:9	32
18:3	32

Tobit

4:12	32

NEW TESTAMENT

Matthew

2:6	19
4:14–16	28
5–7	142
5	166
5:1–2	155
5:5	25
5:6	37
5:9	23
5:13	31
5:14–16	209
5:22–24	18
5:39	25
5:44–48	23
5:44	25, 153, 154
5:45	23, 32
5:47	28
5:48	17
6:5–15	154
6:5–13	164
6:7	28
6:14–15	17
6:32	28
7:16–20	14
7:22–23	14
7:24–27	210
8:11–12	80
8:11	208
9:10	154
9:16–17	168
10	209
10:3–6	80
10:5–6	28, 208
10:6	19, 27, 80
10:7	15
10:8b	22
10:17–18	14
10:20	16
10:23	80
10:24	31
10:25	80
10:25a	15
10:29	17
10:32	17
10:33–39	220
10:35–37	18
10:38	26, 220
10:39	28
10:40	16
10:42	13, 24
11:25–26	24
11:28–30	24

Matthew (cont.)

11:29	25
12:18–21	28
12:30	220
12:33	14
12:38	38
12:48	164
12:49–50	154
12:50	17
13:1	21
13:16–17	24
13:24–30	27, 32
13:34	21
13:36–43	27
13:36	21
13:44–46	31
13:47–50	27
13:57	19
14:14	153
15:4	28
15:21–28	154
15:21	28
15:24	16, 19, 27, 80, 208
16:16	3
16:18	2, 37, 152
18:3–4	24
18:4	25
18:10	24
18:14	24
18:15b	18
18:17	18, 28, 37, 152
18:20	14, 15, 169
18:21–35	22
18:21	18
18:35	18
19:29	14
20:16	29
20:24–28	35
20:25–28	30
21:5	25
21:18–22	153
21:31–32	23
21:31	27
22:10	27
22:11–14	27
22:18–19	179
22:37	153
22:39	153
23:8	18
23:9	18
23:11	30
23:34	16
24:14	213
24:42–51	15
25:5–7	171
25:14–30	15
25:31–46	19, 163
25:40	25
25:45	25
26:28	210
26:39	16
28:16–20	55
28:18–20	210
28:18–19	38, 179
28:18	16
28:19–20	15
28:19	33
28:20	15, 146
28:29	14

Mark

1:7	34
1:10	15
1:12	15
1:14	15, 141
1:15	207
1:17–20	14
1:20	30
1:21	141
1:32–34	23
1:38	141
1:40–45	23
2:10	38
2:14	14
2:15	154
2:16–17	26
3:14–15	22
3:14	14–16, 19, 209

Mark (cont.)

3:20	21
3:21	19
3:31–35	17
3:31–32	21
3:33–35	21
4:1–9	32
4:11	21
4:19	21
4:26–29	32
4:30–32	32
4:31–32	31
4:33–34	21
5:1–20	23
5:21–23	23
5:24–34	23
6:4	19
6:6	22
6:7	15, 16, 38
6:8–11	22
6:12–13	16
6:13	15
6:31–34	153
6:32–44	22
6:34–44	154
7:2–30	28
7:3–4	33
7:22	16
7:24–30	23
8:1–10	22
8:2	153
8:34	26
8:35	28
8:36	21
9:17–19	14, 16
9:35	29, 30, 144
9:37	14, 16, 25
9:38–41	13
9:40	20, 220
9:42	24
10	31
10:13–16	154
10:13	23
10:29–30	17
10:31	29
10:41–45	35
10:42–45	30
10:42–44	144
10:42	31
10:45	144
10:46–52	153
11:9	14
11:17	80
11:25	17, 22
11:27–33	16
12:29–31	153
12:41–44	23
13:6	14
13:9–13	16
13:9	14
13:11	15
13:12	19
13:13	14, 20
13:29–37	15
14:17–21	35
14:20	22
14:26–31	35
14:26	173
14:36	16, 164
14:44–45	34
15:20b–21	16
15:26	28
15:39	28
20:24	24

Luke

1:23	37
1:52	25
4:16	75
4:18	16, 141
4:43	16
5:29	154
5:31	141
5:38–43	23
6:12–16	154
6:12	154
6:20–22	25
6:21	37

Luke (cont.)

6:27	153
6:28–29	25
6:35–36	23
6:36	17
6:40	15
6:40a	31
6:43–44	14
7:12–15	23
7:25–30	23
7:36	154
7:37–39	23
7:38	35
7:39	27
7:45	35
8:3	77
8:26–37	154
8:41–46	154
9:2	15
9:10–17	153
9:11	155
9:17–27	23
9:43	38
9:48	16, 25
9:49–50	13
9:50	20, 220
10:1	16
10:17	14
10:21	24
10:23–24	24
10:27	153
10:29–37	22, 153
10:33	22, 220
10:37	22
11:20	38
11:38	33
11:49	16
12:30	21
12:32	19, 24, 209
12:35–48	15
12:52–53	18
13:23–30	80
13:30	29
14:1	154
14:7–12	29
14:9	27
14:11	29
14:13–14	29
14:21	27
14:24	27
14:25–35	155
14:26	18
14:27	26, 220
14:32	27
15:2	27
15:4	27
15:6	27
17:2	25
17:7	30
17:10	30
17:12	23
17:33	29
18:1–7	23
19:9	27
19:10	141
20:46	171
21:1–4	23
21:12	14
22:19–20	33, 56
22:20	212
22:24–27	35
22:24–26	174
22:25–27	30
22:42	16
24:30	15
24:35	15
24:42	15
24:47	14
24:49	38, 210

John

1:12	14, 141
1:14	145
1:27	34
1:32–33	15
1:43	14
1:49	90
2:23	14

John (cont.)

3:1–21	155
3:2	38
3:18	14
4:7–26	154, 155
4:22	90
4:46–54	28
4:46b–54	23
5:27	38
5:43	14
6:1–15	22
6:28–29	38
6:35	37
6:56	90
6:67–71	19
7:39	15
8:19	17
8:31	90
8:35	90
8:37–47	17
9:2	28
9:18–22	90
9:22	90
9:24	28
10:1–15	20
10:13–16	90
10:16	20
10:25	14
10:26–27	20
11:4	38
11:40	38
11:50–52	90
12:6	77
12:13	14, 90
12:20–21	28
12:25	29
12:27–28	16
12:42	90
12:44–45	16
12:46	90
13–16	155
13:4–15	153
13:8	34
13:13–17	31
13:20	14, 16
13:21–30	35
13:23	87
13:26	22
13:33	24
13:34–35	153
14:9	142
14:13–14	14
14:15	15
14:21–24	15
14:22	21
14:26	15, 16
15:4–5	15
15:4	90
15:5	90
15:6	90
15:7	90
15:9–11	90
15:10	15
15:14	15
15:16	14
15:18–21	16
15:21	14
15:26	16
16:2	90
16:19	21
16:23–24	14
16:23	15
16:26	14
17	154
17:18	16
17:20–21	232
18:14	90
19:17	16
19:19–22	28
19:19	90
20:17	17
20:21	16, 192, 211
20:31	14
21:5	24
21:12–13	15
21:15–17	20
21:20–24	87

Acts

1:4	15
1:8	4, 34, 146
1:15–26	19
1:15	180
2:8–12	80
2:10	80
2:14–36	179
2:38	33
2:41	33, 80, 180
2:42–47	175, 180, 211
2:42	74, 75, 156, 157, 211
2:43–47	179, 211
2:44–45	77, 158
2:46–47	158
2:46	74, 155, 157, 158
2:46a	74
2:47	157, 180
2:47a	74
3:1	74
3:11	74
3:25–26	206
4:4	180
4:32—5:11	77
4:32–35	158
5:12	74
5:14	180
5:17	74
5:42	180
6:1–7	180
6:1–6	61, 77
6:7	77
6:8–10	75
7:59—8:8	81
8:1	211
8:4	211
8:12	33
8:14–17	72
8:36–39	33
8:38	180
8:39	180
9:1–3	81
9:17	146
9:18	33
9:31	152
10	83, 147
10:1—11:18	147
10:40	15
10:48	33
11:19–21	211
11:19	211
11:22–24	72
11:22	152
11:23	59
12:17	73
13:1–3	61, 212
13:14–41	155
14:1	81
15:5	74, 83
15:12–19	212
15:24–29	72
15:24	83
17:1–20	155
17:2–3	155
17:10	155
18:1–4	155
18:1–2	80
18:6	82
18:8	82
18:19	82
19:9–10	172
20:20	172
21	74
21:10	73
21:20–25	73, 78
21:23–24	74
24:5	74
26:5	74
28:22	74
29:17	180
29:18	180

Romans

1:3–4	44
1:7	50
1:16	48, 52
2:4	62
2:10	52

Romans (cont.)

3	49
3:9	62
3:22	49
3:23	49, 62
4:13–18	32
5	49
5:12–21	213
6:3–5	180
6:3–4	33
6:3	55
6:4–9	43
6:4–6	213
6:4	55
8:1	63
8:3–4	212
8:4–5	63
8:10–11	63
8:15	16
8:18–30	65
9–11	44, 52
9:1—10:5	64
9:7–8	32
10	64
10:10	44
10:12	52, 64
10:14–15	64
10:9	43, 44, 54, 64
11:1	32
11:17–24	87, 194
11:17–21	206
11:26	44, 52
12	58, 59
12:1–8	180
12:1–2	56
12:4–5	58
12:6–8	58
12:7	57
12:12–13	59
15:25–27	73
16:1	18
16:3–16	81
16:3–5	159
16:5	51
16:16	34, 35, 50

1 Corinthians

1	54
1:2	50, 134, 179
1:9	33
1:11–12	51
1:13–17	54
1:13–16	33
1:17	54, 64
1:21	52
1:23	65
3:16	138, 213
5:1	62
5:4	56
5:9	62
5:10	63
5:12	63
5:13	63
6:9–11	27
7:10	146
7:12	146
7:15	18
7:40	146
8:6	45
9:5	18
10:20–21	33
10:31	179
11:17–34	180
11:17	56
11:20–22	36
11:20	56
11:23–34	55
11:23–25	33
11:23a	33
11:26	56, 65
11:27	56
11:29	36
11:33–34	56
11:33	56
12–14	159
12	58, 59
12:1–31	180
12:1	64

1 Corinthians (cont.)

12:3	43, 44
12:4–11	58
12:12–30	51
12:13	10
12:27–31	171
12:28	152
14	59
14:5	160
14:6	57
14:26	56, 159, 164, 167, 171, 180
14:30	57
14:33	50
15	65
15:3–5	46, 55
15:9	50
15:10	63
15:20	65
15:23	65
16:1	50
16:19	50, 51, 134, 159
16:20	34, 35

2 Corinthians

1:1	50, 134
1:24	31
2:12	65
4:5	45, 65
5:17–18	142
5:17	146, 213
7:10	62
8:1	50
11:22	32
12:21	62
13:12	34, 35
13:13	45

Galatians

1:3	50
1:6–9	82
1:12	57
1:13	50
1:19	73
2	49
2:1–10	72
2:2	57
2:7–8	83
2:7	82
2:9	72
2:11–14	83
2:16	49
3:6	52
3:8–9	206
3:16–29	32
3:22	49
3:25	52
3:26–28	52
3:27	33, 55
3:28	35
4:6	16
6:16	19

Ephesians

1:1	50
1:4	212
1:22	179
1:23	179
2:10–17	213
2:22	138
3:3	57
4:5	33, 54
4:7–16	180
4:7	59
4:11–16	179
4:11–12	174
4:11	58, 59
4:22–24	213
5:19–20	224
5:19	57, 173
5:21—6:9	53, 223
5:23	51, 152
6:9	53

Philippians

1:1	50, 59
2:1–11	171
2:5–11	144
2:6–11	46, 54, 55
4:22	51

Colossians

1:2	50, 169
1:15–20	47
1:18	51, 152
1:24	51, 179
1:28	57
2:11	180
2:12	180
3:1–4	55
3:3	55
3:4	55
3:5–11	224
3:9–11	213
3:11	52
3:16	57, 173
3:18—4:4	53, 223
4:1	53
4:13	63
4:15	159
4:16	152

1 Thessalonians

1:1	50, 152
2:9	63
2:13	57
2:14	73
4:1	63
4:4–5	63
4:11	63
5:4	63
5:5	63
5:26	34, 35

2 Thessalonians

1:1	50

3:8	63
3:11	63

1 Timothy

3:1–13	179, 180
3:1–7	59, 60
3:1	60
3:2	60
3:3–4	60
3:5	50
3:7	60
3:8	60
3:9	60
3:10	60
3:11–12	60
3:11	60
3:13	60
3:15	50
3:16	47, 54, 55
4	57
4:5	57
4:13	57, 61
4:14	60, 61
5:11	63
5:14	63
5:16	63
5:17–18	61
5:17	60, 61
5:19	61
5:22	61
5:23	43
8:13	60

2 Timothy

1:6	61
2:9	57
4:2	57
4:3	57

Titus

1:3	57
1:5–9	180

Titus (cont.)

1:5	60
1:6	60

Philemon

2	18, 51, 53, 159
5	53
9	53
11	53
13	53
14	53
16	53
19	53
20	53

Hebrews

2:3–4	85
3–4	86
11	86
11:39–40	86
12	86
12:1–2	86
12:2	26
12:22–44	86

James

1:1	19, 73, 78
1:18	213
1:24	78
1:25	78
2:1–4	36
2:1	78
2:2	79
2:6	36
2:8–12	78
2:15	18
3:1	79
3:17	78
4:4	78
4:11–12	78
5:14	79

1 Peter

1:18–19	212
2:1–10	86
2:9–10	206
2:9	84, 86
2:12	84
3:21	34
4:3	84
4:17	86
5:2–4	86
5:3	31
5:13	81
5:14	34, 35

1 John

1:1–3	85
2:18–19	85
2:22	85
3:23	85
4:2–3	85
4:2	85
4:15	85
5:1	85
5:5	85
5:6	85
5:10	85
5:12	85

2 John

7	85

3 John

7	84

Revelation

1:1	87
1:4	87
1:9–20	87
2:9	90
3:9	90
3:20	15

Revelation (*cont.*)

5:9	91
7:4–8	19, 90
7:9–10	91
7:15–17	91
21:12	19, 90
21:14	90
21:24	91
22	201
22:2	91
22:8	87

OTHER EARLY CHRISTIAN LITERATURE

Ambrosiaster

Corpus scriptorum ecclesiasticorum latinorum 81:5–6
                             81

John of Ephesus

Eccl. Hist. IV   101

Tertullian

Apology

50:13   91

EARLY JEWISH AND RABBINIC LITERATURE

Josephus

Antiquities

13.171	74
14.214–15	76

Mishnah

m. B. Meʿsia

7:1	32

m. B. Qam.

8:6	32

m. Ned.

3:11	32

Modern Author Index

Akcam, T., 126, 129
Alexander, P. S., 68, 95
Alexander, T. D., 217
Allen, R. B., 74, 95
Allison, D. C., 24, 39
Amiot, F., 47, 51, 66
Anderson, R., 146, 150
Ascough, R. S., 42, 51, 66

Baker, D. W., 217
Balakrian, P., 126, 129
Baltensweiler, H., 20, 39
Banks, J., 153, 157, 161–65, 167, 168, 176
Banks, R. J., 66, 153, 156, 157, 161–65, 167, 168, 176
Barclay, J. M. G., 96
Barker, K. L., 74, 95
Barna, G., 152
Barrett, C. K., 155, 176
Barth, K., 199, 215
Bauckham, R., 72, 74, 75, 82–84, 87, 95, 212, 215
Baumer, C., 104–7, 115, 116, 126, 127, 129
Bavinck, J. H., 201, 207, 215
Bayer, C. H., 98, 129
Beach, L., 7, 230–32
Beaudoin, T., 137, 148, 150
Becker, A. H., 69, 96
Becker, M., 40
Beker, J. C., 42, 66
Bennington, G., 150
Bennis, W., 186, 189
Berkhof, H., 191, 215
Bikhazi, R. J., 133

Bird, W., 184, 185, 189
Blauw, J., 195, 201, 208, 209, 215
Bloxham, P., 126, 129
Blue, B. B., 155–57, 159, 176, 177
Bock, D. L., 156, 158, 159, 177
Bockmuehl, M., 66, 67
Boda, M. J., 203, 215
Bowers, P., 100, 121, 129
Bowlus, C. R., 103, 129
Boxer, C. R., 112, 113, 119, 129
Boyarin, D., 69
Braaten, C. E., 192, 215
Branson, M. L., 134, 142, 143, 150
Braude, B., 122, 127, 129
Brower, K. E., 26, 27, 33, 39, 40
Brown, C., 177
Browne, L. E., 107, 127, 129
Bruce, C., 130
Bruce, F. F., 50, 53, 66
Brunner, E., 192, 216
Bylsma, B., 181, 182

Capper, B., 77, 95
Carrington-Phillips, W., 8. 225, 232–34
Carter, C., 98, 129
Cary-Elwes, C., 108, 130
Catto, S. K., 69, 75, 76, 82, 95
Cavey, B., 8, 168, 169, 174, 177, 225, 232–34
Ch'en, K., 117, 118
Chao, J., 97, 130
Chester, A., 49, 66, 88, 89, 95
Christensen, D. L., 200, 216
Christides, V., 130
Cileadi, A., 216

Clark, B., 123, 130
Clouse, B., 66
Clouse, R. G., 66
Coenen, L., 151, 177
Cohen, S. J. D., 84, 95
Collins, J., 186, 189
Coloe, M. L., 12, 39
Connell, M. F., 33, 39
Constantelos, D. J., 132
Cooksey, J. J., 113, 130
Cooper, M., 111, 130
Corbier, M., 60, 66
Corrie, J., 217
Craigie, P. C., 198, 216
Cullmann, O., 15, 36, 39
Cuoq, J., 100, 130
Curta, F., 104, 130
Curtis, E. M., 197, 216

Davids, P. H., 78, 95, 126, 176
Davies, W. D., 24, 39
de Villard, M., 100, 132
Dearborn, T., 140, 150
Deeg, M., 108, 130
DeRidder, R. R., 201, 209, 216
Deringil, S., 127, 130
DeSilva, D. A., 154, 177
Dibelius, M., 78, 95
Dittrich, Z. R., 130
Driver, J., 213, 214, 216
Drummond, R. H., 111, 120, 130
Dumbrell, W. J., 196, 199, 200, 216
Dunn, J. D. G., 54, 66, 83, 88, 95
Durham, J. I., 197–200, 216
Dvornik, F., 104, 130

Edwards, R., 135, 150
Evans, C. A., 66, 67

Faroqhi, S., 130
Fee, G. D., 175, 177
Fenske, W., 40
Ferguson, E., 60, 66
Ferguson, J., 60

Ferreira, J., 37–39
Fitts, R., 161, 177
Fletcher, R., 104, 130
Fodor, I., 121, 130
Fowl, S. E., 46, 66
France, R. T., 30, 39
Frankfort, H., 197, 216
Frazee, C. A., 130
Frederickson, S., 141, 145, 150
Frend, W. H. C., 102, 112, 130
Fretheim, T. E., 196, 199, 216
Frost, M., 98, 130
Fujita, N. S., 111, 112, 119, 130

Gallagher, M. P., 136, 137, 150
Galli, M., 97, 130
Galuska, L., 104, 130
Gertz, S., 105, 131
Gervers, M., 133
Gillman, I., 106–8, 131
Goheen, M. W., 9, 194, 216, 236–38
Graber, G. S., 126, 131
Green, W. S., 96
Grenz, S. J., 137, 150
Grillmeier, A., 131
Guant, D., 12, 126, 131
Guinness, O., 182, 185, 186, 189

Hagg, T., 131, 32
Hagner, D. A., 15, 17, 24, 39
Hall, D. J., 98, 131
Handley, M., 103, 131
Harrison, R. K., 216
Hartin, P. J., 73, 78, 79, 95
Hauerwas, S., 98, 131
Hawkins, G. L., 185, 189
Hawthorne, G. F., 177
Heath, G., 7, 227–29
Hedlund, R. E., 201, 216
Hengel, M., 26, 39
Higashibaba, I., 110–12, 131
Hill, C. C., 70, 95
Hirschberg, P., 87, 90–92, 95
Hirschon, R., 123, 131

Holme, L. R., 120, 131
Horrell, D. G., 44, 54, 55, 66
Houlden, J. L., 12, 14, 38, 39
Howe, J., 216
Hsia, R. P., 130
Huston, D. A., 156, 163, 177
Hvalvik, R., 68, 69, 73, 80, 81, 95, 96
Hybels, B., 186, 189

Irwin, B. P., 61, 66
Isicheu, E., 101, 100, 131

Jackson-McCabe, M., 68, 69, 95
Jenkins. P., 99, 113, 114, 129, 131
Jeremias, J., 208, 210, 216
Jervell, J., 73, 95
Johnson, A., 27, 39, 40
Johnson, L. T., 212, 216

Kaiser, W. C., 203, 216
Kee, H. C., 18, 20, 25, 27, 28, 30, 39
Keener, C. S., 80, 95, 157, 177
Keesmaat, S. C., 150
Kentaro, M., 112, 119, 120, 131
Kerkhofs, J., 109, 131
Keung, L. S., 108, 117, 131
Kim, L., 83, 95
Kirwan, L., 100, 131
Kittel, G., 217
Klassen, W., 35, 39
Klimkeit, H.-J., 106-8, 131
Knowles, M. P., 5, 29, 39, 140, 220, 221, 228
Kotter, J. P., 186, 189
Kramer, W., 44, 66

LaCoste, J.-S., 150
Ladas, S. P., 123, 132
Laman, G. D., 120, 132
Lampe, P., 159, 177
Laszlo, G., 121, 132
Latourette, K. S., 108, 132
Leclerq, H., 103, 132
Legrand, L., 203, 216

Lendvai, P., 121, 122, 132
Lévi-Strauss, C., 148
Levtzion, N., 132
Lewis, B., 122, 127, 129
Lewy, G., 126, 132
Liefeld, W. L., 62, 66
Lohfink, G., 194, 204-6, 209, 216
Longenecker, R. N., 52, 66
Lopasic, A., 123, 132
Louw, J. P., 151, 177
Lyotard, J.-F., 136, 137, 150

MacArthur, J., 97, 132
Magonet, J., 216
Marcus, J., 34, 39
Marlowe, W. C., 203, 216
Marshall, I. H., 85, 88, 95, 158, 177
Martin, R. P., 176, 177
Martin-Achard, R., 200, 216
Massumi, B., 150
Masters, B., 122, 132
Matin-Achard, R., 216
McDonald, L. M., 41, 42, 44, 66
Meeks, W. A., 36, 39
Ménage, V. L., 113, 115, 123, 127, 132
Mendenhall, G. E., 198, 216
Merrills, A. H., 131
Michaels, J. R., 95
Middleton, J. R., 136, 150, 216
Minear, P. S., 213, 214, 216
Mirielle, C., 66
Moerman, M., 188, 189
Moffett, S. H., 105-7, 109, 113, 116-19, 132
Moltmann, J., 190, 191, 216
Moule, A. C., 108, 132
Mrázek, J., 66
Mullins, M. R., 131
Murray, S., 98, 132

Nanus, B., 186, 189
Neusner, J., 68, 96

Newbigin, L., 142, 150, 202, 210, 211, 214–17
Nida, E. A., 151, 177
Niebuhr, H. R., 230, 239

Papadopoullos, T. H., 114, 132
Parkinson, C., 189
Paton, D. M., 215
Pattarumadathil, H., 17, 40
Pawelke, M., 9, 235
Pearson, S. E., 53, 66
Peerbolte, L. J., 64, 66
Peters, G. W., 203, 217
Peterson, D., 156, 158, 177
Pitts, A. W., 49, 67
Pokorny, P., 66
Porter, S. E., 2, 5, 11, 33, 39, 41–44, 49, 60, 66, 67, 73, 96, 215, 222, 223
Porter, W. J., 43, 57, 67
Power, J., 192, 217
Proksch, O., 197, 217
Rawson, B., 66, 67
Reed, A. Y., 69, 96
Rexine, J. E., 124, 132
Riches, J., 89, 96
Robinson, J. M., 22, 40
Roskovec, J., 66

Sanders, E. P., 27, 40
Saunders, J. J., 107, 112, 113, 118, 119, 132
Savage, E., 132
Schnackenburg, R., 210, 217
Schoen, U., 103, 115, 120, 132
Scott, P., 37, 40
Shenk, W., 192, 193
Siegwalt, G., 134, 150
Sim, D. C., 96
Simpson, G., 143, 144, 150
Skarsaune, O., 68–70, 95, 96
Smith, D. M., 85, 96
Smith, M. L., 123, 132
Somakian, M. J., 132

Standaert, N., 108, 118, 132
Stark, R., 154, 177
Stevens, G. B., 50, 67
Stone, B., 139, 143, 150
Stott, J. R. W., 157, 177
Stuart, D., 175, 177
Studebaker, S., 10
Surratt, G., 185, 189
Sweet, J. P. M., 66, 67, 96

Temple, W., 215
Theissen, G., 36
Thiselton, A. C., 43, 67
Thompson, M. B., 56, 66, 67
Thompson, R. P., 33, 35, 40
Thumma, S., 181, 184, 185, 189
Torok, L., 131, 132
Toth, W., 104, 122, 133
Tov, E., 66
Travis, D., 184, 185, 189
Treggiari, S., 60, 67
Turnbull, S., 120, 133

Usher, R., 135, 150

Vahakn, D., 130
Van Gelder, C., 149, 150
Vanhoozer, K. J., 136, 150
Vantini, G., 100, 115, 121, 127, 133
Vaporis, N. M., 127, 128, 133
Vistozky, B. L., 69, 70, 93, 96
Volf, M., 134, 150
von Rad, G., 196, 217
Vryonis, N. M., 110, 122, 123, 133

Wagner, P. C., 158, 177
Walsh, B. J., 136, 150
Waterfield, R. E., 127, 133
Wellesz, E., 57, 67
Wells, J. B., 198, 217
Welsby, D. A., 100, 101, 115, 131–33
West, C. C., 215
Westfall, C. L., 6, 73, 78, 85, 88, 96, 215, 225

Whiteley, D. E. H., 54, 67
Wilbert, S., 217
William, T., 133
Williamson, P. R., 196, 217
Willimon, W. H., 98, 131
Willis, W. L., 157, 177
Winter, J., 126, 133
Wittgenstein, L., 67
Wolff, H. W., 196, 217

Wright, C. J. H., 193, 196, 199–201, 203, 217
Wright, N. T., 32, 33, 40, 209, 217
Wuest, K., 179, 189

Yildirim, O., 123, 124, 127, 133

Zdero, R., 153, 158–62, 177

www.ingramcontent.com/pod-product-compliance
Lightning Source LLC
Chambersburg PA
CBHW050345230426
43663CB00010B/1993